GREEN
WARRIORS

GREEN
WARRIORS

*The People and the Politics Behind
the Environmental Revolution*

Fred Pearce

THE BODLEY HEAD
LONDON

First published 1991
© Fred Pearce 1991
The Bodley Head Ltd, 20 Vauxhall Bridge Road, London SW1V 2SA

Fred Pearce has asserted his right
to be identified as the author of this work

A CIP catalogue record for this book
is available from the British Library

ISBN 0-370-31401-8

Photoset by Rowland Phototypesetting Ltd
Bury St Edmunds, Suffolk
Printed in Great Britain by
Mackays of Chatham PLC, Chatham, Kent

CONTENTS

Conservation is not just about saving whales and tigers and rainforests, and preventing pollution and waste, but is inescapably concerned with the future conduct, welfare, happiness and indeed survival of mankind on this planet . . .

Max Nicholson, *The New Environmental Age*

What's good for the poor is good for the environment.

Nigel Cross, SOS Sahel

INTRODUCTION

The Green Alert

In Africa, paramilitary game wardens shoot poachers on sight. They do it in the name of the environment. In Rome, biologists want to rescue the world's disappearing plants. Their chosen method is to bury seeds in a vault beneath the Arctic ice. In Brazil, the government confiscated part of the Amazon rain-forest from Indian tribes – to make way for a nature reserve. In New York in 1989, Margaret Thatcher pledged to the world £100 million to save the rainforests. Environmentalists told her that the money would destroy more forests than it saved. Sometimes it can be confusing being green.

On the catwalk, top models refuse to wear furs and then read in the papers that they are destroying the livelihoods of thousands of Eskimos. In supermarkets, plastic bags full of pulp from the planet's forests carry labels describing them as 'environment-friendly'. In Asia, greens campaign against national parks. On the plains of Africa, rhinos are preserved 'in the wild' behind electric fences and with an armed warden assigned to every animal.

At the start of the 1990s, almost everybody claims to be green. Bush, Thatcher, Mitterrand, even the Japanese say they are true believers. The last years of the century, we are told, will be the decade of the environment, and there are plenty of people after a slice of the action. But perhaps it is time to turn the spotlight on to the green persuaders: the handful of organisations and people in them who set the green agenda and decide which bits of the planet we should worry about. Their influence is everywhere, from the Canadian Arctic to the plains of Africa and the jungles of Brazil. Who are they and where are they trying to take us? This book follows them round the planet that they want to remould. It probes their origins, their motives, their campaigns and their philosophies. Do they want to overturn the consumer society, or just persuade us to buy green? Do they believe in progress and wealth? Should every Chinese home have a refrigerator? Should every Swede hand in his Volvo? As they ask us to save whales and buy green washing powder, do they want our money or our souls?

Times have changed since Greenpeace and Friends of the Earth were formed in the late 1960s by a motley collection of pot smokers, media freaks, draft dodgers and pacifists. Top campaigners in Washington today are powerful green yuppies, with job titles like senior attorney and international vice-president. In London, the City appoints greens to run investment portfolios. In Amsterdam, Brussels and San Francisco, they jet from science conference to campaign meeting to advertising agency. They debate whether the World Wildlife Fund should give up on the African rhino, and whether Greenpeacers would look better on TV buzzing elephant poachers in a helicopter or sending inflatable dinghies to intercept Japanese ships piled high with tropical timber. They consider which eight men should feature as 'rapers of the rainforests' in the next *New York Times* advertisement.

This is no fantasy world. The power is real enough. Green campaigners have shut down the seal-skin trade in Canada; pulled strings to stop the World Bank putting up money for dozens of dams in the Brazilian forests; hounded the nuclear industry pretty much out of business in many countries. The WWF even plays the financial markets, buying the debt of Latin American countries and redeeming it for deals on conservation with their governments.

In the Third World environmentalists are poor, but often equally powerful. They may bash out their newsletters on old typewriters rather than new word processors, and travel by bus rather than Boeing, but they control hundreds of villages in the Himalayas and have managed to shut down the forestry industry in Thailand.

Some greens follow Indian mystics and dig the soil; others keep cans of Fosters in the fridge and hang pin-ups over their computers. Some hug trees; others dine with directors of international banks. Some try to 'think like a mountain'. A few believe that Aids is nature's revenge on our pillage of the planet.

Under the green spotlight, bankers repent and politicians change their spots. Chain stores tell us to buy their banana foot-lotion to save the rainforests. Political battle-lines are being redrawn and old assumptions questioned. If we follow the green warriors where will they lead us?

I

IN LONDON

Uncle Max

There is no clear choice for the title-holder of father of the modern international environment movement. One man with a decent claim to be its uncle, however, is Max Nicholson, the guiding hand behind both the launch of official nature conservation in England and the creation in 1961 of the World Wildlife Fund. Even in his late eighties, there is no mistaking in Nicholson the true colours of an establishment subversive. He has spent some three decades working for the government and, though he is no spy, he is the kind of seriously mischievous character that John le Carré might enjoy writing about.

Max Nicholson was born in Dublin in 1904. After Oxford, he joined the civil service and spent much of the war at the Ministry of War Transport in charge of the merchant cargo fleet. In the late 1940s, from his position as head of the deputy prime minister's office, he devised the future shape of nature conservation and research in Britain, steering into existence the recommendations of an advisory committee called the Wild Life Special Committee, on which he also sat. As Nicholson modestly puts it in his book, *The New Environmental Age*, the committee's recommendations 'accordingly received a more sympathetic understanding than normal in Whitehall, being steered gently through mechanisms which would normally have quietly buried them'.

Foremost among the products of this arrangement was the Nature Conservancy which, from 1949 until a reorganisation of research in the 1960s, was in charge of both British conservation policy and research into the natural living environment. Having shepherded the Nature Conservancy into being, with the issuing of a royal charter, Nicholson drafted a parliamentary bill to broaden its scope. Then, after the removal of its first head, he became, in 1952, director-general of the organisation, a post he held for 15 years. Despite having so adroitly pulled the levers of state power, Nicholson was not seduced by it. He used to tell his managers at the Nature Conservancy, 'If in doubt, try to think what the Treasury would do in such circumstances, and then do just the opposite. That way you will rarely be wrong.' He took to appointing women, Welshmen and even scientists to top jobs. As Chris Rose, one of Britain's top green campaigners of the 1980s, relates: when addressing voluntary environmentalists Nicholson used to warn, 'I tell you never to trust the state. And remember I speak to you as a representative of the state.'

After leaving the Nature Conservancy in 1966, Nicholson continued to cock a snook at Whitehall and published a brutal indictment of its ways in a book called *The System*. That book, his friends believe, ensured that Nicholson will never receive the knighthood that anybody else who had held half his positions could expect.

The Nature Conservancy was the world's first statutory conservation body. Nicholson, its boss, had written for himself a satisfyingly vague job description. He was charged with setting up a network of national nature reserves, but 'the rest of our functions were left somewhat open.' Armed with a board of professors, MPs, fellows of the Royal Society and chairmen of this and that, Nicholson revelled in lots of power and little responsibility. 'Our views and decisions could not be readily gainsaid, especially since no one knew at the time what such an agency ought and ought not to do,' he said.

Nicholson is an ardent amateur ornithologist, and from his earliest days at the Nature Conservancy he feared the effect that modern pesticides appeared to be having on the nation's birds. He lobbied local councils and government departments to limit the new practice of spraying herbicides on to roadside verges to keep back vegetation. His actions, coupled with research carried out by the Conservancy, came a decade before the US and much of the rest of the world was alerted to the dangers to wildlife from pesticides in Rachel Carson's classic book, *Silent Spring*, published in 1962.

At first, however, Nicholson's entreaties were ignored; but in 1960 the public was alarmed by mysterious mass deaths among pheasants and wood-pigeons. Then more than 1,000 foxes died after the spraying of pesticides during the spring sowing of seeds. Nicholson recalls that 'a number of leading agricultural and medical scientists who ought to have known better pooh-poohed the possibility of a connection between toxic chemicals and the deaths of wildlife.' Two months before the deaths hit the headlines, Nicholson had set up a special scientific unit to investigate the effects of toxic chemicals on wildlife. It was then the largest such unit in the world. While scientific proof of the link eluded his scientists for some time, Nicholson was unperturbed. He pressed ahead with calls for the most damaging pesticides to be banned, using all his political wiles to stir up the countryside. 'The appearance of a dazed fox wandering about in broad daylight in the yard of the Master of the prestigious Heythrop Hunt, and the sight of a half-blind fox eating grass, touched a tender nerve in the countryside,' he says. He 'flushed out the hitherto standoffish Masters of Foxhounds and ensured their vigorous and valued co-operation'.

By the end of 1960, he had the tacit support of the makers of agricultural chemicals. The following spring, the deaths were repeated and Nicholson reported to parliament that 'events during the past year have shown that the serious concern felt by conservationists and the urgency which they attribute to this problem were fully justified.' He took on the powerful farming lobby by pressing for a ban on the use of pesticides containing aldrin, dieldrin and heptachlor as seed dressings.

Nicholson had been an important player on the international conservation scene since plans had been revived for the creation of an International Union for the Conservation of Nature, eventually established in 1948. This idea had been in the air for almost four decades: European nations had in fact agreed to set up such a body at a meeting in Basel in 1913. The First World War intervened, and a second attempt fell foul of worsening international relations during the 1930s. While the president of the new body was Swiss and the secretary Belgian, it was Nicholson who had drawn up its constitution, 'obligingly prepared at my request by the British Foreign Office'.

The formation of the union, says Nicholson, 'marked a breakthrough for conservation on to the agenda of inter-governmental business'. But governments, as he knew well, were slow-witted beasts. In nature conservation, he had concluded, non-government, even non-scientific bodies were essential to get things done. While at the Nature Conservancy, he had been the first head of a research council to provide money to voluntary groups. Now, he proposed that the work of scientists at the IUCN should be augmented by a twin body, which would campaign publicly for the environment, arm-twisting governments and, above all, raising funds. As he pointed out in a letter to *The Times*, the IUCN's total budget in 1960 was less than that of the Battersea Dogs' Home in London. Nicholson's invention was the World Wildlife Fund, which is easily the world's biggest and most active independent conservation organisation today. It is at work in most countries of the world, raising funds, protesting for nature conservation and, in many Third World countries, helping governments to devise conservation strategies and management plans for national parks.

Nicholson set up and chaired the committee that established the WWF in 1961. Its other members included Sir Julian Huxley, the head of the UN's science agency UNESCO, whose articles in the *Observer* in 1960 on the perils to African wildlife during the run-up to independence had caused widespread concern. Others were Guy Mountfort, an advertising executive who had come up with the name World Wildlife Fund, and Victor Stolan, a businessman who had come to Britain from Czechoslovakia. Stolan had written to Huxley after reading his articles and proposed the idea of a new conservation body. The fifth member of that original preparatory committee was the man chosen by Nicholson to be the Fund's first chairman, and who eventually held the post for more than 20 years – Sir Peter Scott.

Nicholson says that Scott was at first a reluctant conservationist. He had lived up to the request made by his father,

Captain Scott, in letters written shortly before his death in Antarctica, that his son should take an interest in natural history. Peter Scott's enthusiasm had initially been for shooting. 'At university', remembers Nicholson, 'I would often go to visit him, only to find that he had been off shooting since dawn.' By the late 1950s, Scott had given up hunting and was a renowned wildlife painter; he also ran a bird reserve at Slimbridge in Gloucestershire and was a well-known presenter of a popular TV wildlife show called 'Look'.

But Nicholson, from his position as head of the Nature Conservancy, had a bone to pick with his old friend. 'His TV programme was frankly escapist,' says Nicholson. 'In 1958, I argued with him and with James Fisher [who ran a similar programme on radio] that these birds that they photograph and record might not exist in a hundred years' time if they didn't draw attention in their programmes to the environmental problems they faced.' Scott took this as a personal criticism, Nicholson remembers, 'but he came round, though he did it gradually because he was nervous that his [Slimbridge] sponsors would go off him.' Nonetheless, once Scott had taken up conservation, he was a great enthusiast and campaigned with huge energy.

Scott drafted the famous panda logo for the WWF. He was even better connected than Nicholson and the ideal man to front an organisation destined to have a high public profile. 'Peter moved in élite circles,' says Nicholson. 'To fund the WWF, he wanted to go to fifty or a hundred millionaires and get, say, a hundred thousand pounds off each.' This, in fact, was the original proposal from Stolan, whose earlier letter to Huxley had suggested that 'there must be a way to the conscience and the heart and pride and vanity of the very rich.' In early 1961, the preparatory committee had intended to create the Ark Club, 'a select world fellowship of champions and defenders of wildlife'. But, says Nicholson, 'it turned out that the very rich weren't so keen. So we decided on a more broad-based outfit, but we would recruit princes to give it a special status. We calculated that the millionaires would pay out in order to have the chance of meeting royalty.'

This became known as the Nicholson Plan. It proved a

winning combination and the line-up of founding members of
the WWF, with the maestro Nicholson beaming in the back-
ground, included Prince Philip and Prince Bernhard of the
Netherlands, and Luc Hoffmann of the Swiss chemicals giant
Hoffmann LaRoche, the first of many millionaires. The first
donor was Jack Cotton, a wealthy London real estate devel-
oper, who gave £10,000; then came Shell, one of Mountfort's
clients. Large donations from rich businessmen and their
companies became a feature of the WWF's fund-raising over
the years. And several such donors, starting with Hoffmann,
became active and prominent office-holders. Among the most
controversial of these was Anton Rupert, a South African
industrial chemist who built up the worldwide Rothmans
cigarette empire. His interest in conservation began with a
passion for traditional Afrikaner buildings and extended to
African wildlife.

For the British public, the launch of the WWF was marked
by a six-page 'shock issue' of the *Daily Mirror*. A large picture
of a black rhino and baby was accompanied by the headline:
'DOOMED – to disappear from the face of the earth due to
Man's folly, greed, neglect, UNLESS . . .' Ian McPhail, another
of the founders of the WWF, recalled later that the *Mirror* had
wanted to use a cuddly animal, such as a koala. But McPhail,
as Nicholson's chief PR man, wanted to get across the idea that
even 'uglies' were worth protecting. Sadly, as we shall see, the
campaign to save the black rhino has been one of the WWF's
most expensive and least successful.

Nicholson, like his creation the WWF, is an odd combination of outspoken advocate and cautious mandarin. His
influential role as conservation chief of the International
Biological Programme did not stop him from writing in 1971
that the International Whaling Commission was guilty of
'criminal negligence' in failing to defend the world's whales.
'Their ignorance and their rapacity stand in stark and evil
contrast to the disinterested struggles of so many conservationists,' he said.

When setting up the WWF, Nicholson admits, 'we had to be
quick. Other groups were about to attempt the same thing, but
not on a global scale. If those rival groups had started first, the

whole future of conservation movements would have been different. In particular, people in the US wanted to set up a US-dominated organisation.' A couple of years later the Americans decided instead to set up a US branch of the WWF which, since then, says Nicholson, 'has always tried to go its own way'. Echoing a criticism constantly made about American environmental groups, he says that 'the Americans didn't see the point in a global organisation or a world fund.' Alone among the major national groups, it contributes none of its income to WWF International (most national groups contribute up to a third of their income). Instead, it claims Latin America as its international fiefdom.

One of the prime motivations for setting up the WWF in 1961 was to tap the growing concern in the rich world about what might happen to East Africa's animals as the winds of change brought an end to the European empires in Africa. Huxley, in his influential articles for the *Observer* in 1960, described the region as containing 'a surviving sector of the rich natural world as it was before the rise of modern man'. Says Nicholson, 'The fear was that all hell would break loose on independence, with the national parks such as the Serengeti [set up by the British colonial administration in 1951] being inundated. We felt it was important to get the new African leaders to see the potential for foreign revenues from tourism. We said that they could get as much money from tourism as from digging up the parks to plant coffee. This was considered preposterous by economists at the time, but it turned out to be true.' Huxley claimed that East Africa could make £100 million a year from the tourist trade.

Concern for the African environment was so strong at that time that there were plans to launch a separate wildlife campaign in East Africa. Nicholson's launch of the WWF squashed that idea, too. He argued that Europe had to be the home for the new organisation because both the scientists and the possibilities for raising money were there. Nicholson organised a major wildlife conference in Arusha in northern Tanganyika, which became Tanzania soon afterwards. He says, 'We invited fifty likely future African leaders to discuss conservation.' This was no doubt patrician, but it was supported

by Julius Nyerere, the prime minister of Tanganyika and one
of the more radical of the new African leaders. And, to his
credit, Nicholson always quotes the future African leader who
told him that it was quite understandable for Europeans to be
smitten with anxiety over the future of Africa's large animals;
'after all, they knew what they themselves had done to the
large animals of Europe.'

The formal highlight of the meeting was a ringing declaration, the Arusha Declaration, from Julius Nyerere, which
said:

> The survival of our wildlife is a matter of grave concern to all
> of us in Africa. These wild creatures amid the wild places
> they inhabit are not only important as a source of wonder
> and inspiration but are an integral part of our natural
> resources and of our future livelihood and well-being.

In practice, such sentiments have not eased the tensions
between conservation and the Western-style development to
which the African nations have aspired since independence.
The WWF's early success in intervening to save the white
rhinoceros in Uganda has been followed by a series of near
disasters for large mammals in Africa, such as the black rhino
and the elephant.

Nicholson admits that, in order to win support from African
governments, the WWF has stressed the financial benefits of
nature conservation. In the months before the launch of the
WWF, Nicholson was in constant communication with game
departments in Salisbury, Nairobi, and elsewhere discussing
the potential value of wildlife herds for 'game cropping'. He
hoped that animals killed by sport hunters could provide an
important income for the newly independent nations, and
established the local prices for rhino horn, warthog and
elephant tusks, and hippo's teeth.

The promotion of hunting turned out not to be good for
fund-raising. But for many years, the possibilities for tourism
in national parks has been a mainstay of the WWF's conservation case. Today, it is arguing the commercial benefits of
maintaining the biological diversity of the planet. The con-

servation of the plants of the rainforests is being sold as an investment in potential sources of new pharmaceuticals. Are we chopping down a cure for Aids? the argument goes.

In his later years, according to Nicholson, this pragmatic approach began to irk Sir Peter Scott. 'He became keen on the idea that we had no right to exterminate animals. The WWF always concentrated on losses to mankind, partly because we were already regarded in some quarters as nutcases and we didn't want to attract the "sandalled people". We persuaded Peter to keep a low profile on ethics and he felt sad about that.' But Nicholson believes that in the future ethical issues may come to the fore.

I think that the industrial age has shown its bankruptcy today. People are turning back to find things in the roots of human evolution. Perhaps the environment movement's uncanny success has been due to this great wellspring. Politicians are not attuned to this, because they are so hooked on the modern myths. But many people in the street talk more sense about the environment than people in Whitehall.

That is a view from which Nicholson has never wavered.

Uncle Teddy

Not ten miles from Nicholson's Chelsea home lives another top-notch British green. Teddy Goldsmith is uncle to the radical wing of the international green movement as well as one of its most potent intellectual forces. A few people think he is mad; I have met several environmentalists who believe he is a malign force; but few fail to warm to him personally. In the business world, he is merely an outlandish ornament to the career of his younger brother, the financier and corporate raider James Goldsmith. To greens, he is the founder and publisher of the *Ecologist*, a fundamentalist green journal that passed its 20th anniversary in 1990.

The Goldsmiths were for centuries one of Europe's leading banking families – the slightly poorer cousins of the Rothschilds. Teddy and Jimmy's grandfather, Adolf, came to Britain in the late 19th century and set about becoming British. By 1910, Adolf's son, Frank Goldsmith, was a Suffolk landowner and the young MP for Stowmarket. But anti-German hysteria in Britain at the start of the First World War forced him to flee to France, where he ran a chain of luxury hotels and met and married a girl from Auvergne called Marcelle Moullier, mother of Teddy and Jimmy. Teddy was born in Paris in 1928 and describes his youth as one long holiday, moving between hotels across the south of France. The family returned to Britain (initially to Claridge's) during the 1930s, and by 1950 Teddy was at Magdalen College, Oxford. Jimmy joined him in Oxford at the age of 16 after tiring of life at Eton.

This is one of the moments where Jimmy's biographers notice Teddy. The two of them, says Teddy, spent 18 months at Oxford doing little else but gamble with their friends, who included a man who was to continue to influence their lives, John Aspinall. The difference, even at this age, was that Jimmy gambled with real money, while the others traded in IOUs.

Teddy says today that he became disillusioned with his studies, concluding that the world was going to the dogs and that the study of history was designed to justify the process. After Oxford, he went to Paris where he unsuccessfully started up in business. He soon saw that his brother had greater business acumen, however, and handed over his companies to Jimmy. Teddy then drifted, travelling the world, often with Aspinall who was looking for rare animals to stock his private zoo: Howletts, near Canterbury. Aspinall was leading an extraordinary double life, dividing his time between his zoo and his gambling club, the Clermont, in Berkeley Square, where his rich clients included Jimmy Goldsmith and friends such as Jim Slater and Lord Lucan.

Aspinall's spirit for adventure was turning into a deep love of the wildness of animals, a love which led him into trouble with the authorities in later years after slack safety standards at his zoos led to a series of deaths. Jimmy shared the love of wild things, arguing in the 1980s that, just as predators are essential to the survival of the fittest in the jungle, so his carnivorous activities on the world's financial markets were good for capitalism.

Teddy, meanwhile, was developing his own style of survivalist thinking. He developed an enthusiasm for tribal groups round the world and for ensuring their survival. He read widely on African anthropology and still has a large bookcase of learned volumes on the topic at his Richmond home. In the 1960s, he served on committees for the Primitive Peoples' Fund, now known as Survival International.

His world travels led him to feel a revulsion towards the way that the modern world was destroying traditional cultures. 'I began to realise that the survival of primitive peoples and of the environment were inseparable,' he says today. 'Primitive people were disappearing; so was wildlife, as my friend Aspinall told me. I realised that the root problem was economic development. So I decided to start a paper to explore these issues.'

That paper, the *Ecologist*, was launched in 1970. It was a propitious moment. Other thinkers who are today revered were coming to similar conclusions. One was Barbara Ward, a British economist. She coined the phrase 'Spaceship Earth' as the title for a seminal book published in 1966 on the links between economics and the environment. Ward went on to found the International Institute for Environment and Development in London and was a moving force behind the United Nations Conference on the Human Environment, held in Stockholm in 1972, which led to the formation of the UN Environment Programme (UNEP) and made a number of important recommendations, such as calling for a moratorium on whaling.

For that conference Ward wrote another book with another highly memorable title, *Only One Earth*. She was a brilliant thinker, and an insider, cajoling and arm-twisting in the corridors of the UN. Teddy Goldsmith, on the other hand, was a born outsider, though he, like many in those days, believed that the Stockholm conference could help to usher in a new era of enlightened government. His contribution to the run-up to the Stockholm conference, first published in the *Ecologist* and then in book form, was *A Blueprint for Survival*. The report was written by Teddy and his colleague at the *Ecologist*, Robert Allen. It was launched, somewhat incongruously, at Aspinall's Clermont Club, and amounted to a call for a world order founded not on growth but on stable populations and 'no-growth' economies. That, said Goldsmith, was how native societies lived, and that was the only route to the survival of humans. Despite its call for a world organised around small self-sufficient communities, the report had some highly authoritarian elements, including suggestions for compulsory birth control and abortion and an end to all immigration. Many interpreted it as an extreme right-wing tract. At the launch, Aspinall appeared to welcome the recent floods in Bangladesh, which had killed close to a million people, as a contribution to stabilising population. Nonetheless, the report gained the support of such figures as Sir Julian Huxley and Peter Scott and of organisations ranging from Survival International to the British branch of Friends of the Earth.

Goldsmith called in the report for the formation of a Movement for Survival. This led to the creation in Britain of the People Party, later renamed the Ecology Party and later still the Green Party. And, coming hard on the heels of another apocalyptic report called *Limits to Growth*, which was published in Washington to even greater clamour than Goldsmith could muster, *A Blueprint for Survival* helped to found a strong intellectual case for halting the post-war economic juggernaut.

1972 was a time of high environmental concern round the world. The governments of the US, Britain and many other nations were persuaded to set up new environmental bodies – the Environmental Protection Agency in the US and the Department of the Environment in Britain – and to enact new laws. Other environmental groups were forming in many countries and the Stockholm conference even attempted, disastrously, to co-opt them all into a form of global alliance. 'It took us several years to dismantle that idea,' says Richard Sandbrook, then at Friends of the Earth.

Environmental concern seemed for a while to have entered the mainstream of political debate. In Britain, Goldsmith held meetings with the rising star of the Liberal Party, David Steel, and followed up by accepting a very public invitation to discuss the implications of *A Blueprint For Survival* with Britain's first Secretary of State for the Environment, Peter Walker. 'At that time', he says, 'we genuinely believed that if politicians were alerted to what was happening to the planet, they would do something about it.' But the truth was that 'Walker was only interested in being able to tell MPs that he had seen me.' Teddy has never been invited back by any of Walker's successors.

With legislation, such as Britain's ultimately ineffectual Control of Pollution Act, passed and bureaucracies set up, the heat went out of the environmental debate for a time. The giant hiccup in world post-war economic growth that followed the oil crisis the following year left the world more concerned about the absence of economic growth than its destructive effects. It took more than a decade, and a sustained period of economic growth in the rich Western nations during the 1970s, before green concerns fought their way back towards the top of the political agenda.

For most of the 1970s, sales of *A Blueprint for Survival*, which eventually clocked up 750,000 copies, kept the *Ecologist* solvent, but there was no disguising the fact that few people seemed to want to buy the magazine. Goldsmith decided on one last public gesture. He agreed in 1974 to stand for parliament on behalf of the People Party in his father's old Suffolk constituency. His living-room still contains a charming picture of a smiling bearded Goldsmith leading a group of hippy supporters and a camel (supplied by Aspinall) which is carrying an outsize sandwich-board reading: 'No Deserts in Suffolk. Vote Goldsmith'. He lost his deposit, of course, and retreated for more than a decade to practise what he preached, returning to the land and running the *Ecologist* from farm cottages in Wadebridge in Cornwall. (He kept his flat in Paris, though; he was a Goldsmith, after all!)

The *Ecologist* continued to be read by a small but admiring band and run by a devoted group of bright young greens recruited by 'Uncle' Teddy. It developed and refined his critique of the world. It fanned the flames of concern about the rainforests and educated many budding environmentalists in the belief that if they wished to save the forests they must also save the people who live in them. Goldsmith continued to travel widely, and to give focus to his growing anger at the direction of 'development' projects in the Third World. In Sri Lanka he saw plans to flood large areas for a complex of hydroelectric dams known as the Mahaweli scheme. 'These dams destroy so much in return for a few decades of electricity,' he says. 'I came back from Sri Lanka determined to fight such projects,' and he launched a devastating assault in a book entitled *The Environmental and Social Effects of Large Dams*, published in 1985. He identified for attack the development policies of the World Bank at a time when other environmentalists were only dimly aware of this 'Mr Big' behind their many and various concerns.

In 1989, as his concerns again began to make their way on to the world's front pages, Teddy returned from Cornwall to London, where a constant stream of journalists, film-makers, 'green' industrialists and fellow campaigners began to beat a path to his door. Old friends from the early 1970s were getting in touch again. There was excited talk of Goldsmith dinner parties where natives from the rainforests sat next to top officials from the World Bank. When I joined the throng, he was just back from New York where he had petitioned the United Nations with three million signatures calling for an emergency debate on the fate of the rainforests. The event was captured on film for a TV programme on Goldsmith funded by Ted Turner in the US and Channel 4 in Britain. While in New York, the world's money-making capital, Teddy was also filmed on top of the planet's largest rubbish dump and in a hall full of video games – symbols, he says, of the kind of world to which poor nations should not aspire.

After New York, Teddy went to Washington, a city that seems to like him better than London does. There he met Senator Wychefowler, an old friend and president of the Senate Committee for Forests and Conservation. Wychefowler had organised a meeting on Capitol Hill where other leading senators, including presidential hopeful Al Gore, could hear pleas about the destruction of the Third World's environment. There to tell them the bad news were Teddy Goldsmith and other important campaigners from round the world whose names recur in this book, including Chee Yoke Ling from Friends of the Earth Malaysia, Smitu Kothari from New Delhi, Sunderlal Bahuguna, the head of the Chipko movement of tree-huggers in the Himalayas, Chad Dobson from the Bank Information Center in Washington and Phil Williams, a fellow campaigner against dams, from California. Goldsmith, back from Cornish exile, was in his element walking the corridors of power, and he persuaded Wychefowler to travel with him to Penang in Malaysia for a conference on Third World agriculture.

One of Goldsmith's strengths is that, while enjoying the hurly-burly of campaigning and having a sharp eye for talented young campaigners, he is at heart an intellectual. It is a combination rare in England and may owe something to his French blood. He proudly told me that sales of the *Ecologist* had risen by 200 the previous month, but he also nurtures a growing fascination with philosophy and deep ecology. 'I am looking for the traditional wisdom of society,' he says. While many other environmentalists justify preservation of the environment in terms of science – preserving genetic diversity, saving tropical plants that could provide a cure for Aids – Goldsmith says, 'Perhaps we have to choose between science and wisdom. I can't believe that science and technology leave us better off. The real wealth is nature, which science and technology are destroying.' The *Ecologist* was beginning to run articles on aesthetics, for instance. 'I am looking for a biospheric ethic', he says, 'in which aesthetics and other aspects of life that we tend to ignore will be important. Many of the things that we allow in society and should not, such as destroying forests, eroding soils and depriving people of their land, are aesthetically unpleasant.' He yearns for a world in which it is safe for us to follow such instincts. Indeed, he believes that only such a world is environmentally sound and, in the modern jargon, 'sustainable'.

For Goldsmith, society is deeply corrupted and diseased by economic growth and the consumer society. 'Conventional knowledge', he says, 'is wrong on virtually every issue because it doesn't take account of the fact that it is looking at an aberrant system. It cannot distinguish between a tumour and a healthy organism. Sensible economics, for instance, would be quite different from the economics of today.'

When we spoke, Goldsmith had just published a new book called *The Great U-turn: Deindustrialising Society*. Through chapters on the fall of the Roman Empire and the ecology of health, unemployment and war, he argues that nothing less than the dismantling of modern industrial society can bring salvation. It is a bleak vision of the present, but one shared by many of the more radical environmental campaigners, from the New Age 'deep ecologists' of California to the tree-huggers of the Himalayas. While Max Nicholson's concerns, and those of the WWF, remain largely to conserve wildlife, Goldsmith believes that to save our planet we must save ourselves.

2

ON THE HIGH SEAS

Mind bombs

The intellectual origins of the environment movement are distant. In Britain, there was William Wordsworth and William Morris; in the US, James Audubon and Aldo Leopold. The WWF was the first modern organisation to tap growing international concern about the survival of wildlife. But it was two organisations both launched in the dog-days of the 1960s – the days of peace and love, protest and draft-dodging – that turned saving the environment into an activity we could all take part in. The two groups were Greenpeace and Friends of the Earth; both launched by renegades from the staid Sierra Club in the US, but swiftly taken over by a younger generation.

It is hard to know where the truth lies about Greenpeace. The circumstances of its first ever demonstration in October 1969, when the Vancouver-based outfit was known as the Don't Make A Wave Committee, is a case in point. Here is Robert Hunter, ecology correspondent of the *Vancouver Sun* and one of the Committee, writing in his book *The Greenpeace Chronicle*: 'There were street freaks and Marxists and Maoists and Trotskyites and Yippies and members of the radical Vancouver Liberation Front . . . draft dodgers and deserters . . . ' And yet here he is again, writing in the *Vancouver Sun* the day after the demonstration: 'Who are we? A collection, initially, of very proper and respectable and decently paid and serious and a bit less than illiterate citizens, some professors and some ministers and housewives . . . '

Whoever they were, they were blocking the US–Canadian

border between Seattle and Vancouver. It was the first time the
border had been shut since 1812, so the Greenpeace fable has
it. Their banners read 'Don't Make A Wave, It's Your Fault If
Our Fault Goes'. The concern was that an underground
nuclear test being conducted by the US that day on Amchitka
Island some 4,000 kilometres away in the Pacific could cause
an earthquake that in turn might trigger a tsunami, a giant
wave that could cause a swathe of destruction in North
America. Making his own waves in his newspaper column a
week before, Hunter had claimed that the US was 'taking a
chance of triggering a chain reaction of earthquakes and tidal
waves which would slam the lips of the Pacific rim like a series
of karate chops'.

It didn't of course, and Hunter later admitted that he and his
organisation had never really believed their own propaganda.
'It's not that we had ever lied – that's one thing you must never
do with modern propaganda – but we had painted a rather
extravagant picture of the multiple dooms that would be
unleashed ... tidal waves, earthquakes, radioactive death
clouds, decimated fisheries, deformed babies. We never said
that's what would happen, only that it could happen ...
Children all over Canada were having nightmares about
bombs.' Happily merging his roles as reporter and rabble-
rouser, Hunter had addressed the crowd at that first demonstration, and he admits in his book: 'It was a large and volatile
mob. They didn't want reason, they wanted to be made to
roar. My own will seemed to vanish. Watching the
demonstration on television that night, I was stunned to
discover that one of the demagogues up there ranting and
raging was myself.'

Away from the mob, the Don't Make A Wave Committee,
which turned itself into Greenpeace in 1971, was initially a
rather traditional organisation. Several of its early organisers
were pacifist Quakers and members of the Sierra Club, the
American equivalent of Britain's Ramblers' Club, only larger
and more romantic, as befits an organisation dedicated to
climbing the Rockies and the Sierra Mountains, rather than
to walking the English Pennine Way. In the early days, the
committee met in a Unitarian church. Its most famous and

most used ploy, first brought into play against a new Amchitka test in 1971, was sailing into danger and defying their opponents. The idea was borrowed from the Quakers, who had twice sailed boats towards nuclear testing zones in the Pacific, only to have their vessels seized long before reaching their goals. In 1971, when Greenpeace set sail on its first mission it had one advantage: its Canadian vessel could not be seized by American warships without causing an international incident.

Greenpeace's nuclear protesters were different from their Quaker predecessors in another way, too. Whereas the Quaker tradition of protest had been to bear personal witness to events, Greenpeace tried to make the world bear witness – through news releases, radio reports and, above all, photographs. The mixture proved explosive. As Greenpeace sailed into nuclear testing zones, or later manoeuvred small inflatable dinghies in front of whalers' harpoons and beneath the bows of ships loaded with toxic waste, cameras brought its message to the 'global village' of the TV screen. Greenpeace was the first citizens' group to realise the potential of the moving image. 'We saw it as a media war,' said Hunter. 'We had studied Marshall McLuhan.' He talked of the group as Green Panthers and their film packages on the evening news as mind bombs. 'I saw Greenpeace as an icon, a symbol from which we might affect the attitudes of millions of people towards their environment.' Not surprisingly, then, its first chairman after being reconstituted as the Greenpeace Foundation in 1971 was Ben Metcalfe, someone who had spent time running media election campaigns for politicians; and when he went, Hunter soon had the job.

Even for Greenpeace, keeping in the news was sometimes hard work. Before embarking on a long chase for Japanese whalers across the Pacific in the early 1970s, Hunter had resigned from his job as a columnist on the *Vancouver Sun*. He said:

The advantage of that was simple. The subjective stuff written by columnists is never picked up by the wire [news] services. But the objective stuff of reporters is treated as legitimate news. All I had to do was to make sure I never quoted myself. Instead, I invented quotes, placed them in the mouths of various agreeable crew members, then 'reported' to the outside what they had said. As a journalist, I was, of course, a traitor to my profession. As a 'news manager' for the expedition, I could censor any unflattering realities, control the shaping of our public image, and when things got slack, I could arrange for events to be staged that could then be reported as news. Instead of reporting the news, I was in fact in a position of inventing the news – then reporting it.

In his view the end justified the means: 'If we lost the media's attention, so did the whales.' For Hunter, 'the development of the planet-wide mass-communications system was the most radical change to have happened since the earth was created, for at its ultimate point, it gives access to the collective mind of the species that now controls the planet's fate. One man can now demand the attention of the world . . . If crazy stunts were required in order to draw the focus of the cameras that led back into millions of brains, then crazy stunts were what we would do.' It was for Hunter and the others the ultimate trip, 'far more exciting than anything else that any of us had to do'.

The stories that Greenpeace weaves are so beguiling that, according to one insider, 'News desks will often suppress stories of campaigning cock-ups because they like the Greenpeace image too much.' Moreover, while its arch-rival in many countries, Friends of the Earth, often has an image of brave amateur failure, Greenpeace has over almost two decades maintained an image of swashbuckling success.

To make the image work, Greenpeace needs a clear, simple message. It is good at being against things, but finds being in favour of things harder; and complex issues, such as Third World agriculture or reafforestation, tend to pass it by. It also means that Greenpeace tends to arrive late on the scene, after the issues have been simplified by others and often when a political snowball is already rolling. But there is nobody better at turning that snowball into an avalanche.

Nick Gallie, one of Greenpeace's long-standing British sages, describes the Greenpeace effect thus: 'In media terms, a political and scientific wrangle that has been going on for years is suddenly reduced to a simple headline and picture. It becomes news.' So it was with the whales campaign. The whaling business had been in serious decline long before Greenpeace raised a finger to stop it. In the 1950s, Aristotle Onassis broke every rule in the book of the International Whaling Commission, the club of whaling nations that attempted to impose some order on the industry by imposing quotas on the number of whales that each nation could land. Ships owned by Onassis raced Norway and Britain, the great whaling nations of the day, for declining stocks. Onassis had recruited a team of Norwegian whalers who were in disgrace in their own country for having left to build Hitler's whaling fleet in the late 1930s. At every step of the way he knew he had a secure and virtually unlimited market for whale oil for products such as margarine.

In those days, whaling had social kudos. Onassis brought business moguls and their wives on board his ships to watch the slaughter. On his luxury yacht, *Christina*, bar stools were covered with the white skin from whale scrotums, handrails were made of whalebone and footrests from the teeth of sperm whales.

Even hardened whaling crew members eventually rebelled against the slaughter of young whales and species that in theory were protected by the IWC. Some refused to join his crews because of the frightful and reckless exploitation of the whale stocks. When, in 1956, a detailed Norwegian study concluded that more than half of the whales caught by Onassis's vessels were protected, had been caught out of season, or were less than the minimum size allowed under IWC rules, Onassis accepted that it was time to quit. He sold his vessels to the Japanese.

Amid such chaos on the high seas, and with even the IWC under criticism from scientists for taking a cavalier attitude to the maintenance of whale stocks, the boom was bound to turn to bust. Whale catches were at their highest during the early 1960s, with the IWC quotas permitting the slaughter of tens of thousands each year. And an increasing number of the animals, especially blue whales, dragged into the bowels of the factory ships were immature – a sure sign of trouble. The IWC ignored the evidence until 1964, more than a decade before the first Greenpeace boat set sail for whaling grounds, when 100 Japanese whalers scouring the waters of the Southern Ocean around Antarctica failed to find a single blue whale. After that, slowly and painfully, the hunt subsided, as much due to financial realities as to either the rapidly advancing science of estimating whale numbers or the concerns of environmentalists.

It was during the late 1960s that public concern for the fate of the whales and other sea mammals began to grow. It culminated first in the passing of the Sea Mammals Act in the US and then in a motion passed at the UN Conference on the Human Environment, held in Stockholm in 1972. The conference called on the IWC to impose a ten-year moratorium on whaling. It argued, as did Greenpeace later, that stocks of a range of species needed time to recover from the slaughter of the 1950s and 1960s, when demand for whale oil for margarine and other products had soared.

Greenpeace's love affair with whales began a year after the Stockholm conference in 1973 with a renegade biologist from New Zealand called Paul Spong, who was thrown out of a job at the Vancouver Public Aquarium after publicly proclaiming that a killer whale he had been studying at the aquarium 'wanted to be free'. Spong had some strange ideas, but while the anti-nuclear faction at Greenpeace, led by one of the Quaker founders, Irving Stowe, thought he was crazy, the Tarot-card-reading faction loved him. Spong and Hunter organised a Project Ahab Committee. There was talk, Hunter remembers fondly, of 'organising a "call-in" for whales along Vancouver's English Bay. Hundreds of people would go down to the beach and use telepathy to attract whales from all over the world and provide them with a sanctuary.' The Canadian folk singer Gordon Lightfoot gave Spong $5,000 to go on the road with a Greenpeace Christmas Whale Show – a slides and lecture show containing recordings of whale songs of the kind pioneered in the 1960s by whale biologist Roger Payne for the WWF. He took it across Canada and then to Japan, where he toured 20 cities.

It soon became clear that whales were good box-office in Canada. 'Whale freaks like Spong had a lot of sex appeal in the counter-culture,' says Hunter; and, 'the more radicals we attracted from the counter-culture, the more expensively-tailored politicos we seemed to find ourselves shaking hands with. Trade unionists, mayors, acid-rock groups, yoga societies even, and – perhaps most usefully – boat mechanics joined the cause.' Stowe died unexpectedly in 1974 and, according to Greenpeace's official history, 'in effect . . . the Project Ahab Committee became the new Greenpeace.' The committee set about finding ways to allow the world to 'bear witness' to the slaughter of whales. There is some disagreement about how the idea came about to use fast inflatable boats, known as Zodiacs, to get between whalers and their quarry. Hunter says Spong had the idea after watching film of how the French marine explorer Jacques Cousteau used them to get cameras close to whales. Their official history says they got the idea after the French military used Zodiacs to hound and then board a Greenpeace boat in the French nuclear testing zone off Mururoa in the South Pacific.

Whatever the truth, Spong faced a more exacting task finding out where whaling fleets went. In early 1975, he visited the Bureau of International Whaling Statistics in Norway and, posing as a bona fide whale researcher, obtained maps of the routes of Soviet and Japanese whaling fleets. In April 1975, the first anti-whaling mission set sail from Canada, with 23,000 supporters seeing them off.

Since that day, Greenpeace has been known more for its whaling campaigns than for anything else. On the first trip, a Soviet whaling ship, the *Dalniy Vostok*, was faced with the extraordinary sight and sound of Greenpeacers homing in on the hunt, playing tapes of the songs of humpback whales. The crew responded by shooting a harpoon directly over the heads of their assailants and into a sperm whale. The film cameraman on board got the picture and, after the resulting publicity, no whaling ships tried the ploy again. It was an early and important victory for Greenpeace.

Less commendably, Hunter filled out a lull in the trip by running a wholly fanciful story about the ship sailing to photograph a battle between sperm whales and giant squid rising to the surface at a full moon. 'The struggle between these two immense creatures is probably the most awesome encounter to take place in the natural world,' he quoted a fellow crew-member as saying. Hunter admits, 'As a possible reality it was remote to say the least. But as a news story it was fairly hot stuff.' And it brought more headlines round the world.

Despite such behaviour, the whales campaign was gaining Greenpeace friends. There were many more trips to find whalers in the Pacific. In 1978, the Dutch branch of the World Wildlife Fund paid for the new London office of Greenpeace to send a mission against Icelandic whalers. This was the first of many little-publicised contributions by the WWF, with its staid image and royal patronage, to their more wild-eyed brothers. It was part of a strategy by the WWF of influencing activities at the IWC, which included paying some of the expenses of the leading whale scientist, Sidney Holt, to represent the Seychelles at the IWC.

By this time Greenpeace had identified as its objective the conclusion of a moratorium on whaling at the IWC. Five years before, it would have been doubtful whether most of the campaigners had even heard of the IWC.

Back in the Pacific, some Greenpeacers, complete with a Russian linguist, boarded a Soviet whaling boat and harangued the crew. Another group, led by Spong, drove their Zodiac right up the ramp at the back of a mother ship, where whale carcasses are hauled to be cut up. They climbed on deck and presented the crew with anti-whaling badges. This time, they had a nine-man TV crew from the American TV network ABC in tow.

The opposition was getting tough, too, however. In 1979, the Icelandic government twice arrested anti-whaling campaigners on the high seas. And in 1980, the Spanish authorities held a Greenpeace ship, the *Rainbow Warrior*, in custody for five months, disabling the boat and charging its skipper with interfering with Spanish fisheries. The crew escaped after they smuggled a replacement part aboard and slipped anchor in the night.

In 1983, the *Rainbow Warrior* landed five people ashore at the Lorino whaling station on the Bering Sea in Siberia. They were, predictably enough, arrested. But the real battle was for film of their landing and arrest, taken by a cameraman aboard the *Warrior*. A ten-hour chase followed, during which one member of the crew took to a Zodiac and headed for Alaska carrying the precious film. He was pitched into the water by waves whipped up by the blades of a Soviet helicopter and then winched aboard. But he left the film hidden in the bottom of the inflatable and other Greenpeacers recovered it. No piece of microfilm from a cold war spy can have had such an eventful voyage to liberty. The six arrested crew were eventually handed back to the *Rainbow Warrior* by the light of the midnight sun on the international dateline. It was, says Greenpeace's official history, 'the most publicised Greenpeace event to date'; and the whales never even put in an appearance.

In the years that followed, the campaign subsided, though even after the moratorium on whaling came into force in 1985, Japan and for a while Iceland and South Korea continued to whale, using a get-out clause in the agreement that allowed 'scientific whaling' to continue. In protest, Sir Peter Scott, British delegate to the IWC, publicly returned the Order of the Falcon awarded to him by the Icelandic government. Greenpeace tried to launch a boycott of Icelandic fish, but with little success; and its boats harassed Japanese whalers from time to time, usually en route to another destination – Greenpeace's new permanent base in Antarctica. For the time being, the heat had gone out of the issue.

In the public mind, the virtual end to whaling was Greenpeace's doing. But many campaigners say that Greenpeace hijacked the whale issue. Tom Burke, one of the early whale campaigners at Friends of the Earth in Britain, says, 'Greenpeace have tried to rewrite history, presenting themselves as the people who saved the whales, but the claim just doesn't hold up.' Certainly, there were other and earlier participants. Certainly, too, the industry was on the wane before the campaigns of the conservationists got going. Yet, when all is said, it was the Greenpeace 'mind bombs' that brought the plight of the whales into tens of millions of living-rooms round the world. Greenpeace alone provided the pictures that told the story. Nick Gallie puts it this way:

> A whaling ship, an explosive harpoon, a fleeing whale and between them a tiny, manned inflatable with the word 'Greenpeace' emblazoned on its side – it says it all. The image is a godsend for television news, and instantly hundreds of millions of people have shared an experience of Save the Whales. How many years of petitions and arguing over quotas in the International Whaling Commission could equal that?

By the late 1980s, the only surviving whaling nation of any substance was Japan. Its continued operations, in the name of science rather than commerce, were heavily subsidised for what Jeremy Cherfas (author of *The Hunting of the Whale: A Tragedy that Must End*) believes are political reasons. The Japanese did not want to lose face. Without the politics, he reasons, the whaling would have by now halted altogether. One wildlife campaigner who worked for both Greenpeace and FoE told me: 'In the early 1980s, the word was that the Japanese would give up whaling. Then Greenpeace launched a vitriolic campaign against them and they decided to continue.' Greenpeace certainly realised that it was running into hot water and at one point its international chairman, David McTaggart, called in the sober suits of the WWF to attempt to restore some lines of communication with the Japanese.

In a sense, however, these arguments are meaningless. The crusade to save the whales was essentially a drama in which the whale was a wonderful symbol of the sanctity of life, and its slaughter a crime committed by humans against the natural world. On the face of it, Greenpeace's campaign was directed at gaining and enforcing a moratorium on whaling. It argued long and hard that a moratorium was essential to allow stocks to recover. But it has no intention of ever announcing, 'OK, the whales have returned, let whaling recommence.'

As Patrick Moore, a Canadian stalwart of Greenpeace from the early 1970s through to the mid-1980s, put it, 'We don't think it's a good idea to kill whales. They are a symbol of the conservation of life. Also, they are wonderful things. Whale brains are bigger than ours.' Moore, who counts himself among the more scientific of the Greenpeace pioneers, calls whales 'an alien intelligent life form inhabiting this planet. If you look into a whale's eyes, they display humour. And they can see into each other's bodies, unlike us. Billions have been spent searching for extra-terrestrial life. All that time and energy should have been spent on trying to communicate with whales.'

This kind of stuff is regarded as nonsense by most whale researchers. Whales are about as sophisticated as cattle, they say. But it undoubtedly strikes a chord with many people. 'The scientific debate about whether whales really are in danger of extinction is not one we want to get reduced to,' says Moore. 'The general public is not going to understand the science of ecology, so to get them to save the whale you have to get them to believe that whales are good.'

In the aftermath of Greenpeace's endeavours on behalf of the whale, it is hard to imagine anybody resuming the whaling business on a large scale, whatever the state of the stocks. Alerted to the issue, public opinion in the global village that Greenpeace has addressed so well would not stand for it. And that is the real legacy from Greenpeace's campaign – a matter of morality rather than population biology, of principles not quotas.

A cautionary tale

Despite the media pyrotechnics, Greenpeace still believes essentially in the old Quaker ethic of its founders. It doesn't engage in violence against people or property. Sometimes it bends this rule a little, as when it put a plug into the end of a pipeline discharging radioactive waste from the Sellafield nuclear plant into the Irish Sea. But it was able to win an immediate and grovelling apology and a large charitable donation in 1989, when the prestigious science journal *Nature* suggested in a leading article that Greenpeace had been guilty of ecological terrorism.

One Greenpeacer who bent the rules too far was Paul Watson. He was one of a number of subsequent Greenpeace luminaries who volunteered unsuccessfully for the first boat trip into the eye of the nuclear tests in the Pacific. He was 'a muscular seaman who had knocked about the world on freighters, and who would have been a perfect candidate for the voyage, except that he had North Vietnamese flags stitched to his army jacket, wore Red Power buttons, Black Power buttons, and just about any kind of anti-establishment button that could be imagined,' wrote Robert Hunter. Watson was turned down as 'too radical' for Greenpeace, a label he wore with pride for many years inside and outside the organisation.

Rebuffed, he went off to North Dakota to take part in the uprising of Sioux Indians at Wounded Knee in 1973. He returned as an adopted Sioux warrior called Grey Wolf Clear Water, stuck around and was soon Hunter's 'lead kamikaze' aboard Zodiacs heading for the harpoons. While the others certainly risked their lives, Watson seemed positively to relish the prospect of placing himself in extreme danger. On one whale trip, recalls Hunter, he was about to leap from a Zodiac on to the back of a whale in mid-ocean, when the whale wisely moved away.

Watson then switched his headstrong bravery from saving whales in the ocean to saving seals on the ice-floes off New-foundland. It was his idea to take the Greenpeace media show on to the ice, to film two-week-old harp seal pups being clubbed to death for their pelts by locals and Norwegians landed on to the ice by ship. Again, it was not an original idea. Brian Davies, a Canadian and head of an organisation called the International Fund for Animal Welfare, had been taking journalists to witness the hunt for years. Watson believed that Greenpeace could end the hunt; something Davies had failed to do. Davies was prepared to back him, augmenting Green-peace's meagre income from the sale of badges and bumper stickers in Vancouver to finance the first Greenpeace seal mission in early 1976.

The idea caused some problems internally. Paul Spong, the

inspiration behind the whales campaign, opposed it. But the organisation's leading figures, Robert Hunter and Patrick Moore, came round and at the last moment took charge of the first trip. Watson's plan had been to spray dye on to seals to make their pelts unsaleable. But, when the first vanload of Greenpeacers ran up against angry crowds of seal hunters blocking the road at St Anthony in Newfoundland, Moore and Hunter switched tack. They agreed to throw away their cans of dye in return for the support of the local hunters in a campaign against the professional Norwegian hunters in their boats offshore, who took the majority of the seals. For the New-foundlanders, the hunting was a sideline, though an important one. As Hunter put it, hunting 'was as normal for them in spring as it was to go fishing in summer or to dig up potatoes in the fall'.

The deal may have prevented a lynching, but, says Alan Thornton, one of the volunteers manning the phones back in Vancouver, it caused a furore among their supporters when they heard of the 'sellout' on the TV news. 'It was a bad strategy. They surrendered their power with the dye,' says Thornton. But it also showed up two contrasting approaches within the organisation, with some concerned primarily with wildlife, and others also troubled by the fate of humans, even hunters.

The next offensive against the seal hunters came in early 1977 and was unambiguously Watson's campaign. He headed off for the ice with the claim, 'This year we are determined physically to stop the hunt. Some of us may not be coming back.' Less than a week later, six of them nearly perished after being lifted by helicopter at twilight on to a remote island. The chopper departed before they discovered that they had left their tents back at base. Hunter records that only a tent abandoned on the island by a French biologist years before saved them from freezing to death.

The weather was atrocious and the icepack, normally a flat, unbroken expanse, was that year uneven and broken into small pieces. A veteran war photographer who had been assigned to the story refused to go out on to the ice. But the trip turned into a major media event. The cause was the sudden

arrival from Paris, aboard a helicopter piloted by Swiss environmentalist Franz Weber, of Brigitte Bardot. As Hunter
wrote, 'Until her arrival, the seal-hunt story had been all blood
and death, but now it was blood and death and sex.' Moore
took Bardot out to Belle Island, the final staging post before the
ice, where there had been near-mutiny because Watson and the
others objected to the idea of her presence. But they relented
and she spent several hours at the camp.

Out on the heaving ice-floes, where the swell was around
four metres, there was chaos. All co-ordination had been
abandoned. Only a small party, including Watson and
Thornton, made it to the ships. 'Our tactic of trying to get in
front of the seal boats was quite impossible,' says Thornton.
'When we came across some sealers clubbing the seals and
removing their pelts, Watson began to take the pelts and throw
them into the sea. Then he threw a club in.' This was theft and,
it was later claimed, against Greenpeace's self-imposed rules as
well as Canadian law.

When Watson, wearing a crash helmet rather than the
woolly hats favoured by his companions, reached the ships, he
handcuffed himself to a wire which the sealers were about to
use to haul on board a bale of pelts. Cheering, the sealers
hauled the line in, crashing Watson against the side of the ship
and then five times dumping him into the freezing water. 'He
was lucky to survive,' says Thornton, who pulled him out of
the sea. It took a half-hour argument with the crew of the ship
before they agreed to take on board Watson, who was wet,
freezing and had a dislocated shoulder.

Watson could have been a martyr. Instead, he soon found
himself thrown out of the organisation for breaking the rules
and for allegedly conducting a campaign against the leadership
of Patrick Moore. He was too much, even for Greenpeace. 'He
seemed possessed by too powerful a drive,' wrote Hunter.
'Paul was quite genuine in what he was doing. We were
friends,' says Thornton. 'But he was big-headed. He used to
hurl abuse at the "stupid Newfies". However much you may
think people wrong, you should never humiliate them.'

Soon that drive led to Watson forming a new organisation
called Sea Shepherd, which became engaged in activities that

took him well beyond the law in order to uphold what he sees as a greater law. In the late 1970s, Greenpeace played a large part in uncovering the links between a series of pirate whaling ships, operating outside the rules of the IWC and the nations that subscribed to the IWC's rules. It was a grubby trade. One notorious ship, the *Sierra*, sailed the seas in and out of season, killing nursing mothers, babies, any kind of whale that crossed its path. Environmental investigators found out that it was owned by Norwegians and operated by South Africans under covert Japanese supervision. It sold whale oil to the EEC and whale meat to Japan. But while Greenpeace investigated, Watson took direct action. He had his ship, the *Sea Shepherd*, reinforced with concrete and it rammed the *Sierra* on 16 July 1979, on the eve of a crucial IWC meeting. The *Sierra* survived and was repaired, but the following February it was sunk with a limpet mine in Lisbon harbour. It is widely assumed that *Sea Shepherd* were responsible and Watson has never sought to deny it. Two months later, two Spanish whaling ships were sunk.

In the mid-1980s, Watson crossed swords with Thornton again. Thornton had left Greenpeace and set up an organis-ation called the Environmental Investigation Agency. He was working quietly and diplomatically with the people of the Faroe Islands, in the remote North Atlantic between Scotland and Iceland, to persuade them to tighten controls on the annual killing of pilot whales in their harbour. It was a traditional slaughter, and by now was as much a sport as anything, with some meat dumped and the rest put into local deep freezes. 'We had made good progress,' claims Thornton, 'getting them to agree to new regulations.' Then Watson turned up with the *Sea Shepherd* and there was a confrontation with the whalers. 'There were punch-ups and he was firing flares everywhere,' says Thornton. 'All the progress we had made was lost.'

In Iceland in 1985, two of Watson's volunteers broke into a dockside factory for processing whales run by the Icelandic whaling company, Hvalur. They smashed equipment, includ-ing computers, and switched off refrigerators that contained some 2,000 tonnes of whale meat. They then sank two whaling ships – half of the Icelandic fleet. That night cost the Icelandic whalers around $2.5 million. 'It didn't save a single whale,' says Thornton, 'all it did was unite the Icelandic opposition against us.' Jeremy Cherfas, author of *The Hunting of the Whale* and nobody's idea of a friend of saboteurs, disagrees, however. He wrote that whatever the rights and wrongs of his tactics, 'Watson's *Sea Shepherd* saved more whales directly' than Greenpeace. But perhaps that isn't the issue. In many people's minds, Watson remained associated with Greenpeace, and the occasional libel award to Greenpeace was hardly recompense for the damage it believed had been done to its reputation.

The New Model Greenpeace

Greenpeace's first decade belonged to Vancouver and to Robert Hunter and Patrick Moore. Its second belonged to David McTaggart. By chance, he was a British Columbian, too, though far from either the Quaker or the hippy traditions that dominated the early days. McTaggart was a champion badminton player in the late 1950s, before moving to the US to become a millionaire in the construction business. He built a ski lodge in California called Ski Bear, publicised by a poster of a nude skier, but a gas explosion destroyed the chalet and a legal action brought by an injured employee wiped out most of his assets. 'He fled to the South Pacific with what was left of his fortune, bought a ketch and had been sailing among the islands and atolls since then,' says Hunter.

During a stopover in New Zealand in 1972, McTaggart read a newspaper advert placed by Greenpeace's then chairman and PR supremo, Ben Metcalfe, asking for volunteers to sail into the French nuclear testing zone near the Mururoa atoll in the South Pacific. France had not signed the Partial Test Ban Treaty and its tests were still carried out in the atmosphere rather than underground.

Greenpeace and McTaggart were the perfect match. Greenpeace had stopped the Amchitka tests but was broke. It had no ship to make the Mururoa trip, though there was no mention of that in the adverts. McTaggart had a 12-metre boat that might be up to the voyage, a knowledge of the South Pacific and time on his hands.

From the start, however, McTaggart was a man apart from the rest of the organisation. Though Greenpeace paid the bills and handled the PR, Mururoa was 'McTaggart's trip', says Hunter. It was very nearly his last. In mid-June 1972, as McTaggart and his small crew reached the site for the bomb test, the French navy charged them with minesweepers and a 200-metre cruiser and buzzed them with helicopters and aircraft for eight days. They eventually forced the ketch away from its position downwind of the test zone. As part of the tests, a small nuclear device was exploded. Seeing this, McTaggart tried to re-enter the zone and his boat was rammed and crippled by a minesweeper. The French then 'rescued' McTaggart and his crew from the 'accident', gave them lunch and sent photographs round the world, implying that they and McTaggart were on friendly terms. In the media war, the French had won this round. The tests continued and an angry McTaggart limped home.

The following summer, McTaggart was due back in the test zone with another boat. This time he was to be accompanied by a flotilla of other 'peace boats', including one from the New Zealand Navy sent by the country's new socialist government. The new Australian government of Gough Whitlam was also opposed to the French tests. McTaggart, however, had been delayed in Vancouver by a bitter clash of personalities which led to Metcalfe's resignation. By the time he arrived, in mid-August 1973, the rest of the peace boats had been seized or forced away by the French. He was alone and, as Hunter recalls, 'the French were angry.'

They sent an inflatable boat filled with commandos who beat up McTaggart and his second male crew member. One blow from the butt of a truncheon permanently damaged McTaggart's right eye. A female crew member, who was left unmolested, had taken photographs, which she smuggled in her vagina past French guards. The publication of the pictures embarrassed French generals who had insisted that McTaggart had not been beaten.

Three months later, the French announced that all future
tests at Mururoa would be carried out underground, and
McTaggart had begun a bitter legal battle in Paris to win
compensation. To pay for the case, he had to sell the boat.
Greenpeace itself was broke and any plans to make money
from the sale of the photographs of his beating were scuppered
by Hunter, who had countermanded McTaggart's request and
insisted that the photographs be released to the media free of
charge, for propaganda. It took three years for McTaggart
to win compensation for the ramming of his boat and an
admission from the French government in court that 'it should
not be denied that McTaggart may have helped to persuade
the French government to decide to choose underground
tests in place of atmospheric tests.'

His battle with the French government over for the moment,
McTaggart launched a new crusade to establish Greenpeace in
Europe. It was a move that eventually gave him control over
the whole organisation. Brice Lalonde, who was head of
Friends of the Earth in Paris and later stood as a Green
presidential candidate before becoming an environment
minister under the Mitterrand presidency, had given McTaggart office space while he prepared his case against the French
government. Now Friends of the Earth in Britain gave him a
mailing address in London. But soon, with the aid of former
FoE people such as Pete Wilkinson, Greenpeace had an office
in London. This was followed by one in Paris in 1977 with
Remi Parmentier, yet another ex-Friend of the Earth, in
charge.

Next came Amsterdam, by which time McTaggart had
persuaded the Dutch branch of the World Wildlife Fund to
give him £30,000 to pay for a new boat, the *Rainbow Warrior*,
to launch a campaign against Icelandic killing of fin whales.
Three years later, the same group put up funds for Greenpeace's second European vessel, *Sirius*, which was sold to them
at a knockdown price by a sympathetic Dutch government.

At this stage there was little contact between the different
Greenpeace offices in Europe and North America. Patrick
Moore became president in Canada and tried to set up an
international board. But his efforts to gain control of Green-

peace branches round the world met with opposition, culmi-
nating in his Vancouver office suing the rich San Francisco
office for violation of trademark agreements. McTaggart
struck. As Greenpeace's official history tells it, 'On the eve of
the court case, McTaggart swept into America calling for
unity. He brought together the offices in the US and Toronto,
along with the closely knit groups of Greenpeace Europe,
which he headed, and they confronted the old-timers in Vancouver.' Europe paid the Canadians' debts and all power was
vested in Greenpeace International, to be based in the Netherlands. McTaggart named himself chairman and chief
executive.

In the decade that followed, McTaggart brought a hard-
nosed professionalism to the organisation to harness the bravado of its volunteers and its public image as 'God's navy'.
More remarkably, he managed to achieve this without Greenpeace losing any of its hard radical edge.

During the early 1980s, the dumping of toxic chemicals
became a major preoccupation of the new Europe-centred
Greenpeace, with the Dutch and West German organisations
leading the way. The German headquarters at Hamburg,
headed by Harald Zindler, became formidably equipped, with
a warehouse full of equipment that could be loaded on to
research boats at a moment's notice and sent off into the
Rhine, the Elbe or the North Sea. They found deformed fish,
first in the River Elbe and later in the Rhine and in the German
and Dutch coastal waters of the North Sea. Greenpeace attributes the deformities to chemical poisoning from dumped
waste.

Targets for campaigns included factories in Britain, West
Germany, Belgium and Norway that were dumping millions of
litres of waste from the manufacture of titanium dioxide, a
white pigment. The waste, in the form of sludges dumped at
sea from ships, or liquids discharged from pipes, contained
sulphuric acid and heavy metals. Barges loaded with sludge
were blockaded and pipelines plugged. There were similar
actions on the east coast of the US and in Canada. Titanium
dioxide waste was not perhaps the most dangerous pollutant
around. Its name hardly generated the horror evoked by

radioactivity or dioxin. But it fitted Greenpeace's bill by being discharged from large factories in a number of countries where the organisation had volunteers on hand to take action. In this way local activities could be bound into an international campaign. It also became the forerunner to a more general campaign to reduce pollution of the North Sea.

The 1980s was also the era of the steeplejacks. The idea of climbing chimneys had originated with the German Green-peacers in Hamburg. In 1981, they had scaled a smokestack at a pesticides plant in the city and hung a banner that read, 'When the last tree is cut and the last fish killed, the last river poisoned, then you will see that you can't eat money.' Green-peace signs appeared everywhere in 1984. London woke one morning to find a sign reading 'Time To Stop Nuclear Testing' on the front of Big Ben. 'Give Me Liberty From Nuclear Weapons: Stop Testing' appeared across the Statue of Liberty in New York. In Copenhagen the statue of the Little Mermaid was fitted out with a harpoon through her chest and draped with a bloody Japanese flag and the words: 'She too tried to save the WHALES'. And one day in April 1984, Greenpeace teams climbed the chimneys of power stations in Belgium, West Germany, Austria, Britain, Denmark, the Netherlands, France and even Czechoslovakia, each carrying banners with the simple word 'STOP' as a protest against acid rain. There were also Greenpeace parachute drops, and a balloon wafted over the Berlin Wall.

Behind the publicity stunts, however, the new model Green-peace under McTaggart had undergone a conversion towards science and the more conventional rigours of research. In the old days, scientists had a poor reputation among the organisa-tion's activists. They preferred reading tarot cards instead. Patrick Moore, a moving force in the organisation for the ten years that it was based in Vancouver, was an ecologist. But he avoided involvement in scientific debates. 'We are interested in a conflict of values,' he said. 'You might ask whether the whales are really in danger of going extinct. That is a scientific debate that we don't want things to get reduced to. We believe that wild nature is in trouble. Period.' His friend and arch-campaigner for whales, Paul Spong, runs a whale-watching laboratory on the west coast. Does he publish the results of his research in journals? 'No. He is trying to live and communicate with the whales. He is not working at the level of science,' says Moore.

For Moore, the seal campaign had had little to do with conservation. 'It was an emotional appeal to change the relationship between humans and nature.' In that sense, Greenpeace sometimes appears closer to an animal liberation organisation than an environment group. Certainly Moore veers towards deep ecology, while McTaggart is a more conventional environmentalist. As Thornton, who set up Greenpeace's London office with McTaggart in 1977, put it, 'the Canadians were into a hippy karma way of doing things. McTaggart and I had aspirations to be more organised.'

When Thornton and McTaggart appointed a crew for their first boat to harass Icelandic whalers, they ignored the queues of enthusiastic amateurs who normally made up Greenpeace crews. 'We employed proper engineers and navigators, a bo'sun and the rest,' says Thornton. Wild stories about giant squid battling with sperm whales and hypothetical tidal waves were also frowned on. In place of the off-the-cuff assertions that comprised the analysis of Watson and Moore on the seals issue, Thornton went off to the library of the Canadian High Commission in London and wrote a position paper on the economics, ecology and trade in seals and the seal hunt. It was the first time anybody had done such a thing in the eight years of the organisation's existence, and was a considerable break with the Moore and Hunter school of campaigning. Ironically, while Moore had a doctorate in ecology, Thornton had come to Greenpeace as an aspiring author.

'Looking back, this research was very important,' says Thornton. 'We could give references for the things we said. It gave much more depth to our work.' Thornton commissioned Sidney Holt, one of the top scientific advisers to the International Whaling Commission, to review the data on the catches of fin whales which made up a large part of the Icelandic whalers' catch. 'We did it as a campaigning tool, rather than as pure science,' he says, 'but I think it was the first time that Greenpeace had commissioned scientific research.'

The study provided evidence, from the age and length of caught whales, that the number of fin whales was declining. Ironically, it was just such scientific research into whale populations that Iceland insisted justified its continuing to take whales in defiance of the international moratorium on whaling after 1985.

In Germany, Greenpeace was recruiting scientists to work on its campaign against chemical pollution. One of the founders of the Hamburg office in 1981 was Gerd Leipold, an oceanographic physicist from the country's top lab, the Max Planck Institute. 'I just felt that being a scientist wasn't enough to change things,' he told the organisation's official biographer. Greenpeace was also buying equipment to match its aspirations. In 1985, it added to its growing fleet the *Beluga*, a small firetug fitted out as a mobile laboratory. It could manoeuvre on top of a waste outfall pipe while scientists on board took samples for analysis.

It was, ironically, just as Greenpeace was working hardest to cast off its image as a pirate of the high seas that McTaggart's old enemy from the 1970s, the French government, struck. In an action more reminiscent of Saddam Hussein than of a Western government, commandos under the orders of the defence minister in Paris attached limpet mines to the *Rainbow Warrior* while it was at harbour in New Zealand, preparing to sail into the French Pacific nuclear testing zone. One crew member on board was killed. It was an extraordinary affair and one that brought Greenpeace a lot of international attention. But it was attention that, for once, it did not relish. Ever conscious of the organisation's image, its rising young star, the American Steve Sawyer, told reporters later in the year, 'It has focused attention in such a way that we are caught up with a political scandal, sabotage, terrorism and murder, words which we would definitely prefer not to have associated with our name.'

While improving the scientific quality of his fast-growing international staff, based first in London and then Amsterdam, McTaggart also agreed to set up a research laboratory at Queen Mary College, London, to analyse in greater detail the many complex effluents collected by the *Beluga* on trips on the

Elbe, Rhine and then round Britain's coastline and estuaries. The new commitment to research was attracting attention. In Britain, the Chemical Industries Association sent out a letter to its members warning them not to answer questionnaires from Greenpeace inquiring about effluents. 'Do not underestimate Greenpeace,' it said. 'They have considerable skills in achieving publicity. They also have scientists and engineers. They carry out monitoring exercises and recently succeeded in sealing an underwater effluent pipe.'

The laboratory at Queen Mary College was headed by Paul Johnson, a burly loose-limbed chemist who began working for Greenpeace during the *Beluga*'s 1986 trip round Britain's coasts shortly after completing his PhD at the college. When I visited the laboratory in mid-1989, he was at work analysing samples of sediment from the bottom of the North Sea collected by another Greenpeace boat, the *Moby Dick*. It was part of a prestigious contract with the Norwegian Institute for Atmospheric Research which was investigating how much pollution in the North Sea was the fall-out of air pollution. Johnson also had a deal with the soon-to-be-privatised Thames Water, an organisation much criticised by Greenpeace for failing to clean up the Thames estuary. 'We go on their boats and do periodic fish sampling,' said Johnson. 'We intend to produce a joint scientific paper at the end of it.' In co-operation with biologists, Johnson's laboratory was investigating fish disease in one of the polluted outer reaches of the Thames estuary, near Thurrock in Essex.

He had also analysed soil samples from Greenpeace's new Antarctic station and, awaiting investigation, he had a freezer full of blubber and tissue from seals killed in the previous summer's outbreak of distemper. Johnson's basic analytical tool, a mass electron detector, searches a library of data on 46,000 chemicals looking for a match with whatever sludge it is offered. He specialises in analysing complex discharges, such as one in hand during my visit from Ciba-Geigy's pharmaceuticals works on the Humber estuary. 'We know more about many of these discharges than the companies themselves,' says Johnson. Johnson's is Greenpeace's third laboratory, but the other two are mobile: on the *Beluga* and aboard a bus based in West Germany. 'The problem with the mobile labs is that it is very hard to get their results accepted by other scientists. But here we can have our equipment certified.' Even so, boffins are suspicious people. Johnson remembered with delight a blazing row with the British Ministry of Agriculture's fisheries laboratory over data on PCBs published by Greenpeace. The laboratory refused to believe the figures. 'Actually the analysis had been done for us on contract by another government laboratory at the Institute of Terrestrial Ecology,' he says. 'The fisheries people still won't talk to us.'

On the other side of town, but working for Greenpeace UK rather than the international office, is Jeremy Leggett, a geologist who spent the early 1980s at Imperial College, London, countering Pentagon propaganda and arguing that nuclear test ban treaties could be policed by geologists. He narrowly failed to be appointed as director of FoE in England in 1989. Instead, he was picked by Greenpeace UK's director, Peter Melchett, to be his first scientific director.

Under Leggett, press releases carry references to papers in scientific journals and Leggett has even introduced 'peer review'. Reports are distributed to scientists for comments and corrections before publication. He talked of setting up 'think tanks' and wanted to encourage scientists to speak out on controversial issues. He had persuaded 40 top names, including two Nobel prizewinners, to protest in a Greenpeace advertisement at the British government's promotion of nuclear power as a 'solution' to the greenhouse problem. And he intended to push the case at the next Greenpeace International Council for a campaign against the release into the environment of genetically engineered organisms – a hot topic in the science press but not one to have attracted public attention.

Greenpeace has come a long way from reading Tarot cards and looking for rainbows as it sailed the seven seas in search of whales. But scientists remain on tap rather than on top. According to international director Steve Sawyer, 'our philosophy on issues is extraordinarily pragmatic. We choose the ones we feel we might be able to win.'

Meanwhile, McTaggart's taste for high diplomacy is growing. In 1989, Greenpeace opened an office in Moscow. The popular touch was to the fore. Finance came from a joint venture with Melodia, a Russian state-owned record company. Western rock stars such as Annie Lennox and Peter Gabriel donated music for an album put on sale in the Soviet Union. The company pressed four million copies and the stars, plus assorted rock journalists, were shipped to Moscow for the launch, which grabbed as much media attention in the West as the East.

Greenpeace insisted that it would operate in the Soviet Union as it would in any other country. But it must have been the first national office of Greenpeace set up at the invitation of the state, and with the patronage of a leading member of the host nation's Academy of Sciences, Yevgeny Velikhov. Moreover, Greenpeace staff revealed that they would have nothing to do with green groups being set up in outlying republics, such as the Baltic states, because they were little more than separatist political organisations. Would such scruples operate in other countries? Certainly FoE International was not worried about such considerations, having appointed the Estonian Green Movement as a fully fledged member of the organisation – the only such group in the Soviet Union. After science, now straight politics seemed to be the order of the day at Greenpeace. Had 'God's navy' gone respectable? No wonder there was talk among other green campaigners about Greenpeace entering a mid-life crisis.

A fate sealed

The dispute between Greenpeace and the hunters of northern Canada, which had split the organisation in 1976, had been kept discreetly under wraps ever since the confrontation at St Anthony, Newfoundland. In 1985, however, the tensions raised but never resolved at that time suddenly reappeared. The issue was what to do about the impact on the lives of the hunters of campaigning to save animals.

Greenpeace's photogenic attempts to save seals from their

hunters brought salvation for very few animals and antagonised their hunters. The real purpose of such campaigns, of course, is achieved either when legislators act or purchasers of the hunters' furs are shamed into closing their cheque books. Greenpeace's success in saving seals came not on the ice-floes of Canada but in the corridors of Brussels. In 1983, feeling the heat of public opinion, ministers of the European Community, the largest market for seal skins, voted to ban imports of the skins of harp and hooded seals, the two main species in the Canadian hunt.

It was one of the first conservation actions by the European Community. Initially the ban was for two years, but in 1985, as concern grew that it might be lifted, the British environment minister William Waldegrave revealed that in less than two months 'the British government has received more than 56,000 letters from all over the world from people concerned about the survival of seals after the ban expires.' The ban was renewed and then made permanent in 1989. In the ministers' meetings, there was some talk about threats to the survival of the seals – but the real concern was the extent of public hostility to the continuation of the hunt. The issue was ethics rather than conservation.

After the initial ban in 1983, the bottom had fallen out of the market for seal pelts, and sales and prices plummeted round the world. The hunters had no market and they were angry. The following March, on the Magdalen Islands in the Gulf of St Lawrence close to Newfoundland, they destroyed a helicopter belonging to Brian Davies's International Fund for Animal Welfare, and the Canadian authorities seized a Greenpeace plane.

Sympathy for the hunters began to grow. Radical journals normally sympathetic to environmental causes began to portray the plight of the 'noble' hunter. Two anthropologists wrote a striking piece about life among seal hunters on the Magdalen Islands for the *Whole Earth Review*, a magazine with deep green origins. They complained of the 'Bambification' of nature. You've seen the photos of doe-eyed baby seals, they said; well, after a month these pups are abandoned by their mothers – 'So much for motherhood.'

Clubbing is bloody but painless. 'An urban society which no longer butchers its own meat is easily shocked at the sight of blood,' but 'sealing is the rite of passage to adulthood for men in these villages.' The hunters were the true ecologists, the article said, keeping nature in balance by controlling the numbers of seals – each of which gobbles down more than a tonne of fish a year. Seals had to be managed – 'and that means killing them humanely, killing them young, when they can be caught on the ice, and before they eat their tonnes of fish.'

There were sneers, too. The 'armchair ecologists' and 'toxic environmentalists' espousing a 'new paganism' were getting rich on the suffering of seal hunters. Anti-sealing contributions rang the cash register for Greenpeace and 'Brian Davies travels with the jet set, alongside such ardent environmentalists as Brigitte Bardot. Pretty good for a small-town humane society volunteer.' Such redneck sentiments were hardly original, but you didn't expect to read them in the journals of the counter-culture.

Liberal pressure groups were also crowding in. Canadian Indians had formed a group called Indigenous Survival International to fight their corner. And during 1985, ISI's representatives gained publicity by attacking 'extremist animal rights groups' who were 'undermining the maintenance of traditional lifestyles that harvest renewable resources'. Hunting sounded a bit different put like that.

Some of Greenpeace's replies to this unaccustomed criticism sounded shrill and uncharitable. Moore told one of my colleagues in an interview for the *New Scientist*:

> The politicians of the North in their polyester suits perpetuate the myth of traditional culture. They are taking advantage of the noble savage syndrome. The tragedy is that the average Indian people think they are living a traditional lifestyle. At public meetings they tell you that their people are eating seal meat in their homes that night. But if you go to the Hudson Bay supermarket they've got their shopping carts filled with instant pizza mix. Sure, natives should have a place in the wilderness, but should they be allowed to bring their rifles and snowmobiles with them?

Greenpeace managed to duck the backlash over sealing, partly because the battle was largely won at that point, and partly because most sealers were poor white fishermen rather than Inuits, on whom the label 'Keep Off, Native Culture At Work' sat rather better. But the conflict between the rights of native hunters and their prey would not go away. It reached flashpoint not over sealing, but over trapping for furs. Despite campaigns by Friends of the Earth in the 1970s, London remained a major centre for the world fur trade, and the Hudson's Bay Company maintained important auction rooms there. In 1984, Greenpeace in Britain had launched a powerful campaign against the fur trade. Its centrepiece was a poster and cinema advertising campaign featuring a photograph by the well-known fashion photographer David Bailey. It showed an elegantly dressed woman dragging behind her a fur coat with blood streaming from it. The copyline, written by Bryn Jones, a former *Daily Mirror* journalist who was now Greenpeace UK's director, read: 'It takes up to forty dumb animals to make a fur coat. But only one to wear it.' It was a powerful image and brought the organisation contributions and grief in large and equal amounts. Many Greenpeace women were outraged by the sexism of the poster. Equally irate were the national offices in Canada and Denmark which had become sensitive to the 'natives' issue and were building links with the Inuit communities in Arctic Canada and Greenland.

Journalists in 1985 were sniffing an anti-Greenpeace story, and the campaign against furs, which had so far been confined to Greenpeace's London office, was clearly vulnerable. Stuart Wavell, a reporter for the *Guardian* – probably the paper read most by Greenpeace's British supporters – felt guilty that he might have misled his readers in an article the year before about the launch of the campaign. He put on his snowboots and set out for the trading posts of the North West Territories' fur trappers at Fort Rae near Yellowknife close to the Great Slave Lake. It was from there that Indians headed north beyond the treeline to set traps for caribou and white foxes, muskrats and beavers, sable and lynxes. They eat the meat and sell the furs to traders such as the Hudson's Bay Company. Their economies depend heavily on the fur trade.

'I spoke to chiefs, development officers, priests and politicians. I also met trappers on the Stagg River,' Wavell wrote in a long, hard-hitting article. 'They were unanimous in their belief that Greenpeace's anti-furs campaign would be disastrous for the Dogrib [a grouping of about 1,400 Indians] and sections of the Chipewya, Slavey, Hare and Loucheux Bands with whom they have combined as the Dene Nation.' Cindy Gilday at Yellowknife told him, 'We thought Greenpeace were the hope for the world in their concern for the environment, animals and their Indian brothers. Now they are attacking our way of life.'

George Erasmus, who represented the Dene Nation at Indigenous Survival International, demanded and got talks in Greenland with Greenpeace chiefs. Back in London, they were displaying an instrument which showed the cruelty of the fur trappers. It was the leg trap, a crude device in which an animal – whether fox or muskrat, lynx, caribou or beaver – could spend days alive and in agony before being killed and collected by hunters. Erasmus agreed it was cruel, but said, 'When you put it all together, they are picking the weak spots and building on them. They used the emotive issue of the killing of seal pups to shut down the whole seal hunt. That drastically affected the culture of native people. Now they are doing the same thing with fur – the concept of cruelty to animals caught in the leg trap. Through that one crack in the wall they are going to try and ban all fur in Europe.'

Whatever the rights and wrongs of the matter, the politics were clear. Greenpeace in London had got itself into a head-on clash with American Indians, whose myths had inspired many of the organisation's founders and one of whose legends had given the name to Greenpeace's most famous ship, the *Rainbow Warrior*. The London office, however, was adamant that it wanted to continue the campaign. That summer, Pete Wilkinson from the London office told me, 'The UK will not back down. We respect the lifestyle of the indigenous people, except that generally they are not indigenous. They don't live in igloos and their pelts go on to the international market. If they want the benefits of twentieth-century living, they must accept its morals.' In any case, he said, the campaign was aimed against

the international traders. This claim seemed at odds with
Greenpeace's publicity material, which was either about
trapping or about the 'dumb animals' who wore the products.

Something had to give and the McTaggart machine moved
into town to limit the damage. Before Greenpeace's annual
international council meeting in Britain that autumn,
McTaggart's young American lieutenant Steve Sawyer told the
press in the kind of civil service tones that Greenpeace saves for
its own affairs: 'The fur campaign was not something that the
rest of the organisation was behind, and it grew to the point
where it spilled over the borders of the UK in ways which were
unacceptable. There's nobody in the organisation who will say
that means we are in favour of the leg-hold trap or anything
like that. But that particular battle, and particularly the terms
of reference within which it was framed, is not one that we
want to take on at this time internationally.' More pertinently
he added: 'The way it was getting framed in the press was
Greenpeace against the people in Greenland and northern
Canada.'

Greenpeace UK was unceremoniously told to shut down the
campaign. When its staff refused, they were fired along with
their director, Bryn Jones, and told that they could reapply for
their jobs, but under a new boss. He was Lord (Peter)
Melchett, a young green-minded peer who farmed in East
Anglia using ecological methods, and who had been a junior
Labour minister in the 1970s. Unlike the leg trap, McTaggart's
kill was instant. Jones was gone. Mark Glover, who ran the
furs campaign, stalked off to set up a new organisation called
Lynx, based around Jones's and Bailey's original 'dumb animals' poster. Wilkinson accepted a new assignment – six
months' exile on a boat that tried and failed to set up a
Greenpeace camp on Antarctica. It was, perhaps, McTaggart's
nearest equivalent to the salt mines.

For the fur hunters and their families the die was already
cast. Greenpeace may have moved on, but it had substantially
reinforced growing public revulsion at the slaughter of animals
for their fur. In the three years that followed Greenpeace's
campaign, demand for furs fell in Britain by three-quarters and
dropped by 90 per cent in Holland. This was ironic since, as

one Canadian observer noted, Dutch farmers still killed half a million muskrats in leg traps each year to protect their crops.

As animals liberationists unconnected with Lynx or Greenpeace firebombed stores selling furs, the Hudson's Bay Company announced in 1989 that it would close its great London auction house. And in 1990 Harrods closed its fur department. Glover's Lynx organisation, which opposed terrorist tactics, talked of a campaign against ermine in judges' robes. It opened a shop in London's Covent Garden, selling clothes emblazoned with its stylish artwork, and ventured Stateside with an office in Los Angeles to cash in on a revolt against furs among Hollywood stars such as Kate O'Mara and Liza Minelli. Lynx's famous David Bailey poster would have to compete there with another animal rights slogan based around the horrors of the leg trap: 'Get a feel for fur; slam your fingers in a car door.' American fashion designers followed a British example of refusing to use real fur, while *Elle* magazine adopted a 'no fur' policy and Zsa Zsa Gabor sold her large collection of fur coats. The EEC announced plans to ban the import of furs from countries that use the leg trap and called for fur from trapped rather than farmed animals to be labelled. Green consumers were on the war-path and a trade that had once handled 40 million pelts a year was now down to perhaps 10 million.

Surveying the scene, Hugh Brody, author of several books on the Canadian Indians, said that the effect of the campaign 'has been dramatic and by and large uncontrollable. The economic basis of hunting families and, in the eastern Arctic, of whole communities collapsed.' He recalls that it was earlier intruders from the south that first forced native peoples to enter the fur trade; before that they had taken animals mostly for their meat. Over the decades, the hunters reorganised their lives to suit the needs of the European fur market, becoming dependent on the trade in skins. 'Their concern with the environment and love of nature ensured that even the peak of the fur trade did not result in the extinction of a single species.' He calls the 'moral righteousness' of the campaigners a 'new example of southern, imperialist intrusion'.

3

THE FoE FACTOR

Centre half and left wing

Friends of the Earth in Britain began life one hot August night in 1969 amid sand-dunes on a remote coastline in Ireland. There Edwin Matthews, an American lawyer based in Paris, met Barclay Inglis, a retired Scottish businessman who had been a director of the Milk Marketing Board. This unlikely pair shared a love of wildlife and were both members of a party organised by a local hotel to crawl in the Irish sand watching seals.

Inglis discovered that night that Matthews was a friend of a prominent American environmentalist, David Brower, who had very publicly resigned as executive director of the venerable Sierra Club – a conservation group made up largely of peole who walked the Sierra Mountains of the American West. Brower, who already had behind him a glittering career opposing plans for dams in the American West, was inspired by the new radicalism of the student campuses and, like many of the new wave of environmentalists round the world, saw the strident consumer advocacy being pioneered by Ralph Nader and his 'Nader's raiders' as a model. He had tried to radicalise the Sierra Club but failed. So, almost exactly at the time when disaffected members of the Club in Canada were launching Greenpeace, Brower quit to set up Friends of the Earth in the US.

Brower wanted an international organisation and had decided to set up national chapters of FoE round the world, appointing Matthews as his European talent scout. One of Matthews's first catches was a young Frenchman called Brice

Lalonde, who formed FoE in France and later took a post as environment minister in the administration of François Mitterrand. Inglis, by contrast, saw his role as encouraging the development of young British environmentalists. He and Matthews settled on three green-minded student activists to launch Friends of the Earth UK: Jonathan Holliman, Richard Sandbrook and Graham Searle. Unlike Lalonde, none have become household names, but all three remain influential figures in the environment movement today. The London office of FoE is, two decades later, the most important in the FoE family and the host to the FoE International office.

In those early months, Jonathan Holliman wrote the first British green consumer guide – two decades before a new version hit the bestseller lists. Today he works for FoE's office in Japan. Richard Sandbrook, plucked from the presidency of the student union of the University of East Anglia, is today the director of the UN-backed International Institute for Environment and Development in London. But FoE's first director was Graham Searle, who had a reputation as one of the cleverest of the new student radicals. He had been student president at King's College, London, doing deals at a time of student unrest with the principal, General Sir John Hackett, who came to academia after being Commander-in-Chief of the British Army on the Rhine. Searle then became full-time vice-president of the National Union of Students under the presidency of Jack Straw who 20 years on was a member of the Labour Party's front bench.

Brower's publisher, Ballantyne Books, gave Searle a room in the back of its London office in King Street, and a part-time job reading science-fiction manuscripts. Searle combined this with running FoE. At an early stage, Searle and Lalonde had persuaded Brower that each national office of FoE should have considerable autonomy – something which to this day sets them apart from the centrally controlled Greenpeace. Searle's plan was to create a small professional lobbying organisation, emphasising the virtues of sound research. Nobody wanted a mass membership, and 'it certainly wasn't democratic,' says Searle, who kept the power of hire and fire to himself. At one point, he imposed a rule that none of his growing staff could talk publicly on any subject until they had first spent six months on research.

Searle set his new organisation three campaigns. It won two of them, yet is best known for the one that it lost. Its first victory, one of the first by environmentalists against aspects of the fur trade, was against London's place as a world centre for furs from rare big cats. Searle's first wildlife campaigner was Angela King, a woman who is variously described by friends as 'a self-effacing woman from Dorset' and 'a fashion designer from New York' (both descriptions were true). Opposition to the furriers had surfaced during the 1960s, but FoE carried out detailed research into the international trade and successfully lobbied for an Endangered Species Act. In March 1972, it persuaded the British government to ban imports of furs from tigers, snow leopards and clouded leopards.

Searle, who was a geologist, also decided to take on Rio Tinto Zinc, the world's largest mining company, which wanted to dig the biggest copper mine in the world in the Snowdonia National Park in North Wales. He hired a former employee of RTZ and between them they so harried the company and the government that in September 1973 the scheme was abandoned.

What first put FoE on the map, however, was its demand for the return of the returnable bottle. By the early 1970s, the days of the 'tuppence back' on bottles of beer and pop were numbered. As a scientist, Searle had explored the energy-saving potential of returnable bottles with his energy campaigner, an American mathematician friend of Brower's called Amory Lovens. 'We weren't worried about the recycling of the glass,' says Searle today. 'It's only sand, after all, and wasn't an issue. But in energy terms, it made sense for the bottles to be returned, cleaned and re-used.' Searle knew well enough that energetics is not a populist issue – but a sense of waste is. FoE hit the front pages for the first time when it collected up some 1,500 non-returnable bottles and dumped them one morning on the doorstep of the biggest British manufacturer of drinks in non-returnables, Schweppes.

'The idea came up at a lecture I gave at the Institute of Contemporary Arts [ICA] in London. After my talk on energetics, somebody asked what they could do. I said we should campaign for recycling. And somebody in the audience suggested returning bottles. From the audience we collected two hundred bottles and things went from there.' Searle had on his books a young man called Pete Wilkinson, who possessed a licence to drive heavy goods vehicles. His truck showed up outside Schweppes London HQ one Saturday morning in May 1971 and 60 volunteers posed for cameras while delivering the bottles. A bemused caretaker and a large coterie of journalists were told by Searle that, 'In five years, Britain could produce enough bottles to build a pillar to the moon.'

FoE's unofficial biographer, Joe Weston, says, 'It was a new form of protest in Britain; it was peaceful yet confrontational; it was witty and at the same time made a recognisable and serious point about the wastefulness of the throwaway society that Britain was becoming.' But it never became the basis for a successful campaign to bring back returnable bottles. This was largely because the manufacturers responded to the pressure on them by promoting bottle banks. Customers could throw used bottles into skips for crushing and melting down to provide the raw material for new bottles. Says Searle, 'If sand was the issue that would be fine. But smashing up bottles and re-forming them uses just as much energy as making new glass. It is not what we had in mind.' Chris Rose, one of FoE's campaign strategists during the 1980s, believes that the initial publicity was almost too good. 'The trouble with a really successful publicity campaign such as that is that the public automatically assume after a while that it succeeded. You cannot persuade people that the Schweppes bottle dump was a failure. But the campaign did not stop the tide against returnable bottles.'

It did, however, launch FoE in fizzy campaigning style, though that brought its own problems. On the Monday morning after the dump thousands of people were on the phone wanting to join FoE. 'The organisation did not really want members and could not have a membership under its structure as a limited company,' says Weston. Meanwhile, all over the country enthusiasts were setting up dozens of local and entirely unofficial Friends of the Earth groups. It took many months to vet the groups and authorise the use of FoE's name.

By 1973, Searle had itchy feet. 'A danger with voluntary organisations', he says, 'is that people stay too long. I said I'd stay for two or three years. We had won cat skins and RTZ. It was a good point to leave.' He did, but not before coming up with a ruse to balance the books. Through the anti-furs campaign, Searle had met John Aspinall, the right-wing conservationist friend of the Goldsmith brothers, who owned the Clermont Club in Mayfair. There he set up a meeting at which Searle could ask for money from Aspinall's rich clients, who included James Goldsmith, the financier Jim Slater and the banker Lord Rothschild.

'Aspinall suggested that I bait them, because they would enjoy that,' says Searle. 'So I did. I attacked their investment policies for damaging the environment. I attacked their mining houses and the James Bay [hydroelectric] development in Canada. They grilled me in return. They had a good time and passed the hat round. I got fourteen thousand pounds. During backgammon afterwards, John suggested that I bet it all. I didn't, which was a great sadness. But it wasn't my money.'

James Goldsmith did not contribute to the 1973 hat-passing that night, but a few years later he helped pay for the expensive and time-consuming opposition launched by FoE to the Windscale nuclear reprocessing plant.

Many of Britain's sharpest environmental campaigners owe their apprenticeship to FoE, and a good many of them have landed up at Greenpeace. One of the first acts of the British branch of Greenpeace, when it was formed in 1977, was to poach Pete Wilkinson. A working-class boy brought up in Deptford, South London, he had begun his green career as one of the early appointments of Graham Searle and played left wing to Searle's centre half in their local football team. 'Wilks' was the one with the HGV licence, who had driven the truckload of Schweppes non-returnable bottles, and he drank at The Cheshire Cheese, a spit-and-sawdust pub off Fleet Street, with the *Daily Mirror*'s industrial editor of the early 1970s, Bryn Jones.

This link got the environment and FoE on to the front pages of Britain's most popular paper. Jones, fed with beer and ideas over lunch, made whaling a national issue just in time for FoE's first big rally on the issue in Trafalgar Square in 1972. And he brought nuclear waste to the attention of the British public in 1975, when FoE was fighting hard to force a public inquiry into the government's plans for a new nuclear reprocessing plant at Windscale (later renamed Sellafield in a vain attempt to expunge its appalling image, which had been generated largely by Wilkinson and Jones).

In October 1975, Jones told his readers in bold black type on the front page of the *Mirror* about a PLAN TO MAKE BRITAIN WORLD'S NUCLEAR DUSTBIN. It was a fine phrase, picked up from an article written earlier that year by FoE's nuclear expert, Walt Patterson. An American who had settled in London with his British wife, Patterson remembers Jones's piece well: 'Factually, it was so riddled with inaccuracies. But it hit the fan.'

Patterson won his public inquiry and set to work collecting evidence for the hearings. That work became FoE's most exhausting task for the next three years. Wilkinson, whose speciality was action rather than research, left to join Greenpeace's first London office, then being set up by the Canadian seals campaigner, Alan Thornton. Thornton had moved to London the previous year to campaign in the world centre for trade in seal pelts. His work had swiftly outgrown the desk he had been given in the offices of the British Union for the Abolition of Vivisection. So he and McTaggart moved to a small corner office with one phone five floors up in a liftless building off Whitehall.

From the start, Wilkinson's anti-nuclear campaigning at Greenpeace had a more gung-ho populist style than the relatively cerebral FoE as it prepared for the Windscale inquiry. 'We always researched our facts very carefully and erred on the side of understatement,' says Patterson. 'Greenpeace at that time was slapdash in its research and you could never accuse them of understatement.' During the subsequent Windscale wars, and skirmishes over nuclear waste, which ran on well into the 1980s, the contrasting styles of Wilkinson (who later

recruited to Greenpeace his old drinking friend Bryn Jones)
and FoE were very clear.

FoE embraced the public inquiry system, pouring resources,
including cash from James Goldsmith, into a rigorous case
against the reprocessing plans. FoE has always believed that
such public hearings are one of the few arenas in British public
life where complex arguments can be fully aired and government servants held to account. Friends of the Earth's arguments won widespread admiration at the Windscale hearings,
at that time Britain's longest ever public inquiry. But, while
Patterson graduated to become an internationally respected
authority in nuclear matters, FoE lost the battle and the new
plant was built. FoE's director at the time, Tom Burke, remembers, 'We pioneered things there, getting an inquiry and then
winning all the arguments. But the lesson we learned was that
it is the politics, not the arguments, that matter.'

Wilkinson at Greenpeace believed public inquiries were
fixed from the start. He preferred direct action. Thornton had
proposed a campaign against secret dumping of barrels of
nuclear waste by Britain in the Atlantic Ocean. Wilkinson set
out to locate the dump site, eventually stumbling on it after
noticing on a map of the Atlantic Ocean an area marked
'dumping zone' off the coast of Spain. He soon had inflatables
buzzing the annual British dumping operation. He found the
British nuclear authorities almost as violent as McTaggart had
found the French. One memorable photograph shows a fragile
inflatable having large drums of waste dropped on it, while
men aboard the nuclear vessel played high-pressure hoses at
the Greenpeace crew. 'The drums were missing us by inches
and there's this man on board shouting "It's your funeral." It
was unbelievable – we thought somebody was going to get
killed,' remembers Wilkinson.

The issue of the annual dump was developed into an international scandal by McTaggart's growing Greenpeace
European empire. Having grabbed public attention with its
derring-do on the high seas, the organisation took its case to
the scientific community and won the support of the only
regulatory authority, the voluntary London Dumping Convention, for a moratorium on dumping. The British authorities

felt exposed and when Wilkinson brought into play his trades union contacts and persuaded the National Union of Seamen to refuse to dump waste from boats in the Atlantic Ocean, the British suspended dumping.

With that disposal route for nuclear waste closed down, Wilkinson returned to a campaign launched by Greenpeace in 1979 against the nuclear reprocessing plant at Windscale. The plant was run by British Nuclear Fuels, which had already shown itself a determined opponent. In 1979, it had gone to the High Court to obtain an injunction preventing Greenpeace from interfering with ships bringing spent nuclear fuel from round the world to the reprocessing plant. When the actions continued, it had McTaggart, Wilkinson, Thornton and Greenpeace itself all fined for disobeying the injunction.

This time, Wilkinson declared his intention to try to close the plant, one of the largest nuclear operations in the world, and in November 1983, he attempted to place a bung in the end of the pipe discharging radioactive water into the Irish Sea off Windscale. For Patterson at FoE, the pipeline was dirty but of no great consequence. For the amphibious Greenpeace it was a lethal and potent symbol of destruction – and the most vulnerable point of the top-security and partly military Windscale operation. But BNF was not about to be rolled over by Greenpeace. Its extensive intelligence-gathering network had got wind of the plan. 'I still don't know how they found out,' says Wilkinson today. The company welded an anti-bung device, made up of two fierce prongs, to the end of the pipe. Then it set loose its lawyers. Wilkinson and Greenpeace found themselves in a long and wearying legal battle as BNF attempted to slap a series of injunctions on them preventing them from interfering with the pipeline. For some time, Wilkinson played a bizarre game of cat and mouse, moving flats almost daily in an effort to prevent BNF from serving him with a writ.

At one point, Greenpeace refused to give assurances in court that it would leave the pipeline alone. At which BNF applied to the courts for a sequestration of all Greenpeace's assets. In the end, Greenpeace paid around £50,000 in fines before giving up the bung battle. In 1986, it returned to the issue – very publicly

giving itself two years from 1986 to 1988 to force the closure
of the plant. But it failed to make any impression, despite
defying the legal injunctions again in June 1987, and inserting
inflatable rubber balls into the pipe. BNF threw copies of the
injunctions on to the deck of the Greenpeace ship, *Sirius*,
during the operation. Five months later, a Dutch member,
Hans Guyt, began three months in gaol for his part in breaking
those injunctions. Despite all the effort and the huge public
concern about the plant, this was one battle that Greenpeace
could not win. Some insiders say that the legal counter-attack
mounted by BNF depressed McTaggart, who feared that the
entire organisation could be hamstrung if other companies
combined to adopt similar tactics.

A forgotten feature of these nuclear battles is the contrasting
views on safety issues of Friends of the Earth and Greenpeace.
During the 1970s, FoE made little of the pollution or safety
hazards of nuclear power. (Indeed it is surprising to discover
that, despite its large portfolio of diverse campaigns, FoE
concerned itself remarkably little with any pollution issues
until it began campaigning on acid rain in the 1980s.) For
Greenpeace, on the other hand, the insidious threats of radia-
tion loomed large from the start. 'Save the Humans: No
Nukes' was one of its campaign slogans.

Patterson at FoE remembers the arguments of many other
environmentalists giving evidence at the Windscale inquiry
that radioactive waste from the Windscale pipe might be
accumulating on mudbanks in the nearby Ravenglass estuary
or contaminating sea life. 'So they might,' he says today. 'But
I've never been too concerned about nuclear seaweed. There
are hazards, but they are generally no worse than other
industrial hazards. I said that at the Windscale inquiry, men-
tioning lead in exhausts as one example, and I was heavily
criticised for it by other groups. At the inquiry, Friends of the
Earth was talking mainly about the problems of radioactive
waste management, about the dangers of weapons prolifera-
tion [fed by plutonium produced during the reprocessing] and
economics. On all three counts we have been borne out by
events. I think investment bankers are finding out today, in the
early 1990s, the things that we told them about in the 1970s.'

Frustration with their failure to dent the British nuclear industry led to a certain recklessness at Greenpeace by Jones and Wilkinson, who began to see conspiracies everywhere. In 1984, there was mounting public concern about the safety of flasks that carried nuclear waste on the nation's railways from power stations to Sellafield. There was talk that a railway accident could cover whole cities with fallout, making them uninhabitable. To stem the tide of speculation the state-owned Central Electricity Generating Board planned a spectacular public demonstration. It staged an accident, in full view of TV cameras, in which a train ran at 100 mph into the side of a flask. The flask was undamaged. But Greenpeace's George Pritchard called foul. He publicly alleged that engine mounting bolts had been removed from the locomotive for the demonstration, so reducing the severity of the impact on the nuclear flask. When challenged, he admitted to having no evidence for this charge and was later forced into making a full written apology.

Such embarrassing gaffes compounded unease felt at Greenpeace International by McTaggart and his new young American protégé, Steve Sawyer, about the British operation, which culminated, after the furs affair, in the purging of Jones and Wilkinson's departure to set up a permanent Greenpeace camp in Antarctica. After that task was completed, at the second attempt, Wilkinson retired from the fray to write his memoirs of 18 years in the environmental front line. From Schweppes to Sellafield and the South Pacific, nobody had done more to raise the green flag in Britain.

A kind of victory

The London office of Friends of the Earth is opposite a warehouse for civil service forms. Round the corner, the local pub has a large reproduction at the door, depicting a 19th-century whaling boat harpooning its prey. There's nothing like a daily reminder of your enemies.

It was a humid June day, the height of Britain's long, hot,

'green' summer of 1989. The receptionist was handling three calls at once and the campaigner I had come to see – Andrew Lees, an indefatigable harasser of any element of authority within range – was at the start of a 45-minute phone conversation with a business correspondent from Fleet Street. He had been up until 2 a.m. that morning gutting and refining his interpretation of yet another leaked document from his current prey, the soon-to-be-privatised water authorities. Now he was making sure Fleet Street got the message.

I sat and waited at reception. By the time Lees was free, I was walled in by deliveries of large cardboard boxes. Some contained hundreds of save-the-rainforest sweat-shirts, which were selling like crazy all over the city; others contained posters and leaflets advertising something called Arts for the Earth. This was a joint venture with the *Telegraph*, whose middle-class readers of south-east England were growing twitchy about their government's desire to build motorways, high-speed rail links and entire new towns in the green belt. That summer, the paper ran an environment story at the top of the front page almost every other day. It was happy to join forces with people whom a couple of years before it would have called cranks. This alliance had produced an art exhibition entitled 'Waters of Life' at the Snape Maltings near Aldeburgh in Suffolk, one of Britain's most fashionable arts venues. For, as the *Telegraph* reached out to the greens, so the muesli and sandals brigade were making a bid for the support of the yuppies.

The reception noticeboard on that June day, however, revealed that nothing much had changed at the heart of FoE. There were pleas for the return of lost cycle clips; various polemics ('Breastfeeding is an environmental issue'); a poster for the Gandhi Summer School, and several chalked-up requests for lifts to Glastonbury for the midsummer hippy festivities that weekend.

Lees was now off the phone and gasping for a cigarette. Up on the roof of the Friends' dilapidated five-storeyed building, half the staff were puffing away (smoking is banned indoors, of course). Lees – like most of the campaigners – was tall, white, male and well-spoken. He won his spurs with FoE as a volunteer in Norwich, turning a farmer's plan to drain a patch of water meadow on the edge of the Norfolk Broads into a test case for the government's commitment to protecting the countryside. Now on head office's 80-strong payroll, Lees seemed to be on TV or in the papers almost every day, gesticulating fiercely as he offered new disclosures about filthy rivers or poisoned tapwater. He had spent the previous six months running a campaign to demand that Britain's water be cleaned up, skilfully exploiting the media's sudden interest in what is normally a backwater topic, in the run-up to the privatisation of the water authorities. He didn't halt the sell-off, but he made such a dent in the government's £30 million advertising pitch that ministers completed the sale only after handing out more money in grants, indemnities and debt write-offs to the water authorities than they took in the sale itself.

Lees's bludgeoning zeal was convincing subeditors all over the country that the minutiae of European directives on drinking water were the stuff of hot news. Yet, despite the column inches, he seemed at odds with his boss, the successful director of FoE through its late-1980s renaissance, Jonathon Porritt. While Lees is the grammar-school pugilist, Porritt is the thinking man's green and, like his counterpart at the head of the UK branch of Greenpeace, Lord Melchett, an aristocrat.

An Old Etonian and son of a former Governor General of New Zealand, Porritt says he first 'communed with nature' when he spent a teenage summer chopping down trees in New Zealand. Whereas Lees thrives on conflict, Porritt, despite a radical 'deep green' ideology, believes, as one former colleague put it, 'in the ability of decent chaps to sit down and reach a civilised agreement'. A man at the *Telegraph* told me, 'We were looking askance at first at the idea of a tie-up with Friends of the Earth. But the management all said that Porritt was different. He was one of us.'

While Lees was burning the midnight oil on his exposés, Porritt was a regular on the radio, sitting beside Cabinet ministers on 'Any Questions' and choosing his favourite music on 'Desert Island Discs'. After five years in the job, Porritt was about to leave FoE for a career as author and TV presenter and, perhaps, to return to a leading role in the Green Party. His replacement was to be David Gee, a former leading trades union health official who had switched from the reds to the greens after falling out with his superiors. 'Personally, I'd prefer to be a plumber's mate than a philosopher's mate,' said Lees tartly. It'd been a long day.

June 1989 was Britain's greenest month. On the 15th, the Green Party swept up 15 per cent of the vote in elections for the European Parliament. And a PR firm announced that in a poll two-thirds of the British public said they would pay more for environment-friendly products. Of the two events, the second was rather more important to industrialists. Soon every product seemed to have some magic green ingredient.

Dyed-in-the-wool greens didn't know whether to laugh or cry. Was this victory? Tom Burke, who had been the first director of FoE to make *Who's Who*, said it was. 'Britain has gone green,' he told me. 'Not everybody realises it. But what did greens think winning would be like? Did they expect a parade with everybody saying Well Done? Secretly, I think a lot of campaigners did.' Others saw only commercial opportunism. Jonathon Porritt, Burke's successor in the late 1980s, said, 'Green consumerism is a target for exploitation. There's a lot of green froth on top.' Business was putting the con into conservation.

The deep green *Ecologist* magazine saw defeat. The language of the green movement had been taken over by the consumer society. 'Underlying the current green consumer boom is the idea that, with careful housekeeping, we can somehow have our cake and eat it,' the magazine boomed. This was 'no different to a belief in perpetual motion'. Consumerism was the problem, not the solution.

John Elkington, a long-time environmentalist and author with Burke of *The Green Capitalist*, had helped to start the bandwagon rolling the previous autumn with a bestselling book, *The Green Consumer Guide*. He argued that the consuming public could exert a 'positive influence . . . through our spending power'. Many campaigners had fumed puritanically that he was making money out of the environment business, like the makers of the products he was recommending, and some industrialists gasped at the rates charged by his consultancy business, SustainAbility, to point them on the path to a green and profitable future. Even Elkington's friends made double-edged comments. Richard North at the *Independent* newspaper said, 'Everyone always knew that he would be a success. He was wearing proper business suits when most of the eco-freaks hadn't found their way to the Oxfam shop for their first tweed jacket.'

Elkington was not to be deprived of his success. Sure, he said, ozone-friendly aerosols and phosphate-free detergents were only a beginning. But green consumerism was getting the message to a whole new audience, and you had to start somewhere. But critics said that he was trying to have it both ways. The point was reinforced weeks later when, having agreed in an interview that supermarkets were 'a cancer on the high street', he published *The Green Supermarket Guide*.

Everybody in the green movement, whether for or against the consumer society, had their favourite horror story of companies chasing the green premium. Friends of the Earth, hedging its bets on the big issue, offered the Green Con award. Rover, the car maker, won an early gong from FoE, as well as rapped knuckles from the Advertising Standards Authority, for a claim that one of its cars was 'capable of running on unleaded petrol. This means it's as ozone-friendly as it is economical.' The ASA quietly pointed out that lead damages babies' brains, not the ozone layer. 'We were green with ignorance,' pleaded Rover.

The ASA also hauled BP Oil over the coals for claiming that its 'Supergreen' brand of lead-free petrol caused 'no pollution to the environment'. How about contributing to urban smogs, acid rain and the greenhouse effect, for starters? And Citroën was told off for an advert for its new diesel-powered car which claimed 'while you're looking after the pennies, you're also looking after the planet; diesel is lead-free.'

The German firm AEG claimed that because its dishwasher used less water and electricity than some competitors, it was kinder to aquatic life. 'This contribution to the environment may seem minute. It isn't. If you're a newt.' Entertaining too was a firm of furriers that advertised its fox-fur coats as environment-friendly. The company argued that the

manufacture of artificial fur releases chemicals that damage
the ozone layer, whereas killing real foxes does not.

The German battery-maker Varta had seen the green trend
early, grabbing market share when it launched a mercury-free
'green' battery in Britain in 1988. Its competitors were struggling to make up ground. Duracell introduced its 'green' range
of long-life batteries, claiming that they contained no cadmium, a metal which, like mercury, is toxic. Smelling a green
rat, a trade newsletter called *Green Gauge* investigated. It
found that 'long-life batteries in Europe have contained no
cadmium for at least seven years. Duracell claim that it is valid
to say that the new range is cadmium-free because "consumers
believe cadmium is commonly present in batteries".'

The same newsletter had unearthed the embarrassing story
that Procter and Gamble's new green washing powder, Ariel
Ultra, had been tested on rats. It was turned into a front-page
lead for the most noisily green of the tabloids, *Today*, which
announced: 'Animals died for green soap suds . . . Mice and
rats were force-fed with Ariel Ultra until they died to check
that the detergent is safe for families.' The publicity undermined a £2 million launch the following week for the product.
'Ariel washes green' said the full-page adverts, though the only
specific claim it made for the powder itself was that it contained '30 per cent less chemicals'. What did that mean?

Washing, presumably because of its connotations with
cleanliness, was a fruitful area. Millions flocked to pay extra
for phosphate-free detergents made by Ecover and Ark, even
though water scientists insisted that phosphates in rivers came
mostly from fertilisers rather than washing powder. Washing-
up liquid was also advertised as phosphate-free, even though,
as the Royal Society of Chemistry pointed out, 'This product
never contains phosphates anyway.'

Then there was the 'green nappies war'. It was started by
Peaudouce, a Swedish company. In 1988, Sweden had been hit
by a public panic over the revelation that the standard
bleaching process for the pulp that makes up the absorbent
padding in disposable nappies can produce tiny amounts of
dioxin. A small amount of this can get into pulp mill effluent
that enters rivers. An even smaller amount might stick around

in the nappy. Baby's bum might be at risk. Peaudouce was well placed to meet this concern, having introduced a new pulp plant using a different chlorine-free, dioxin-free process. Indeed its advertising subsequently did much to introduce people to this new threat. London advertising agents Connell, May and Stevenson were soon covering hoardings with pictures of happy sleeping babies and copylines such as 'Green peace'. Peaudouce's share of the market jumped from 8 to 13 per cent.

As other firms leapt on to the dioxin-free bandwagon, Peaudouce tried to keep its green edge in the market by announcing a plastic lining to the nappy that was '81 per cent biodegradable'. Soon, it said, the glues that held the lining in place would be biodegradable, too. ENDS, a decade-old environment newsletter, decided to get to the bottom of the matter. It found that while the Peaudouce chlorine-free bleaching process was indeed dioxin-free, in tests its effluent killed more fish in rivers because it contained more of other pollutants.

Another booming business in the environment-friendly late 1980s was green investment services. Here, too, there was growing concern that there was as much hype as substance in some claims. Experience in the US had suggested that many of these environmental funds were investing in industries that most environmentalists had high on their hate lists. One review found that 'for the most part these funds invest in firms specialising in toxic and hazardous waste clean-up, air and water pollution control and . . . incineration plants.' The Environmental Awareness Fund, for instance, listed among its investments the manufacturers of nuclear power plants, waste incinerators and waste management firms that had featured in complaints from environment groups. The survey, in the journal *Catalyst*, concluded, 'These companies are not out to heal the Earth – they are set up to cash in on the booming waste industry. They . . . directly benefit from the production of waste – so do their investors. We should be channelling our investment dollars into ways of minimising the production of waste.'

In Britain, where the *Independent* newspaper said that more

than 150 financial products bearing an environmental label
had been launched during 1989, there were similar stories. The
first green personal equity plan, the Fellowship Trust, included
in its original portfolio shares in two companies which raised
hackles.

One was Rentokil, a pest-control firm that uses large
amounts of pesticides that are frowned on by many environment groups. The other was Coalite, which, while manufac-
turing smokeless fuel, had an unsavoury reputation for
creating serious air and water pollution around its factories.
Other noted polluters in its portfolio were Allied Colloids,
Leigh Interests, a large waste disposal firm, and Yorkshire
Chemicals.

The editor of ENDS, Marek Mayer, said, 'It doesn't look as if
some of the funds have done their homework.' But his journal
accorded generous space to one fund, the Merlin Ecology
Fund. Its head company scout was a well-connected green
campaigner, Tessa Tennant, most noted for bringing chic to
the green cause with a Green Ball in London in 1986. Merlin,
like its American counterparts, featured companies in the
clean-up business more than pollution-free manufacturers,
but its more sophisticated research enabled it to avoid firms
with a bad reputation in green circles.

Some may have wondered, nonetheless, what either an
advertising agency, Abbott Mead Vickers, or the owners of the
Safeway supermarket chain were doing in the portfolio. Safeway, it turned out, had come top in John Elkington's *Green
Supermarket Guide* and Elkington was an adviser to Merlin.

In North America, where the market for 'ethical investment', both green and otherwise, is more developed than in
Europe, some environment groups have become directly involved in the green consumer business. During 1989, 14 US
environmental groups joined religious groups and public pen-
sion funds in establishing the Valdez Principles fund, named to
commemorate the Exxon Valdez oil spill. In Canada, a group
called Energy Probe had set up its own Environmental Mutual
Fund, which featured among Canada's top ten mutual funds.

But arbitrating between various companies' claims to their
greenness is a thankless task that environment groups would

do well to avoid. There is no consensus about what to measure. Elkington went out of his way to praise the responsibility of many multinationals, including the oil giant Shell, for its efforts to mitigate the impact of its activities in Europe and North America. But others point to the nature of Shell's businesses. It is among the world's top five traders in oil, the planet's largest source of air pollution. It is one of the biggest of the new giant global seed companies, at a time when these companies' products are under attack from environmentalists for undermining peasant agriculture in the Third World. And in 1990 it came under sharp attack in Thailand for a scheme to plant large tracts of Thailand with eucalyptus trees.

ICI, another winner of Elkington's bouquets, is a prodigious polluter of Britain's waterways and was the last of the world's top manufacturers of CFCs publicly to accept the case that they were damaging the ozone layer.

One of the most dangerous mistakes for environment groups has been to endorse products themselves. When Canada's Pollution Probe (no relation to Energy Probe) agreed to endorse and take royalties from sales of biodegradable nappies and other products sold by Loblaws, part of the giant Canadian conglomerate, Weston, staff resignations and public protests led to the resignation of Probe's director, Colin Isaacs. Isaacs had appeared personally in some advertisements. Was he reaching out to industry, demonstrating that the environment and profits could go together? Or was he undermining one of the environment group's strongest assets, its absence of economic self-interest?

The WWF has for many years allowed its logo to be used on products without attracting much criticism. 'The customer feels he is helping nature by buying our products,' said one manufacturer of tissue paper quoted in WWF publicity. It wasn't very clear whether the WWF went along with this view or whether, as its brochures to companies suggest, it viewed the endorsement as a straight business transaction. But the WWF may be increasingly called to account by other green groups suspicious of its many formal and informal links to big business. Pat Adams at Probe International in Canada (which is related to Energy Probe but not Pollution Probe) got angry when the WWF entered into an agreement with Petrocan, the Canadian oil giant. They collaborated on a book on Canadian endangered species, which was handed out at petrol stations. The names of the two organisations appeared together on TV advertisements and, in return for being allowed to use the WWF name on its products, Petrocan gave money to the WWF's biodiversity project.

The problem, says Adams, was that 'at the time Probe International was receiving many complaints from environment groups in Ecuador about Petrocan building a road right through the rainforest to get at oil.' Adams complained to the WWF, which agreed to intervene in Ecuador. 'It put pressure on its partner, Petrocan, to take steps to ensure that illegal settlers did not invade the rainforest around the road.' The WWF came out of the controversy smelling of roses, says Adams.

In London, some greens worried that consumerism was subverting their work. One newspaper supplement ran a spread on the 'young, gifted and hippest fun things around'. There was a Guardian Angel, an up-market club bouncer, a Staffordshire bull-terrier, lots of Chanel, lots of leather and a copy of the 'hottest green manifesto from Ark'. Copy these fashions, it said, 'and you too could be crucial for five minutes'. Well, that was about as long as Ark lasted on the scene.

Ark was launched in 1988 as an attempt to combine consumerism with environmentalism. It was the brainchild of Bryn Jones, the former *Mirror* man and director of Greenpeace in Britain. Sting and Anita Roddick of the Body Shop put up cash. At the launch, as one newspaper put it, 'Dustin Hoffman was photographed on intimate terms with the new [green] washing powder.' Ark marketed its own brand of phosphate-free washing powder, opening the way to a massive scramble for the new green washing market a year later. It attracted rock stars and, perhaps fatally for Jones, the board was augmented by Isaac Tigrett, the American founder of the Hard Rock Café in London. Jones said later, 'I wanted a democratic environmental movement with a commercial arm. Isaac, as a commercial man, wanted an environmental arm that would give the products credibility . . . even the smallest decisions became a trial of strength.'

It ended in tears. Jones's first campaign, a dramatic prediction that the greenhouse effect would raise sea-levels by five metres by 2050, was shot down as alarmist even by other greens. Then Chrissie Hynde – singer with the Pretenders, ardent vegetarian and Ark convert – told a journalist who asked about her green credentials that 'I have been firebombing McDonald's'. It was a stupid joke, especially as the commercial end of Ark was then preparing plans for a chain of 'veggie-burger' houses. Then someone did firebomb a McDonald's. Jones wanted Hynde to resign from the board. Tigrett wanted her to stay on. There were injunctions and Jones, who had mortgaged his house to help launch Ark, bailed out.

At Ark, business and greenery did not mix. But in the summer of 1989 everybody wanted to think differently. In central London the shop window for the green movement is the London Ecology Centre, in Covent Garden, the heart of chic consumerland. The place is a monument to the new greenery. Out have gone nearly all the books. I found a couple of picture books on whales and seals and, of course, *The Green Consumer Guide*. The shelves were taken up instead with piles of boxes of 'environment-friendly' washing powder and washing-up liquid. There were save-the-rainforest T-shirts and postcards and pain-free cosmetics. The days when greens wanted to feed their heads seemed to have passed.

4

IN AFRICA

To catch a poacher

When Alan Thornton took his lunch box to the Canadian High Commission in London in 1976 to read the files on seals, he became the first Greenpeacer to conduct serious deskbound research for a campaign. In the decade that followed he perfected the business of investigation as both bookworm and sleuth. After leaving Greenpeace in the early 1980s, he formed a new organisation called the Environmental Investigation Agency as a vehicle for his work. From a small office in Islington, North London, round the corner from the British offices of both Greenpeace and Friends of the Earth, he set out to avoid the headline-hogging style of Greenpeace and pursued anonymity. 'It's hard to do undercover work if you've had your photograph plastered all over the papers,' he says. 'So we keep a low profile. The trouble is that if people haven't heard of you, it can be hard to get funding.'

The pay-off for quality research can be considerable, however. And the man who sold his first piece of writing (on seals in 1976) to the doyens of investigative journalism at the *Sunday Times* is now, in effect, running his own Insight team. The high-point so far has been a two-year investigation into the international ivory trade, which triggered an escalation of public concern that led to the ban on the trade introduced in January 1990.

The EIA's work is a shrewd mixture of painstaking litera-ture searches and cloak-and-dagger bravado with a 16-mm camera. The ivory inquiry, funded by the Animal Welfare Institute in the US, began with a six-month study of published information about the ivory trade. But such information was sparse. By the late 1980s, four tusks out of every five in the market were poached. Some of the best clues to the nature of the trade came from court reports in local papers – a Zimbabwean caught on the Botswana border carrying tusks hidden in a Tanzanian truck, for instance.

Thornton, a tall soft-spoken Canadian, remembers that work started 'when I met someone who told me about an ivory-smuggling boat doing a run from East Africa to Dubai.' It was a good tip. Dubai was the home at that time for a processing factory for poached ivory, run by a Mr Poon. Thornton claims that the factory was at one time 'responsible for the deaths of a hundred thousand elephants a year'. It yielded some of his most memorable film – captured when he persuaded the owner of a neighbouring factory to raise his photographer on a fork-lift truck high into the air for a peep over the wall. The pretext was that he needed footage of an adjacent Black & Decker factory for a film on trade in Dubai. The film formed the basis for a three-part story on ITN that was sold round the world and forced the closure of the factory. 'We usually try to sell such film, but this time we decided to give it away to get maximum distribution. It was vital, but it must have lost us tens of thousands of pounds,' he says.

For many campaigners that coup would have been sufficient. Thornton was pleased by it. 'It was well known in the trade that a Dubai factory was a major centre for the trade. But nobody had bothered to gather the evidence and make something of it.' But he had a greater ambition. 'There is no point in putting the spotlight on a few poachers, the odd trading link, or even one factory. If you shut them down, another quickly opens. Such scandals have come and gone before. We decided that we had to get in deep. It was necessary to uncover the whole trade, the people who ran it and those who had permitted it to flourish. We didn't go public for a full year. We didn't even tell other environment groups what we were doing.'

The result, when it was finally published in full in the autumn of 1989, was a devastating piece of investigative journalism called 'A System of Extinction'. Here was the Poon family, based in Hong Kong, the world's main trading centre for worked ivory, supplied with ivory from the notorious factory in Dubai, which was also owned by the Poons. Here were the Japanese firms that financed the Poons, and the front companies and trading routes that took poached ivory from Africa via Europe and Singapore to Hong Kong.

Thornton named other major figures, such as the Lai family, also from Hong Kong, and Wang Kuo Tong, who has links with French-speaking Africa and whose ivory often travelled through Belgium. Then there was the Pong family, for whom, he claimed, Chong Pong has operated from Pretoria for 30 years, trading in ivory taken from throughout southern Africa. There was the whiff of political scandal, with Pong charged with operating with some kind of official sanction because of his role in sanctions-busting imports and his alleged close relationship with the security services. Also named as a leading figure in the trade was Anthony White, a former member of the Rhodesian secret services, who in 1980 attempted to blow up the Zimbabwean guerilla leader, Joshua Nkomo.

In the Zimbabwe of 1989, too, Thornton's investigations revealed evidence of soldiers poaching in Hwange National Park and their role in protecting the local ivory traders. He claimed that South Africa used poaching as part of a deliberate policy to destabilise neighbouring countries such as Mozambique. Two rebel groups backed by South Africa during the 1980s, Unita in Angola and Renamo in Mozambique, poached ivory to finance their activities.

With photographs and copies of ships' manifests, false passports and company shareholders' lists, Thornton and his colleagues provided detailed documentation for many of the vague claims that environmentalists had made over the years about the operation of a clandestine business that had killed an estimated 2,000 elephants each week for the previous decade.

But perhaps Thornton's most remarkable material relates to the operation of the secretariat to CITES – the Convention on International Trade in Endangered Species. He showed how the CITES secretariat, far from maintaining a civil service ethic, had, under its secretary-general Eugene Lapointe, lobbied against the growing calls for a ban on the ivory trade. And he showed how its activities, notably in offering periodic amnesties for stockpiles of poached ivory, had often served to strengthen the monopolies of the top Hong Kong trading families. 'Thanks to Lapointe,' he alleged, the families 'achieved control of the international ivory trade, pushed ivory prices through the roof and caused further destruction of Africa's elephants.'

Thornton launched a sustained attack on one of CITES' consultants, Ian Parker, for opposing a ban on the ivory trade. Besides being the author of several respected books on the ecological role of elephants, Parker claims to have shot several thousand elephants himself. Thornton accused him of 'carefully concealing' his business connections with the legal ivory trade and of a 'clear conflict of interests' that had been ignored by Lapointe.

Missing from the report, however, is Thornton's anger about the role of the World Wide Fund for Nature (WWF) and its sister organisation the International Union for the Conservation of Nature and Natural Resources (IUCN) in the tragedy of Africa's elephants. These bodies were the traditional post-colonial repositories of expertise on the conservation of African wildlife, and their advice was accepted by most African governments. And yet they had held the line for almost three decades against growing calls for a ban on the ivory trade. They argued that such a ban would drive the trade underground, and they believed that the legal ivory trade was an important source of revenue for African countries, and could help to pay for more wardens in national parks. But instead they had presided for almost a decade over a boom in the trade in poached ivory, a boom only possible under the camouflage created by the existence of the smaller parallel legal trade.

Because of the failure of the WWF to take its responsibilities seriously during the 1980s, Thornton says, 'the public simply did not know about the slaughter going on in Africa.' The IUCN, as the repository of scientific expertise about the state of the elephants, 'should bear the brunt of the criticism for the failure to act. They prevaricated for ten years, refusing to acknowledge the failure of their policy to promote "sustainable use" of this resource.' Thornton lobbied hard with friends at the WWF in the US and in East African capitals throughout early 1989, using unpublished material from his researchers. There was, he said, no alternative to a ban. While there was a large market in the rich world for ivory there would always be people willing to risk their lives to satisfy it. The problem could never be solved in Africa. It had been created outside the continent, and had to be solved there.

On 18 July 1989, President Daniel Arap Moi of Kenya brought Nairobi's international press corps to a national park in the middle of his country. There he set fire to a pyre of some 2,000 elephant tusks – roughly 12 tonnes of ivory – seized by his park rangers from poachers who had been killing the elephant population in the park. He wanted to demonstrate the new-found determination of himself and his new director of wildlife and conservation, the anthropologist Richard Leakey, to stamp out the booming trade in illegal ivory. The trade had reduced Kenya's elephant population by perhaps three-quarters during the 1980s.

For some, the bonfire was a futile and ridiculous gesture. Moi could have sold the ivory on the open market for almost £2 million in much-needed hard currency and paid the wages for more park rangers. Economists said that the destruction of so much ivory would simply force up the market price, encouraging poachers to take even greater risks with his rangers in search of their fortune. To most conservationists, however, it looked like a clear message to the poachers that their days of clandestine support from within Moi's administration were numbered. What was beyond doubt, was that Moi's fire provided a telling symbol of the failure of conservation policies adopted over more than three decades, since before independence, in the national parks of East Africa.

1989 was the year of the elephant. While the greenhouse effect, shiploads of toxic waste, and spectacular election successes by various green parties across Europe all briefly hit the headlines, none had the staying power and sheer emotional appeal of the African elephant. The story broke publicly in June with the publication of a new estimate, commissioned by the WWF, of the elephant population of Africa. The study concluded that numbers had halved in the previous decade, to around 600,000 animals. At least 70,000 elephants were being shot each year, mostly by poachers supplying a vast international trade in ivory from the elephants' tusks. About half of the ivory ended up in Japan. As one paper put it, 'The greatest mammal ever to have walked the earth is hurtling towards extinction.'

The small print of the report revealed that the new estimate of the elephant population was not quite as unexpected as the publicity suggested. It was a little under 20 per cent lower than previous estimates – comfortably within the margins of error for studies of this sort. Part of the reduction was due to a new way of estimating the numbers, but most was due to increased poaching. At the beginning of the 1980s, there had been widespread reports that East Africa's game reserves were overstocked and the elephants were becoming a menace. But the hue and cry that developed around the survival of elephants in 1989 had as much to do with politics as population biology.

There was the pressure created by Thornton's revelations both about the ivory trade and the operation of CITES. This helped to convince the Tanzanian authorities that existing policies had to change. There was the politics of the Kenyan game reserves. Moi was panicking as much about gangs in his national parks threatening tourists as about the decline in elephants. A series of well-publicised murders of white tourists and a zoologist, combined with the tales of poaching, were giving prospective $200-a-day tourists the impression that the parks were just a little too wild and untamed for their safety. Tourist revenues were threatened.

And there was the politics of the WWF. The rich American arm of the organisation, with an income approaching $30 million a year from public donations, had been stung by pictures in the US press showing dead elephants with the message that the WWF supports the ivory trade. Several thousand American supporters of the WWF had resigned over the issue.

Since the days of Huxley the WWF, especially in Europe, had held to the view that the key to protecting elephants was not to ban trade in ivory but to control it, largely by strict policing of national parks in which most elephants lived. But

African governments and their advisers from the WWF could not devise effective ways to police the reserves, nor could they find ways of persuading their citizens that the elephants were worth more alive than dead. Thornton's report exposed in gory detail the size of the multi-million-dollar industry that had flourished under their very noses.

The pressure for a change in policy at the WWF was building up. As one insider put it, 'The new information on the size of elephant populations provided the excuse they needed to make the change.' The abrupt policy switch came in June 1989. It was only two months since the WWF had joined with other bodies, including African governments, to launch a four-year African Elephant Action Plan aimed at improving policing of key elephant populations. It had specifically excluded a ban on the ivory trade. Now that policy was to be turned on its head. A lot of people inside the WWF from both sides of the argument were seething about the manner of the change. The fund-raisers in the US, the Europeans felt, were determining conservation policy. The tail was wagging the dog.

Soon Western governments, including Britain and the US, added their voices to calls for a ban. The move was then pushed through a meeting of CITES. By the end of the year, the Japanese, the biggest importers of ivory products, had announced that they would pull out of the trade and even the piano-makers Steinway had said that they would no longer fit ivory keys to new pianos.

The great U-turn on elephants was ungraciously accomplished. At the CITES meeting, WWF staff joined in the general outrage that the large Japanese ivory industry was funding the CITES ivory unit, which had for several years helped to police the international ivory trade. They rather ignored the fact that five years before, the WWF had helped to organise this funding, boasting to general approval that it had agreed to channel the money through its Japanese office.

Unabashed at such setbacks and determined to regain the high moral ground in the elephant business, the WWF also made its pitch for cash. It held eight simultaneous press conferences round the world to publicise its report and relaunched an amended African Elephant Action Plan. 'At least £12 million is needed urgently,' WWF said. It expected to raise some £500,000 during 1989 to help save the African elephant. Most of its money would be spent on Africa's national parks.

The ban on the ivory trade came into force in early 1990 and caused an immediate and spectacular drop in trade, with many reports of traders in poached ivory shutting up shop. However, a loophole opened when the British government announced that it would allow six months for the sale of 670 tonnes of ivory, the world's largest stockpile, held in Hong Kong. Angry campaigners said that this stay of execution for the remains of perhaps 70,000 elephants would allow the syndicates time to switch to an entirely illegal trade.

Unconvinced that the demand would be shut down, East Africa rounded up poachers. In late 1989, 4,000 troops went on a little-publicised swoop through Tanzania, arresting some 2,000 poachers and seizing huge quantities of ivory. And Kenya was gearing up to intensify its war on the poachers.

In announcing its revised African Elephant Action Plan in late 1989, the WWF revealed that it had recently provided 'funds to maintain and operate five aircraft used in anti-poaching operations in the giant Tsavo National Park in Kenya', and was about to step up the number of anti-poaching rangers in the Selous Game Reserve in Tanzania, home of Africa's largest population of elephants.

So what were these anti-poaching operations that the WWF was helping to pay for? A month after Moi made a bonfire of poachers' tusks, *Today* newspaper in London helpfully sent one of its reporters, Gerard Evans, for an on-the-spot report on the activities of Kenya's new director of conservation, Richard Leakey. The article was terrifying – and not only for what it told about the carnage among elephants. It raised serious questions about the propriety of what was being undertaken in the national parks of East Africa in the name of the WWF.

According to Evans, the score after two months of Leakey's new 'get tough' game of hide and seek with poachers was one dead elephant and 30 dead poachers. '*Today* was invited to witness the new Kenyan fighting rangers, equipped with 200 of the latest German-made G3 assault weapons, a fleet of 50 new army trucks, spotter planes and helicopter gun ships,' Evans reported. Game wardens were being 'moulded into paramilitary fighting men with shoot to kill orders' by Sandhurst-trained Captain Henry Manlenya. Evans called the operation 'more akin to the Green Berets than Greenpeace'. Quite so. This was not conservation, it was civil war.

As Evans remarked without a hint of disapproval, 'Concern for the elephant population is restricted largely to the grim reality that if the holidaymakers stay away, the stability of Kenya is threatened.' Money talks louder than elephants. The former warden of a Kenyan national park had calculated that year that each elephant in his park was worth £40,000 each year to the nation in tourist revenues.

The enemy, so far as the Kenyans were concerned, were the Somalis who live in large areas of the remote Northern Frontier Territory of Kenya, an area which many Somalis regard as properly part of a Greater Somalia. They come poaching with AK47 rifles and, according to some reports, use the money gained from selling tusks to buy more arms for their own civil war within Somalia.

The Somalis have a bad reputation throughout the Northern Territory. It has been bandit territory since colonial times – a remote region where Richard Leakey, in his other role as the country's chief anthropologist, once had charge of more than 1,000 square kilometres of 'protected area'. Human fossils were scattered in profusion and nobody could so much as lift a rock without Leakey's permission. George Adamson, the 'lion man' of the Kora National Park who was shot dead in the bush in mid-1989 as the counter-attack against poachers began, may have been killed by Somalis. He once said, 'The Somalis are the most destructive people on earth. They've turned their own country into desert and will do the same in Kenya.' As Bill Woodley, head warden of the Tsavo National Park said of dead Somalis gunned down by his rangers, 'Serves them right, too.'

Others take a more sympathetic view. Marcus Colchester spent six years at Survival International in London fuming at the number of times that the WWF turned up on the wrong side in his battles to help cultural minorities round the world. He says, 'In north-east Kenya, the authorities have never recognised any autonomy for the local Somalis. They fear the annexation of the land to create a Greater Somalia, and so there has been a heavy regime up there, with emergency legislation in place since before independence.' The Somalis, he says, have been excluded from the development of the country, deprived of their land, their liberties and sometimes their lives. In 1984, Survival International documented the death of 124 people in the area at the hands of police. Now, it seems, park rangers have joined the front line. For Colchester, 'Somali dissatisfaction is at the root of the poacher problem in Kenya. If the Kenyans had worked with the Somalis, giving them political rights and grazing rights, there would be far fewer problems.'

Richard Leakey's bloody war against the poachers, backed with equipment and donations from the WWF, is the unacceptable face of an approach to conservation that tries to separate people from animals. It is an old issue.

Huxley's original appeals for action to save African wildlife, made in a series of articles in the *Observer* newspaper in 1960, clearly saw the natives, notably the Masai in Kenya and Tanzania, as being in conflict with their natural environment. Masai cattle were 'rapidly reducing large stretches of land to dusty semi-desert,' he wrote. Nowhere in his articles did he wonder at how East African wildlife survived in such profusion and for so long in the face of these perfidious natives. Nor did he consider whether the arrival of Europeans, who took much of the best Masai land for themselves, might have been part of the problem.

The crisis between conservation and people in East Africa was discussed at a conference of conservation and development experts at the end of 1988 in Arusha, Tanzania, the scene of Julius Nyerere's ringing declaration 17 years before that an independent Africa would be safe for wildlife. The scene was appropriate for other reasons, too. It is the heart of the game reserve region of East Africa. Nearby are such famous reserves as the Masai Mara, Amboseli and Serengeti National Parks. Arguably, a film made in the late 1950s, 'The Serengeti Must Not Die', did as much as anything to generate the public

concern for African wildlife that launched the WWF. The
entire region was also once the undisputed land of the Masai,
pastoralists who for centuries moved around the plains with
their cattle. Far from obliterating the wildlife, they lived
peaceably within one of the greatest wildlife areas in the whole
world. Yet white colonialists and their successors, after drastically reducing the numbers of many animals through hunting,
felt the need to establish game reserves and move the people
from the land. Initially, the idea was to create hunting lands,
but later conservation became the cause. In Tanzania alone,
more than 25,000 square kilometres of Masai land is now set
aside for wildlife. At the same time as the wildlife parks are
being put out of bounds to their former owners, other parts of
the Masai lands are being encroached on, with government
encouragement, by farmers with ploughs. The Masai are being
inexorably fenced in.

The result is conflict, between the Masai and the farmers and
the Masai and the park rangers. A report from the Arusha
conference concluded that 'disenchantment with conservation
has antagonised [the Masai] and made them less willing
defenders of the wildlife they once so well preserved.'

The Serengeti region contains at least half of all the wild
animals in Tanzania and Kenya and is perhaps the most
prolific area for large animals in the world. At its heart are the
protected areas, such as the giant Serengeti National Park in
Tanzania which extends into Kenya, where it is called the
Masai Mara.

Over the years, conservationists have repeatedly sought to
extend the reserves, to separate the Masai and the wildlife yet
further. Huxley in 1960 called for the creation of a giant Masai
National Park – a piece of Orwellian Newspeak, since it
would have restricted the independence of the Masai still
further. As recently as mid-1988, the Masai were thrown out
of the Mkomazi where they had lived since long before the area
was declared a game reserve. Elsewhere, wildlife has been
given extra protection in various 'buffer zones' and 'dispersal
areas'. Rarely are local people consulted about the creation
of these buffer zones.

A paper presented to the Arusha conference concluded that

'the conventional insular and often autocratic approach to conservation has taught the Masai to exercise the utmost caution and suspicion in dealing with protected area authorities. They view the innovations floated under the names buffer zones, dispersal, conservation and management areas as mere disguises to secure continued free utilization by wildlife of range resources on what remains of their land.'

During the 1950s, the Ngorongoro highlands in Tanzania, east of the Serengeti, were the centre of a bitter dispute over demands that the Masai be expelled from the entire highlands. The debate had almost as much heat as that generated today by concern for the fate of the Amazon rainforest. Under pressure from conservationists, the British administrators told the indigenous people to leave both the Serengeti and the Ngorongoro regions.

The Masai refused to go and, fearing a replay of the Mau Mau rebellion going on across the border in Kenya, the authorities looked for a compromise. The British governor, Sir Richard Turnbull, zoned the Serengeti as a national park, but agreed to allow the Masai to use the Ngorongoro area. He told a meeting of the Masai Federal Council in August 1959, 'It is the intention of the government to develop the [Ngorongoro] crater in the interests of the people who use it. At the same time, the government intends to protect the game animals of the area. Should there be any conflict between the interests of the game and the human inhabitants, those of the latter must take precedence.' His promises were reinforced by the views of Huxley who believed that national parks 'would strengthen the position of the Masai in the Kenya of the future, where they will be competing for prestige and political power with the Kikuyu and Bantu tribes'.

Such optimism seemed to show little understanding of the extent to which the Masai relied on their environment to survive. Today, the Masai are deprived of the water sources of the western Serengeti on which they used to rely, and are prevented from cultivating their land. 'The majority of families in a community of previously well-off pastoralists are falling destitute at the hands of conservation,' the Arusha conference heard. Most have received no cash compensation for the loss of their lands. The colonial authorities advised the WWF that there was no need or duty to give natives a part of the income from the tourist trade in the national parks. Nor were there jobs. A recent survey of the Ngorongoro conservation area found that of 280 employees of the conservation area, only seven come from the local community. The Masai are reduced to gathering honey to make into honey beer, to illegal cultivation of land where they can get away with it and, of course, to becoming ready recruits in the service of the poachers.

Meanwhile, the Nogorongoro crater is not, as Turnbull promised, being used in the interests of the Masai. They are not allowed in. The crater is a large extinct volcano covered by grassland that was used by the Masai's cattle at the end of the dry season, when other sources of food approach exhaustion. Today no humans are allowed to enter through either of the two entry points, except by government bus. As the author Patrick Marnham put it in a penetrating essay on the area:

> The African crater came to an end when the Masai, who had enriched its life, were banished from it. Now that has been succeeded by a European crater, empty of man as an inhabitant, but seething with man as a day-tripper . . . But nothing could be more forced than the pretence that Ngorongoro is in some way preserved from human influence. The magnificent display of unspoiled nature is as artificial as a safari park in the grounds of an English stately home.

In Marnham's view those who sought to meet the challenge of the famous wildlife film of the 1950s that 'The Serengeti Must Not Die' have killed it in order to save it.

The tragedy is that the people who sustained and nurtured Africa's greatest wildlife reserve are being steadily alienated from it and forced to see the animals in it as their enemies. When Moringue Parkipuny, a Masai leader and Tanzanian MP, joined American Indians at a conference in the US to discuss the common fate of native peoples in the 20th century, he spoke of how the newly independent nations of Kenya and Tanzania have over the past 25 years 'pushed out people who had lived in harmony with wild animals' in the name of

defending the new national parks. 'The wild animals are free to
graze as much as they want outside the parks . . . but the Masai
are not allowed to go with their cattle inside the parks,' he said.

The WWF offers African nations the idea of national parks
as a way to preserve wildlife, while earning foreign exchange.
The Masai see things rather differently. 'Money is being made
by the local government,' said Parkipuny, 'the governments of
Tanzania and Kenya, local enterprise and international capi-
talists. But the people [the Masai] who have made certain
historical contributions to the survival of these animals, they
don't get a single cent.' The Masai, he said, 'are turning against
wild animals because now they have been brought up to
realise that the main cause of their suffering is wild animals.
They say that it is better that these wild animals disappear.'

Finally, he turned his attention directly to the 'international
wildlife conservation organisations based in the US', naming
the WWF and others as 'active in supporting and propping up
the anti-people preservation strategies in East Africa. These
organisations have not come round to recognising the link
between indigenous culture and the survival of the wildlife
heritage in the developing countries.' People who support the
WWF 'make their contributions with the understanding that
the money is going to be put to good use to protect ecological
species. But that money is being used to destroy indigenous
cultures.' It is a charge awaiting an answer.

Alan Thornton, from his rather different perspective as a
Western defender of elephants, finds common cause with the
Masai. He too believes that the WWF's great experiment in
establishing national parks to protect African animals has
failed. Centrally imposed conservation strategies simply do
not work, he says. 'We have to move towards putting native
people in charge of their wildlife.' They understand the importance to their survival of elephants and the rest of the
wildlife far better than Huxley and his successors can ever
hope to. He sees no contradiction between this view and his
determination to shut down the ivory trade. Far from it. The
creation of the international ivory market is an important part
of the disruption from outside that has overtaken life on the
plains of Africa. 'If the market remains, there will always be

people prepared to kill elephants and officials willing to be bribed to look the other way. You have got to close the market,' he says. 'We have stressed all along the responsibility of the consumer nations in stopping the slaughter.'

Parks and people

All over Africa, peasant farmers and nomadic peoples have been cast as enemies of their own environment. In 1989, Survival International sent urgent protests to Quett Masire, the president of Botswana, after his government announced plans to expel tribal people, including Bushmen from the Central Kalahari Game Reserve. The reserve, which is about the size of Switzerland, was established in 1961, five years before independence, in part to protect the traditional life of the Bushmen. Today, Masire says that the few hundred Bushmen and Bakgalagadi in the reserve, who rely for their livelihood on hunting wild animals and gathering wild plants, 'pose a threat to the wildlife'.

Survival International has another explanation for the move to expel the Bushmen. The majority population of Botswana, the Tsawana, are cattle rearers. In recent years, thanks to loans from outside aid agencies such as the World Bank, some of them have become very rich by carving giant ranches out of the country's grasslands, which were until recently communally owned. These new beef barons include the president himself and most of his government.

There is growing evidence that overgrazing by cattle on these ranches is damaging the fragile soils. Yet, despite the risks and a long series of defaults on previous loans, the World Bank in 1985 approved another $10 million to the Botswana government for more ranches. Confusingly, it called the project the 'Tribal Lands Grazing Policy'.

Botswana's growing cattle industry has taken a heavy toll on both the wildlife and the lives of the Bushmen and other people farming in a traditional manner, forcing them into ever smaller enclaves. The barons' beef goes for export mostly to the European Community, which provides privileged access to its markets, but requires in return guarantees that the meat arriving at European ports is free from foot and mouth disease. To meet that demand, Botswana has erected more than 1,200 kilometres of fences to keep the ranch cattle apart from wild animals. The fences now block the migration routes across the plains of wildebeest, antelope and other game. Hundreds of thousands of animals have died as a result. 'When touching pictures of dying wildebeest started appearing on television screens there was an outcry,' says Survival International. But, rather than tear down the fences, the government announced plans for improvements to the protection for animals in its game reserve – by ridding the reserve of its human inhabitants.

Throughout Africa, communities living traditional lives, harvesting the natural produce of the land, are being evicted from the most fertile land by farms and plantations, often growing crops intended for export. Then, under pressure from environmental groups such as the WWF and with an eye on possible revenues from tourism, governments create national parks and reserves that squeeze native people yet harder. The basic tenet of Huxley's case for national parks in Africa – that they would enrich the natives – is rarely seen. Whether the battle is played out in the rainforests, between foresters and shifting cultivators, or on the grasslands between cattle ranchers and nomadic pastoralists, the end result is often conflict also between conservationists and the people who know best how to live in harmony with their environment.

During the 1980s, the WWF began to acknowledge these dangers. A series of internal assessments of the effectiveness of the WWF's conservation projects has shown that the success-ful ones are those that involve most deeply the local people. But these genuine attempts to learn all too often founder on the Fund's need to work through government agencies, which insist on central control and often wish to 'tame' native people by bringing them under national legal and taxation systems and to integrate peasant farmers into the mainstream cash economy.

The WWF's publicity still tends, its critics claim, to 'blame the poor' for the destruction of their land. One leaflet, *Wild-lands and Human Needs*, published in 1988, says that 'much

of the Earth's remaining biological diversity is in rural areas of
the tropics where the poorest of the poor struggle to draw their
livelihood from the land . . . The driving imperative of the poor
to overexploit otherwise renewable resources is perhaps the
most direct threat to wildlife and wildlands.' But what exactly
is this driving imperative?

Studies by the IUCN show that in the poorest and most
environmentally vulnerable region of Africa, the Sahel,
population is not growing fast in rural areas and that the real
pressure on land comes from the annexation of the best
farming land by big farms growing peanuts, cotton and other
export crops. Nonetheless, the WWF sticks rigidly to the view
that there need be no conflict between conservation and
economic development in such regions. Its critics say that
when conflicts do arise, the first to suffer are native peoples.

A good example of the WWF's impact on Africa is the
1,200-square-kilometre Korup National Park in Cameroon,
where the WWF regards its plan to integrate economic development and conservation in and around the park as a
text-book example of how to get it right. The park is one of the
most important rainforest reserves in Africa. During the last
ice age, as other rainforests dried out, the Korup survived and,
partly as a result, today it contains a vast variety of wildlife,
including 400 species of trees, 252 of birds and 52 of large
mammals, such as leopards, elephants and chimpanzees. It is
home to almost a quarter of Africa's species of primates. The
forest is in a remote, previously undeveloped, part of
Cameroon close to the Nigerian border. It was first reached by
road only in 1986. The intention is to develop the region
without destroying the forest.

The park is a joint venture of the Cameroon government and
the WWF, a product, says the Fund, of its desire to involve local
people in preserving their environment. Yet, despite much talk
of local consultation and of education programmes for the
natives, the project bears the hallmarks of a solution imposed
by outsiders. Project plans talk of designing sustainable farming methods for local people. But there are already signs that
both development and conservation could be at the expense of
many local people.

Mark Infield, a conservationist involved in the project, described it at length in the *New Scientist* in 1989. He said:

> To begin with, most people were enthusiastic about the park, believing that it was an important development. When they realised that [economic] development would be banned in the park, interest flagged. Many began to have even stronger misgivings when they learnt of plans to relocate some of the villages. Conflict grew when villagers discovered that they would have to stop hunting before they developed other ways to earn money. The Korup project is working to defuse the conflict.

It is hard to see how such a conflict can be defused. Hunting is an important local occupation, with 'bush beef' one of the main sources of protein. The Cameroon government intends to resettle the thousand people still living inside the park, though a project that drew up plans to relocate villages without involving those concerned at the earliest stage hardly sounds promising. Infield warned, 'Local people must be convinced of the benefits of retaining forest outside the park . . . If hunting and trapping remain illegal, farmers will eliminate wild animals from their land because they damage crops.'

Meanwhile, in early 1990, Western journalists returned from a WWF-sponsored visit to Korup with stories that timber companies were moving into the fringes of the forest, cutting timber for export. 'The WWF pleaded with us not to report this because it would upset the Cameroon government,' one of the journalists told me.

After more than 25 years of missionary zeal in promoting national parks in Africa, the WWF in 1987 conducted a pioneering study into what the natives thought about its endeavours. The results reveal the extent of the Fund's problems in reconciling its ideas with the realities of life in Africa.

The story begins with a series of internal checks during the 1980s on the success of the Fund's conservation initiatives round the world. The studies revealed that the successful projects are almost always those that involve the local people most deeply. The failures are characterised by conservation being imposed – frequently at the point of a game warden's gun. So the Fund has been putting greater effort into educating the people on whose land nature reserves and national parks are established.

Sally Zalewski of WWF France spent two years finding out how people in rural West Africa responded to the men in four-wheel drives who button-holed them in the bush with slide shows and panda stickers. Did these conservation road-shows help to persuade the people of Senegal and Gambia to report poaching and work to preserve elephants and other animals in neighbouring national parks?

Her findings, recorded as 'WWF project 3714: Elaboration of a system to evaluate the impact of a wildlife public aware-ness and education policy in developing countries', have shocked those who have read them. She found, for instance, that after more than a decade of visits from the 'green mis-sionaries', over a quarter of those interviewed knew nothing whatever about the nearby national park. Of the remainder, she says, almost half 'manifested a negative attitude' to the park. Less than a third had a 'positive attitude'. When asked why the government forbids hunting and fishing in the parks, 55 per cent said they did not know and only 21 per cent identified nature conservation as the reason. Says Zalewski, 'The future of the parks is compromised by these negative attitudes.' It leads 'to poaching, or, when this becomes too difficult, to a complete lack of interest in park activities leaving it wide open to poachers coming from outside'.

Her analysis seems to be borne out by events. She found that 74 per cent of the people living near Niokola Koba National Park in eastern Senegal did not know the purpose of the park, the highest 'don't know' count recorded in the study. It is an area where poaching is rife and often perpetrated by people crossing the border from Guinea Bissau.

This is doubly embarrassing since the WWF's mobile edu-cation unit is based near the park at Tambacounda and, says Zalewski, the people there have 'had the most intensive education programme, with two equipped audiovisual mobile units and a full-time education officer'. Niokola Koba and

Saloum, a coastal national park in Senegal, are the two areas where the WWF education programmes have been most intense. Yet they also record the highest scores for 'negative attitudes' to the parks.

Western conservationists and Africa villagers clearly have very different perceptions about the environment and the threats to it. A recent study by the International Union for the Conservation of Nature and Natural Resources (IUCN) identified elephant poaching as a key problem in Niokola Koba. But among locals only four people out of the 160 interviewed agreed that poaching was the most serious threat to the environment and wildlife. Three times as many saw the national park itself as a serious problem in their daily lives, by harbouring wild animals that damaged crops, for instance.

The local people there and elsewhere were worried about drought, loss of trees and bush fires. Says Zalewski, 'It is essential to identify [conservation] priorities in terms of the worries and concerns of the villagers in their daily lives in order to establish realistic and workable development and education programmes.' This, WWF workers increasingly realise, must be a major priority for their activities in the 1990s.

There is, however, a potentially serious conflict of interest here. The WWF fund-raisers back in London, Washington and Switzerland 'sell' the WWF around issues such as elephant poaching rather than on preventing bush fires or mitigating drought.

Even apparently trivial issues show up the yawning gap between African and Western perceptions. Westerners may know and love the WWF panda symbol. But, though it is plastered on the Fund's cars and equipment and appears on its films, few African villagers questioned by Zalewski remembered it. 'It quickly became apparent that the panda symbol was a totally strange visual concept for these African villagers,' she said. 'They were curious to know what it was, where it lived, did it exist in their country, and could it be eaten.' Not, perhaps, quite the message the WWF had in mind.

Zalewski divided the answers to her most important question, 'What is the purpose of a national park?', between those who had seen the WWF film presentations and those who had not seen them. Of those who had missed the film, 61 per cent were vague or did not know about the park's purpose. Far worse, the figure rose to 75 per cent among those who had seen the film. Even those who said they knew what a national park was for appeared to have been confused and turned off by the film. Before seeing the film, the great majority said the park was for nature protection or tourism. Afterwards, they said it was for 'government use'. 'The film presentation appears to have a negative impact,' commented Zalewski.

This fascinating study raises wide questions about conservation education in rural Africa. Though education has been part of the WWF's brief in Africa since its formation in 1961, Zalewski says that 'little assessment of the effectiveness or the benefits has ever been carried out'. But, rather than distributing Zalewski's report in a gesture of glasnost and inviting outside opinion on how to respond, the WWF has kept it under wraps, and not put on record its conclusions from the study. Zalewski herself concludes that, 'The concept of a Westerner, carrying out environmental education or awareness programmes in developing countries, is presumptuous. As has been proved many times over, rural populations in developing countries are very aware of their environment and indeed have lived in harmony with it for centuries.' The lesson is clear. It is Africans who should be giving environmental education courses to the WWF.

Often the best way of conserving African environments would be to improve the standing of the rural poor and native communities within African society – to break the dominance of city élites, and then leave the people who live on the land to conserve it. As Nigel Cross, the British director of SOS Sahel, which helps to fund tree-planting schemes in the Sahel argues, 'What is good for the rural poor is good for the environment. What is bad for them is bad for the environment.' But even conservation schemes imposed from outside need to be far more creative if the WWF is not to end up presiding over the destruction rather than the preservation of Africa's unique wildlife.

The *New Scientist* reported one such creative development in Zambia. There Richard Bell, an African biologist in charge of a development project in the Luangwa Valley, told the magazine's reporter:

> The institutional nature of conservation was established during the colonial period; it has strong paternalistic and racist elements to it, and is itself a large part of the problem ... What has happened is that the control of natural resources has been progressively taken away from rural communities by central government bureaucracies, and the benefits flowing from them have also been progressively concentrated in national treasuries. In effect, a wall has been created between rural communities and the resources among which they live.

The purpose of Bell's project, like that of a number of similar schemes under way in neighbouring Zimbabwe, is to give the animals back to the people. The reasoning is simple. In Zambia, and throughout Africa, elephant numbers began their current, most critical decline only when, in the name of conservation, they were taken out of the hands of the local people and 'protected' by governments in national parks and reserves. Governments themselves were quite incapable of protecting them; but communities could, and would, provided it was in their interest to do so.

Bell estimates that from 1973 to 1986, when his project started, poachers had taken from the Luangwa Valley ivory worth about $500 million. Most of that money finished up in the hands of ivory traders and corrupt government officials. The local law-abiding farmers received little money, but cared even less about the poaching since they had no stake in protecting the elephants. Now they do. The wildlife is theirs. The project charges fees for hunting licences and safari concessions. So far, no elephants have been hunted, because, says Bell, numbers have not recovered sufficiently from the poaching days. But he figures that the local people now have an interest in halting the poachers. He is angry that the ban on the ivory trade could upset the plans, though the ban does not prohibit trophy hunters, provided they do not attempt to sell their ivory.

The rhino has always been at the forefront of WWF campaigning. The front-page splash in the *Daily Mirror* which launched the Fund in Britain in 1961 urged readers to join the crusade, 'If you don't want the phrase "dead as a dodo" to be replaced by "dead as a rhino"'. During the three decades since, although the WWF alone has spent millions of pounds on protecting the black rhino, its numbers on the hoof in Africa have fallen from 100,000 to around 4,000. By all rational standards, the campaign has been a disastrous failure. The rhino has suffered from the loss of its habitat, and from a sharp increase in the poaching of horns, which began in Kenya in the early 1970s.

Rhino horn is used to make handles for ceremonial daggers popular in North Yemen and to make traditional medicines in south-east Asia and India, where it is widely regarded as an aphrodisiac. While trade in rhino horn is technically banned by CITES, it persists more strongly than ever. As poachers risk death to harvest their raw material, the price of powdered rhino horn is said to have reached $40,000 per horn in Taiwan, a major trading centre.

The question is: Would the losses have been worse without the WWF? Many experts, including some involved with the very first campaign three decades ago, believe that most of the Fund's efforts have been misplaced. They believe that the two mistakes at the heart of campaigns to save the black rhino, and also the African elephant, were the alienation of local people from their national parks, giving them no interest in preventing poaching, and the concentration almost entirely on preventing poaching rather than trying to shut down demand for rhino horn in the world outside.

As early as the mid-1960s, some insiders wanted to switch to an assault on the trade in rhino horns. One idea canvassed at the time was to employ former police officers with experience in uncovering drug trafficking. It never happened. The formation of TRAFFIC (Trade Records Analysis of Flora and Fauna in Commerce) provided some numbers on the trade, but little more, say insiders. 'They are just boy scouts and girl guides,' said one. At a meeting in 1987, it was fund-raisers rather than conservationists who insisted that the rhino be kept as the subject of a major campaign. They saw a continued source of income in the public's response to one of the most potent images of the WWF: fighting the war against the poacher. As the campaign continued into the late 1980s, less than 20 per cent of spending was on efforts to combat the trade – a one-man operation begun in 1985 and funded year-to-year. Poachers remained the central target. But as one insider put it, 'Shooting and imprisoning poachers has had no effect, so why go on wasting money at the wrong end? Is WWF to buy 4,000 armoured cars to protect the remaining rhinos?'

That is roughly what some people in Africa have in mind. In 1989, a London-based organisation called Rhino Rescue launched an appeal for money for a rhino sanctuary at Laikipia in Kenya. The sanctuary opened in 1986 on a cattle ranch and had around 40 black rhino protected behind 74 kilometres of fence carrying 7,000 volts and with one armed security guard per rhino. The aim of the new appeal was to pay for more armed guards to protect more rhino, and to install infra-red cameras to monitor them at night. Similar high-security rhino ranches have been established elsewhere in Kenya and in Zimbabwe.

Esmond Bradley Martin, the resident rhino expert for the IUCN and WWF through the 1980s, believes that 'the only way of saving the rhino in Africa north of the Zambezi is to put them behind fences.' This sounds like a description of a zoo rather than preservation of animals in the wild. It does, however, meet one criticism of the WWF's policy towards policing herds of large mammals in national parks – that resources had been spread far too thinly to be effective. Bradley Martin puts the cost of maintaining an effective high-security rhino sanctuary at around $3,400 per square kilometre per year or $6,200 per rhino.

While the sanctuaries should be able to save a few dozen or even hundred animals, they can never do more than that. In the Lower Zambezi Valley in Zimbabwe a sanctuary on a former cattle ranch, set up in 1985 and funded by the WWF, houses ten black rhino. It lost one, but 'saved' the other nine. However, in three years in the bush outside, more than 250 rhinos were killed by poachers.

There have been other ploys suggested. The WWF briefly considered starting a rumour that rhino horn contains anthrax spores. More seriously, in Damaraland, Namibia, in 1989 the park authorities began cutting off the horns of rhino in an effort to thwart poachers. It was an interesting experiment, but probably not one that can be followed successfully elsewhere in Africa. Damaraland is a virtual desert. Poachers can see that a rhino has no horn before taking aim to shoot it. Elsewhere, rhinos live in dense bush and would generally be shot before the hunter knew they were shorn of horn. Rhinos use their horns to defend themselves and their calves against predators such as lions and hyenas. So in many places you'd have to kill the lions first. Also dehorning is expensive, especially since the horns regrow and would have to be cut again within three years. Dehorned rhinos might not be to the liking of tourists in East African parks, where rhino are a leading attraction. And there is a fear at the WWF that its donors might not like the idea of funding such mutilations.

The sanctuary has the advantage for the WWF of meeting public perceptions of what saving animals is about. It reinforces one of the central images of the WWF – its heroic fight against the African poacher. So, whether or not sanctuaries provide the last stand for the black rhino, they undoubtedly appear as a last stand for the old-style conservationists on which the WWF's original successes were built. Rhino Rescue is partly under the WWF umbrella. Its supporters include the WWF's two princes, Bernhard and Philip, and, according to a long laudatory article in the *Sunday Telegraph* in 1989, its British base of support is at the Shikar Club in London, a watering hole for old colonial hunters, where one old African hand, Maurice Coreth, passed round the hat before himself heading off to spend some time in charge of a Kenyan sanctuary. The irony is that, to preserve an ideal of separating man from nature, animals are being protected behind high-voltage fencing. This, as one WWF hand put it, 'is failure disguised as a success by its cost'.

Tragedy in the Sahel

The WWF is setting up nature reserves in some of the most arid parts of Africa. Yet even in the drought-stricken Sahel region on the edge of the Sahara its concern remains largely for animals rather than for the fate of the herdsmen. And, where its projects extend to a specific concern for humans, the priorities are generally economic development of a kind that does little for the indigenous people.

Its flagship project in the region is the Air and Tenere National Nature Reserve in the Air Massif, an island of wildlife in the desert margins of Niger. Here, as in Korup, the WWF is attempting to reconcile the conflicts between the native people, its brand of conservation and the interests of a national government intent on 'development'.

John Newby, the WWF's representative in the republic, says that 'it would certainly be easier to evict the human population' from the reserve and concentrate on protecting its rich variety of cheetahs, ostriches and gazelles. But instead, the WWF and the Niger government decided to let the region's 3,000 nomadic people, largely Tuareg herders, carry on living in the reserve, which is twice the size of Switzerland. Under the project, however, 'legislation will control a wide range of activities in an attempt to promote sustainable land-use and natural resources practices,' says Newby. Controlled activities will include hunting, protecting cattle from predators and gathering wood.

But is the WWF sure that it knows more about how to conserve resources than the Tuareg? What do the Tuareg think about the state of their environment? Is the WWF sure that the government, whose staff will police the reserve, is more interested in conservation than in bringing to heel the troublesome nomads?

There are laudable aspects to the project. The area has suffered from drought. Recovery will be helped by the planting of trees and the re-seeding of valleys with grasses. But the backdrop to the work is the continued destruction of the way of life of the Tuaregs, who have survived in the area for thousands of years without the benefit of Western know-how.

Before the French colonialists arrived in West Africa, the Tuareg ruled the land that is now Niger. The French defeated them after many battles and allowed Fulbe cattle herders and Hausa farmers to move on to their lands. With official encouragement, Hausa farmers have in recent decades taken their ploughs far into the pastures of the desert margins, fencing off grazing land for fields all along the road from Niamey to Agadez, almost to the edge of the reserve itself. The Tuareg are being hemmed in. Their traditional means of livelihood – herding camels, goats and sheep, irrigating small fields around water holes and operating the surviving camel train routes across the desert – face threats from outsiders that have only been intensified by two decades of drought.

The Air project has two components: the protection of the area's wildlife and, grafted on to that during planning with the Niger government, schemes to 'develop' the area. It is a textbook WWF scheme. The aim of the development is to offset the impact of new rules to conserve wildlife and to reduce the locals' dependence on 'destructive' use of the land. The result may be to impoverish them, diminish their control of the land that they understand better than anyone else and, finally, should the economic development bear fruit, to put the wildlife under a new and more deadly threat.

First, the conservation. An area comprising roughly an eighth of the entire reserve, some 10,000 square kilometres, is to become a 'strict nature reserve' with most human activities banned. While Newby believes that this is essential to conserve wildlife and natural resources, he says that many of the rules that the government already imposes are unjustified. For instance, to protect the few species of animals at genuine risk, such as the addax and dama gazelle, the government has banned all hunting since the 1960s. It is illegal for herders to protect their animals from attack by predators such as the ubiquitous jackal. Now the government wants to ban the collection of wood even though, says Newby, most herders are good at conserving trees by taking wood sparingly, and many of the poorest will be hit hardest by the ban.

The development likewise seems to offer little to the Tuareg. The major idea to bring money into the area is tourism. The scenery and animals are spectacular. But the few tourists who already reach the reserve do considerable damage, says Newby. They 'harass wildlife and pillage prehistoric sites'. And the Tuareg whose land they invade see none of the money they bring. 'As in many isolated, exotic places,' he says, 'the local people are often the last to benefit.'

In theory, the project, like Korup, is a flagship for local participation in conservation. That may sound fine from the WWF headquarters in Switzerland. The practice is different. Says Newby, 'Project design is supposed to be done with the people, and project proposals passed to them; this is rarely adhered to.'

At the start of the project in 1986, Newby wrote that it provided 'an excellent opportunity for the rational management of natural resources'. Three years on, he was less optimistic. In a few small areas on the vast reserve, local schemes, from planting trees to installing small dams to protect from floods, had been successfully established. But he doubted their long-term viability. 'Given the poverty of the Sahelian nations, the capacity of governments to undertake all manner of work depends greatly on the presence of outside assistance and projects – projects which are in theory destined to disappear.' He wrote of 'nepotism, graft, self-aggrandisement and political expediency' and warned that without more fundamental reforms, 'it is unlikely that short-term gains and benefits can be sustained.'

The Air Massif, like much of Africa, seems hopelessly caught between tradition and centralised government control. The losers are both the people and their environment. The WWF may say that the wider issues are beyond its control. But to the Tuareg, it must appear that the WWF has joined the forces that oppose them and their environment. The WWF's aims of wildlife conservation would be better met by curbs on the spread of sedentary farming than on hunting, and by the withdrawal of government-controlled park rangers and the reassertion of control by the Tuareg, the acknowledged masters of the desert environment.

One of the most challenging analyses of what is going on in the Sahel came in 1989 from the WWF's sister organisation, the IUCN, in a report called, dryly, 'IUCN Sahel Studies 1989'. The report embodies many of the tensions and inconsistencies that have bedevilled thinking among environmentalists about Africa. The study began, says the IUCN's director-general, Martin Holdgate, as a review of the Sahelian environment in the wake of the drought of the mid-1980s. But it turned into an analysis of the relationships between humans and their environment in a region where those relationships are at their most raw and fragile.

At the heart of the matter is a single problem: Are the conservation policies of national governments, as advised by the WWF, part of the solution or the problem in the Sahel? Part of the report gives one answer; part the other.

The conventional pro-government view is given in an early chapter from the World Conservation Monitoring Centre, an organisation based in Cambridge, England, that was once owned by the IUCN but is now jointly run by the IUCN, the WWF and the UN Environment Programme. The chapter places Africa's wildlife in conflict with the human inhabitants of the Sahel. Even when those people are living on the edge of starvation, it comes down in favour of wildlife. It describes the Niokolo National Park in Senegal, for instance, which 'has been extended seven times' and where 'disaffected local people now engage in a great deal of poaching.' The language tells the story: the local people are engaged in hunting, as they always have been, but following the creation of the park, they become described as poachers.

During two decades of dry weather, punctuated by two severe droughts, many nomadic herding communities in Chad, Niger, Mali and Burkina Faso have faced prolonged crises. Cut off by invading farmers from the pastures they once used in times of drought, they have migrated towards 'the millions of hectares of protected areas [which they see] as potentially rich settlement areas'. Such migrations must be halted by firm action from the authorities, says the WCMC. 'There is all the more need for governments to recognise the value of protected areas and to take seriously their responsibility to exert control

in situations where national interests conflict with individual
or local interests.'

While the WCMC has detailed proposals for protecting
everything from flamingoes in Ethiopia to leopards in Somalia,
it has no view about how to save the endangered peoples of the
Sahel. And it has one law for natives and another for the
government. In Chad, it observes without comment that military activities have decimated the oryx and addax in two
national parks. Then it proposes tough 'anti-poaching activities' against local people in the parks. Similarly, oil exploration
'will have considerable impact' on the Sudd region of Sudan,
which it calls 'the most important inland wetland in Africa',
containing perhaps as many large mammals as are found in the
Serengeti region. There is no suggestion, however, that the
exploration should be halted.

The WCMC calls for new reserves in Chad 'to include the
seasonal migration route of elephants', but proposes no such
right for nomadic herders, whose rights to migrate, it says,
should be curtailed in the interests of conservation. It tells the
government in Mali that it should 'control human settlements
within reserves [and] discourage grazing of cattle and livestock
within reserves, even in times of drought. This puts added
pressure on wildlife populations when they too are stressed.'
Perhaps it is time to establish an international union for the
conservation of people.

Three chapters later in the study comes the case against such
divisive conservation strategies. Jeremy Swift of the Institute of
Development Studies at the University of Sussex criticises the
'idealised visions' of European and North American conservationists being imposed on African people, often by their own
governments. He backs the herders against both the devel-
opers and the self-appointed conservers of their lands. 'A few
people', he says, 'have become richer and more powerful as a
result of [development], but many, especially poor people,
have been dispossessed of their traditional access to pasture,
water and trees, and made more vulnerable to drought and
famine . . . Conservation is probably best achieved by giving
local institutions the incentives and power to manage their
own resources.'

Swift goes on to describe how the local people traditionally live in harmony with their harsh desert surroundings. Their systems, he says, have been ignored and second-guessed by Western scientists and African administrators, who have nationalised and privatised the common pastures and suppressed traditional land laws.

At the front of the IUCN's report, there is a call for the Sudanese government to set up a game reserve in the Red Sea Hills to give protection to the Nubian ibex, gazelles and other animals. At the back of the report, Swift describes in detail the traditional land law of the Beja people, who live in those hills. There is a complex of communal rights to land, water and vegetation down to individual acacia trees, designed to preserve social and ecological harmony. The establishment of any game reserve would undermine that land law, and replace it with national laws.

Recent research, says Swift, 'has shown that native resource tenure rules are much more sophisticated in many rural societies in farming, fishing and herding economies than had formerly seemed to be the case'. Why not work with the grain? he asks. 'Pastoral territories are composed of several different elements, including grass, shrubs and trees, surface and sub-surface water, different types of salt deposits, wild animals and other useful resources. The same area may have different rights attached to it from one season to another. Particular rights may be attached to the fruits of a tree, but not to its leaves, or the seeds of a grass (collected as human food) but not to the grass stems and leaves once the seeds have been collected . . . Particular groups of herders have the right to graze pasture in sequence, each group for a specified period of time after one group and before another.' How can central governments begin to compete with this sophistication? By sending in teams of park rangers to police bans on hunting, wood gathering and grazing, Swift's friends at the WWF and the IUCN may be doing much more harm than good.

The debate about how to preserve the common pasture lands of Africa is summed up in the phrase 'tragedy of the commons'. The phrase was immortalised by an American named Garett Hardin. He said that common ownership of a resource, such as land, encourages its overexploitation and ecological decline. If nobody owns the pasture, but every farmer has his own cattle, then the rational thing for each farmer to do is to increase his herd.

This theory is the accepted wisdom of the WWF and of African governments and Western development agencies. It dovetails conveniently with their zeal to 'develop' traditional societies by creating private property and introducing them to money. The take-home message is that private ownership is good for the environment, while common ownership is bad. Hardin's case, written primarily about Africa's grasslands, can be heard repeated today on every issue from saving the rainforests to planting eucalyptus on Indian 'waste land'. It certainly underpins the WWF view that legal frameworks, in the form of national parks, rangers and guns are needed to conserve Africa's environment. Most particularly, it has helped the arguments of African governments that they should take charge of common pastures and forests.

But as Hardin himself has protested, the theory applies only when social controls have broken down. In Africa, says Swift, loss of social control of commonly owned land is usually a result of government intervention, rather than the trigger for that intervention.

Throughout history pastoral communities have survived by imposing sophisticated rules of behaviour to meet the needs of both the environment and its nomadic herders. By intervening, governments have destroyed those customary rules and the societies that enforced them. 'A tragedy of the commons is effectively the result of government action,' Jeremy Swift says. It may be too late to return entirely to the old order, he agrees. But these traditional rules, deeply embedded within the pastoral communities of Africa, offer a far better chance of survival for the people and their environment than those solutions that are imposed and rely on central governments for their implementation. The separation of traditional communities from their land and its wild animals, whether in the name of conservation or anything else, is likely to lead to disaster for both the people and the animals.

Peasants and profits

The famine in Ethiopia in 1984 brought a remarkable out-
pouring of worldwide public concern. The rock star Bob
Geldof and his Live Aid organisation spent a year raising tens
of millions of pounds and travelled the world, festooned with
TV crews, chastising governments and officials for their failure
to prevent the tragedy. In late 1990, famine loomed again as
drought found the people of the northern highlands of
Ethiopia still unable to feed themselves. What had gone wrong
in Ethiopia?

The droughts were serious, but hardly unique. The prime
culprit was the soil of the highlands, where 80 per cent of the
country's 40 million people live. The government said that the
highlands were losing three billion tonnes of soil a year as wind
and water ravaged a land devoid of vegetation. Half the
farmland was classified as 'severely degraded' and the government's head of soils and water claimed that on 20,000 square
kilometres the soil was gone for ever.

Too many farmers were trying to win too much food from
the soil, it said, and it announced plans to step up a project to
move 1.5 million people from the highlands to fertile but
unused land in the south of the country, where they would live
in model villages and farm on model farms.

Was this cynical social engineering by a brutal Communist
regime, or a bold strategy to break out of a cycle of environmental decay and famine? Most aid groups had little time for
such questions. They were concentrating on alleviating immediate suffering. And their own projects for helping the
Ethiopians to recover depended on the co-operation of a
government that was highly suspicious of Western agencies of
all sorts. Environmentalists, of all people, ought to have had a
view. Yet they too were mostly silent. 'I'm not sure exactly
what we could contribute,' one top environmentalist told me.
Given the tales of ecological holocaust coming from across the
continent, one would have thought quite a lot. But perhaps
saving whales and elephants is easier.

One of the few environmentalists to bite the African bullet
was Pat Adams, head of Probe International, a Canadian

group that has pioneered investigations into the effect that aid from Canada and elsewhere has on the environment. 'Little did the world know,' she wrote after the Ethiopian famine, that in 1984, 'we were helping to rescue victims of earlier aid efforts.' Adams's version of the Ethiopian tragedy begins in the 1960s with the UN Food and Agriculture Organization, a lumbering bureaucracy based in Rome that is charged with helping poor nations to grow more food. The FAO proposed converting large tracts of the fertile Awash valley in Wollo, central Ethiopia, into plantations to grow sugar-cane, cotton and bananas for export. Part of the project involved building dams on the River Awash to provide water for farms and hydroelectric power for the country's capital, Addis Ababa.

It was one of many grand projects launched in Ethiopia and elsewhere in drought-prone Africa during the 1960s and 1970s to generate foreign exchange from cash crops. The irrigated fields of the Awash valley were given over almost entirely to multinational companies and, like similar schemes elsewhere in the country, received heavy subsidies, through exemptions on import duties for tractors, pesticides and ferti-lisers. The drain on the public purse for such investments was considerable. By contrast, at this time peasant agriculture, a matter of life or death for most Ethiopians, was receiving just 1 per cent of public spending.

The FAO helped to persuade the World Bank and its sister agency, the African Development Bank, to provide loans for the project. Writes Adams, 'Before the construction of the dams, the valley's rich floodplains – a mixture of savannas, swamps and forests nurtured by the biannual floods of the Awash River – had supported 150,000 people. But with the damming of the river, flooding decreased dramatically. As the valley bottomlands became arid, the land could no longer support its inhabitants.' About 20,000 people were thrown off their land to make way for the plantations. Many more could no longer survive, since their water had been taken from them. The Afar tribe suffered the most, moving with its livestock on to the lands of its neighbours in the surrounding hills. Soon the tribes were at war and, worse, the soils of the crowded highlands became overused.

'When the rains failed in the early 1970s and again in the early 1980s', writes Adams, 'the people, bereft of their former resources, became wards of famine relief stations.' A scheme designed to increase the wealth of a nation had caused the impoverishment of its most vulnerable citizens through the destruction of their environment. It is a pattern which Adams sees at work around the world. Indeed she fears it may be about to happen again to the same people.

The Ethiopian government's first response to the famine was to plead for foreign aid to settle more than a million of the highlanders on spare land in the south of the country. But, writes Adams, 'the project, which Ethiopia tries to justify on environmental grounds, is already having disastrous environmental effects. To settle the 1.5 million people from the highlands, most of Ethiopia's remaining forests are being cleared, robbing that country of scarce fuel and fodder and of a barrier to the encroaching desert.' Ironically, too, back in the highlands, the Ethiopians wanted to replace peasant farming with state-run plantations of fodder crops. The destruction of Ethiopia's traditional peasant farming communities would be complete.

Adams is a development economist who studied in Britain at the University of Sussex and later worked as a consultant in Africa. Today, there is still a slight air of the old colonial about her. The sensible shoes, beads and hair-do would pass muster at any East African expat cocktail party. But that experience has forged an exceptionally tough mistrust of the whole aid business. 'When I was in Africa,' she says, 'I realised that the aid people, especially the development banks, were, through their projects, taking power away from people such as the Afar who were best able to take decisions about their own land. They were giving it to governments, who took all the wrong decisions. It wasn't development, it was people taking advantage of money.'

She left the aid business, she says, 'after I became involved in a so-called model agricultural village project in Ghana . . . As if these people didn't know how to farm!' When I met her at her office in Toronto, she was at work on a book arguing the case that Africa's debt crisis had a silver lining in that it stopped governments borrowing more money for destructive projects.

Disillusioned, Adams switched to the environment. She admits that 'it was not until I worked in the environment community that I thought hard about how decisions are taken.' The new generation of environmentalists that has grown up in Western countries since the late 1960s had always been in the business of 'picking apart' the decision-making processes that damage the environment. So it came naturally to them to do the same in the Third World. Environmentalists, she says, were far quicker than aid groups to realise that even the most philanthropic aid projects were unlikely to succeed when imposed from outside. Genuine democratic decision taking was essential if aid was to work.

Adams is being charitable to environmentalists, most of whom avoid Africa and shun the politics of development. Her brand of environmental thinking, stressing democracy and the importance of native peoples to the preservation of the environment, owes as much to the work of anthropologists and civil rights activists. Many of her own ideas come from collaboration with the defenders of indigenous peoples such as Marcus Colchester, a campaigning anthropologist at Survival International during the 1980s. Colchester is credited by many (not always approvingly) with persuading the British Overseas Development Administration not to back aid for Ethiopia's resettlement programme.

Nonetheless, Adams is right that most aid agencies, even those with an interest in the environment, take what they would see as a more pragmatic view about democracy in Africa. Nigel Cross of SOS Sahel admits: 'Actually, we don't work anywhere where there are democratic governments. Our view is that these are people with environments that can be improved and that we can help.'

Whatever the importance of democracy in decision taking, there is growing agreement that many of Africa's environmental and human problems arise from the excessive power placed in the hands of central governments based in capital cities far away from the majority of their people. It has proved one of the most lasting, corrupting and damaging legacies of the colonial era. Those governments, dominated by urban élites and egged on by Western development agencies, have sought riches for their countries by borrowing heavily to invest in schemes to develop industry and mechanised agriculture geared to export crops. Their promotion of such schemes, in preference to assisting peasant farmers to grow food, does much to explain the declining food production in Africa over the past 20 years, the continent's growing debt and reliance on aid and its disintegrating environment.

In the Sahel region of West Africa – stretching from the Atlantic coasts of Mauritania and Senegal, through Mali and Niger to Chad – farming for food is being driven out by government enthusiasm for the production of peanuts and cotton. It began in the final years of the French control of the region. While the British catastrophically failed to establish groundnut (peanut) plantations in Africa, the French made a big, and initially laudable, success with peanuts. Throughout the drylands of West Africa, farmers alternated crops of millet for food with peanuts for profit. It worked well because the farmers, knowing their own soils, left the fields fallow for up to six years after each crop cycle. But after the Second World War French demand for imports of edible oils expanded and Paris pumped in aid money for fertilisers, pesticides and capital equipment to establish plantations to meet that demand. Farmers reduced fallow periods and began to take their ploughs further north on to land on the margins of the Sahara which they had previously left to nomadic herdsmen, such as the Tuareg, who relied on it to survive during times of drought.

Meanwhile, peanuts got the good land and food crops were forced to the fields nearest the desert. Food production stagnated during the 1960s, and began to decline during the 1970s, as average rainfall declined. The seeds of the great famines of the 1970s and 1980s had been sown.

Nigel Twose of Oxfam has studied the causes of the famine of the early 1980s. He says that 'during the past two decades, the Sahel has had a consistent record of failure in food production for local consumption, but of steady success in the cultivation of export crops. Half of the cultivated land in Senegal is used to grow peanuts.' While nomads and poor farmers starved in the early 1970s and again in the early 1980s, the amount of land, investment aid and subsidies set aside for peanuts and cotton in countries such as Mali, Chad and Senegal kept on growing. The crops were often grown on state-run farms while, says Twose, 'the poorer food-producing peasants were left to manage as best they could on marginal and overexploited lands.'

In Senegal, the government passed a law in 1964 effectively banning the traditional six-year fallow by taking away ownership of land from farmers who did not plant for three years. This too increased production of cash crops, but led to a decline in grain yields.

Meanwhile, the nomadic cattle herders and their traditional pastures on the desert margins also suffered. The five million pastoralists of the Sahel need to travel long distances in order to find nourishment for their cattle throughout the year. Rain comes in short, sharp and infrequent showers. The herders are expert at finding the small patches of pasture that have benefited from the showers. And at the end of each dry season, the pastoralists head for the wetter lands where farmers grow crops. There, despite the traditional antagonisms between the two groups, the cattle were once allowed to drink at wells, graze on stubble and to manure the ground before moving back towards the desert when the rains came.

Post-war 'development' funded by European aid programmes broke down these arrangements in many places. Farmers moved north into the pastures. And shallow wells where the cattle traditionally watered were shut down and replaced by larger, deeper boreholes. This effectively reduced the amount of pasture on which they could graze, since, during the dry season, cattle can walk no more than 30 kilometres from water. The Tuareg were on the retreat in Niger; the Peul herders gave way to the Wolof and Serer farmers in Senegal, and so on. When the droughts came, hundreds of thousands of pastoralists sold their cattle and headed for relief camps or jobs in the cities of neighbouring countries such as Côte d'Ivoire and Liberia.

Many of the development projects designed to alleviate the perils of drought and desertification after the famine of the early 1970s actually made the crisis of the early 1980s worse. In particular, money to combat the spread of deserts was put into cash-crop farms that put still greater stress on the desert margins. It was part of an ambitious 'dash for growth'. But during the 1980s, peanut sales, which once made up three-quarters of Senegal's export earnings, slumped with falling world prices and declining yields from exhausted soils. The peanut economies are now unable to pay off the loans that financed those projects. Yet a report for the World Bank published in 1989, on creating 'sustainable growth' in Africa, advocated more investment in export crops. All the time the real victims are the poor – and the environment.

5

FROM THE EAST

Opening the floodgates

Janos Vargha, a Hungarian biologist, wanted to stop a dam
being built on the River Danube. In so doing, he helped change
the course of East European history in the mid-1980s, playing
an arguably crucial role in opening the way to the overthrow of
Stalinist regimes from East Berlin to Bucharest. Vargha defied
the Hungarian authorities for half a decade, organising a
clandestine group called the Danube Circle to oppose the
dam-builders. He was for three years the Circle's only spokesman because the others were too afraid of losing their jobs or
of imprisonment. But he remained free and by mid-1989 the
dam was cancelled and the floodgates of reform had opened in
Hungary and on across Europe.

The Hungarian and Czechoslovak governments had harboured plans since 1951 to generate electricity from the
Danube. In 1977, their two leaders, Janos Kadar and Gustav
Husak, signed an agreement in Budapest, the Hungarian
capital, to build a complex barrage scheme along 150
kilometres of the river, much of which follows the border
between the two countries. Upstream, there would be a dam
feeding the entire flow of the Danube along a canal to a huge
hydroelectric power plant at Gabcikovo, to be built by
the Czechs. Downstream, on the scenic Danube Bend, at
Nagymaros, the site of an ancient Hungarian capital, the
Hungarians would build a smaller dam.

The operation of the dams would together have completely
changed the flow of the river. Water would have poured
backwards through the town of Gonyu for long periods. River

levels would rise by up to 16 metres along some stretches and lower by six metres on others. Vargha argued that such massive disruption would destroy the ecology of both the river and the surrounding countryside. Untreated sewage from the filthy river would pour into natural underground water stores in gravel beds and limestone rocks which supply most of the country with clean water.

For most Hungarians, Vargha was the first man to defy the regime openly since the Soviet tanks rolled into Budapest after the popular uprising in 1956, and his protest soon showed, even to outsiders, that the tides of change were at work in Hungary. One of the first to sense it was Andras Biro, a journalist who left his country in despair in 1956 and travelled the world for organisations as varied as the United Nations and Robert Maxwell's publishing empire. I met him in Budapest during late 1989. He was able, for the first time in three decades, to talk freely in a city bar about the evils of the state. 'I returned home in 1987', he told me, 'because I could see that things were changing.' Vargha and the Danube Circle were the visible sign of that change. 'It was an extraordinary thing for Janos [Vargha] to do. The Circle defied the government. They diminished the fear of the people so that tens of thousands of people were prepared to put their names to a petition opposing the dam.' He did that at a time when the Circle was still illegal, meeting every week in secret and communicating with its supporters by samizdat [underground] newsletters.

Vargha's campaign prized open the cracks between the Stalinists and reformers within the Communist government and gave political opponents of the government the courage to speak once more. 'The breakthrough to political change here occurred when the government suspended work on the dam,' says Biro.

Typical of the silent opponents of the government who were galvanised by Vargha was Anna Varkonyi, an environment journalist, and one of Vargha's earliest soul mates. Her interest in green issues had been first stirred by the UN Conference on the Human Environment held in Stockholm in 1972. She remembered the publication of Barbara Ward's famous book,

Only One Earth, in Hungary in 1978, and recalled the way that the Communists had translated and initially approved for publication Rachel Carson's *Silent Spring* in the mid-1970s. They considered it a handy indictment of Western abuse of the environment, until 'a comrade from the ministry of agriculture' called the publishing director and pointed out that it might stir up opposition to Hungary's own pesticide-saturated prairies. Publication was halted and only reconsidered in 1989.

Anna Varkonyi revered the work of Jocsik Lajos, a scientist who had pioneered environmentalism in Eastern Europe in the 1970s. 'He had wanted to foster co-operation among people in the Danube Basin, but his idea had fizzled out.' Varkonyi joined *Buvar*, an environmental magazine. Its name means 'explorer of nature', but, being under state control, its explorations were tightly circumscribed. In an effort to break out, she made contact with Western environmental groups, including Austrian greens. 'At the time', says Varkonyi, 'there was nobody involved in the environment here except the Young Communists, who were active in local environmental questions.'

In 1978, the government had set up a National Authority for Environmental Protection, with a liberal called Gyorgy Gonda in charge. 'We at *Buvar* tried to be a shop window for the National Authority,' says Varkonyi. Meanwhile, Gonda fostered the launch of ecology clubs in Hungarian universities. These clubs, like *Buvar*, were politically safe. But some, notably the ELTE Nature Conservation Club, established at the ELTE University in Budapest in 1984, later provided a raft of support for Vargha's radicalism.

In 1980, Janos Vargha, dispirited by his work for the National Academy of Sciences, joined *Buvar*. 'When Janos joined us, we became radicalist,' says Varkonyi. He wrote an article about the ecology of the Danube and the likely impact on it of the dam project. Since Hungary had signed a deal with Czechoslovakia in 1977 for the construction of the dam, it had emerged that the plan would involve digging a new bed for the Danube on Hungarian soil and ceding the land to the south of the new bed to Czechoslovakia. It also became known that the bankrupt Hungarians wanted the Austrians to build their dam – and in return take most of the power from it for the first 20 years.

Vargha's article criticising the dam scheme got as far as the printers before, as Varkonyi remembers, 'someone from the magazine's advisory board stopped it. Janos still has the page proofs.' She later got the article printed in another weekly magazine, *Uj Tukor*. Its publication, she says, was the real start of the Danube movement.

Scientists such as Vargha voiced their opposition through official channels in the early 1980s, but made little headway. In May 1984, as plans for the dam progressed, Gyorgy Gonda backed *Buvar* staff in their opposition. But he was sacked in May of that year and, days later, Janos Kadar imposed a ban on public speaking on environmental issues, and a news blackout on progress on the dam.

The Danube Circle was formed in August of that year. It met every Tuesday in Vargha's parents' house in Buda, the hilly half of Budapest on the west side of the Danube. Varkonyi was one of the original members of the Circle. During its first weeks, the Circle collected 6,000 signatures for a petition sent to the government, opposing the Hungarian dam at Nagy-maros. The secret police confiscated many pages of the petition before it was delivered. In December the first edition of the samizdat *Danube Circle News* appeared.

Meanwhile, Varkonyi's contacts with Western environmental groups bore fruit. In September, the Austrian greens called on their government to halt negotiations with the Hungarians for financing and construction of the Nagymaros dam. The Austrian greens were already in the midst of an angry campaign to halt construction of another dam on the Austrian section of the Danube at Hainburg, and that Christmas they occupied a wood that was to be cut down to make way for the dam. Stung by public support for the protest, the Austrian government cancelled the Hainburg project. One consequence was that the Austrian government increased its resolve to fund Nagymaros. This was tantamount, said the greens, to exporting Austria's environmental problems, and they redoubled their opposition to both dams.

Vargha published a detailed environmental impact study of the Nagymaros dam in June 1985. Later that year, he was awarded the Right Livelihood Award – the alternative Nobel prize. His determination to aim for the highest standards of scientific rigour in his campaigning work turned his crusade virtually into a full-time job. 'Janos risked almost everything,' says Varkonyi. 'He had no money for several years.' Vargha had left *Buvar* for a job as the editor of the Hungarian edition of *Scientific American*, called *Tudomany*. That proved short-lived. In 1986 he abruptly found himself out of a job. 'I wasn't exactly sacked,' Vargha told me, 'the job just ceased to exist.'

The campaign continued with even greater vigour during 1986. In January, Vargha called an open press conference at the Zoldfa Restaurant in central Budapest at which greens from Hungary, Austria and West Germany all spoke against the dam. Such an event was unheard of in the Eastern bloc at that time. The police kept watch but allowed the event to proceed. A few weeks later, they arrested and interrogated Vargha and others when they announced plans for a march through Budapest. Despite official threats, some 200 West Germans, Austrians and Hungarians went ahead with the demonstration. They were met by tear-gas and clubs. The brutality of the police brought protests from the European Parliament, though not from Western governments. Further petitions and public demonstrations followed. Austrian greens were arrested for handing out leaflets at Budapest's metro stations.

When Karoly Grosz became Hungarian prime minister in 1987, he announced plans to speed up construction of the Nagymaros dam. But the political tide was beginning to turn. In May 1988, a week after a crucial Communist Party conference, Vargha organised a mass demonstration against the dam. 'There was an extraordinary feeling of elation and liberation about that march,' remembers Varkonyi. Later that summer, contractors started to excavate the river bed at Nagymaros, and in September, some 50,000 people marched through the streets of Budapest to demand a halt. In the days afterwards, the Danube Circle collected 150,000 signatures demanding a referendum on the dam. Some kind of political

Rubicon appears to have been crossed that summer. In October, there were for the first time demonstrations to mark the anniversary of the 1956 uprising. And soon Imre Pozsgay had replaced Grosz on a tide of support for that uprising.

Hungary's new revolution was under way. Vargha's opposition to the dam was being joined by thousands and then tens of thousands of people with grievances of all kinds against the administration. The Stalinists, cracking before the pace of demands for reform, halted work on the dam in May 1989 and began negotiations with their Czech comrades to cancel the Czech half of the scheme.

I met Vargha at his home in the village of Pilisborosjeno, a jumble of newly built houses working their way up the once-wooded hillsides outside Buda. He, like many of his fellow citizens, had fled from the smog caused by the millions of ancient two-stroke cars that clog Budapest's streets. The city is the most Western of Eastern Europe's capitals. It has the traffic jams of the West, but the filthy, polluting car engines of the East – the worst of both worlds.

On a Sunday afternoon he was busy with two colleagues poring over the screen of his word processor to correct the detail of a new report. On the hills behind his house, prosperous young city-dwellers were queuing up to hang-glide over the village and into the few remaining fields. Central planning has not done much to control the haphazard urban sprawl visible all round Budapest.

On TV each night while I was there, the new session of parliament could be seen organising the voluntary demolition of the one-party system, the first East European state to do so. Free elections were announced one night. On another, the system of Party officials operating as super-shop-stewards alongside management in every factory, office and laboratory, was summarily abolished. How big a part had Vargha's rebellion played in triggering this transformation? He is not sure, but he is clearly a politically astute man as well as a scientist and environmentalist. 'For some years,' he said, 'I was almost the only person who believed that the dam would not be completed.' While his own concerns were largely for the ecology of the Danube valley, he realises that many of his fellow campaigners were more concerned about a loss of national sovereignty. The Czechoslovaks would take a little Hungarian soil, and the Austrians would take the dam's electricity. Other allies simply wanted to join any vehicle for opposition to the Communists. Inside the government, too, the dam was a pawn in another game.

'I realised three years ago that, post-Kadar, the Danube question would be an issue in the subsequent fight for power.' The reformist wing had begun a battle against the great state-owned industrial conglomerates. 'First, the reformers took on the mining conglomerate, then the water lobby.' Water engineers have gained huge power in many Communist states. Their monolithic dams, canals and irrigation schemes suit the desire of central planners to conquer nature. 'The energy and water lobbies represent the Stalinist structure,' Vargha said. 'Water projects here are paramilitary, centralised, undemocratic and monolithic – just like the state. In a country where decisions are taken in hunting lodges and long corridors, and with local people having no say, the power of these élites is huge.'

So when Vargha opposed the Nagymaros dam, he found himself taking on the state itself. But he also found powerful allies among the emerging reform movement within the Communist Party itself.

In mid-1989, at the moment of victory, Vargha had resigned from the Danube Circle, plunging the now-legal environmental group into crisis as it sought to find a new direction for its activities. His reasons may evoke sympathy from many ecologists in the West. Once, he said, 'the Circle had a good scientific reputation, but now I am surrounded by people who are not interested in gaining knowledge. They want glory and success in daily politics. They want to march, produce leaflets, hold press conferences. But they lack data and analysis.'

Now that the samizdat days were passed, the Circle had been boarded by newcomers. Some of those that Vargha liked least had also formed a Green Party. There was much dark talk during my visit about these interlopers, many of them from the Youth Environmental Council, an organisation set up by the

Communist Youth. And some of Vargha's friends believed that the formation of the Green Party was a Stalinist plot to divide the political opposition. If so, it failed totally.

Vargha, meanwhile, was taking his own place in the new party political scene, as the chief architect of environmental policy for the new Alliance of Free Democrats. Would he take a government job? Maybe. But he claimed to be less interested in government than in the revival of civic life in Hungary. For 30 years, citizens' activities of all sorts, from nature rambles to mass demonstrations, were deemed to be political – and politics was the monopoly of the Party. Its officials oversaw and attempted to control or prohibit everything. For Hungary to become a democracy again, it was important to create an undergrowth of societies, clubs, trades unions and groups of all sorts, untrammelled by Party oversight and the need to be sanctioned by the authorities. This, he felt, was as much a part of democracy as electing democrats to parliament.

Vargha found himself at the centre of a civic movement that extended far beyond the environment. He introduced me to Gyorgyi Mangel from the newly formed Independent Trade Union of Science Workers, which had battled to remove Party officials from their positions of power inside laboratories. And I met Istvan Rev, a streetwise organiser of the Blue List, a loose alliance of activists, many old-timers from the Danube Circle, who want to help set up myriad citizens' self-help groups around the country.

Vargha's idea is to catalyse rather than control. 'Many people want to unify the green groups, since the local groups are mostly very weak,' he says. 'But we must leave them to find their own way. We need free sources of green ideas that are not influenced by political bodies. We need to experiment.'

Many environmentalists who through the 1980s pinned their hopes on links with Western green groups were hoping that those carefully nurtured contacts would now flower. I met Zsuzsa Voltanyi, a young veteran of the 400-strong ELTE Nature Conservation Club at the ELTE University. The club produces an English-language environmental newsletter, *Greenway*, which is circulated in several East European countries. She, like Anna Varkonyi, had been to conferences in the

Netherlands. She and her colleagues had links with Greenpeace in Hamburg. The club's leader, Laszlo Karas, was Friends of the Earth's contact in Hungary. 'We will eventually form a Hungarian FoE group,' she said. It would help them to campaign on such issues as Austrian toxic wastes being brought to Hungary for burial. 'We are afraid that as economic links with the West grow, Hungary could become an environmental colony for the West, taking their waste and doing their dirty jobs.'

Vargha agrees. 'There is a misbelief amoung Hungarians that democracy will solve the ecological problems. This is not so . . . Stalinism has made the situation more serious here. But that is all. After the celebrations, there will be grave days in Hungary for the environment, especially since we have not got the money to clean up the mess left by the Stalinists.'

Vargha wants to set up an ecological research institute, probably financed from abroad. It will look at new ecologically sound ways to develop the ailing Hungarian economy. The massive state farms – modelled all too visibly on the US prairies – have proved an ecological, social and economic disaster. They have destroyed as many Hungarian villages as President Ceausescu wanted to eliminate over the border in Romania; and they have contaminated with nitrate the drinking water of hundreds of villages. There are, say environmentalists, dozens of cases of 'blue baby syndrome' caused by nitrate poisoning each year. A new agricultural plan based on peasant farming is desperately needed and Vargha would like to dedicate himself to that task.

I left Vargha at his favourite café beside the Danube and headed for the train that would take me back through the hedgeless prairies of northern Hungary to Austria. He was in deep discussion with Jan Zdarsky, a visiting Czech environmentalist, who was setting up an ecology society in Prague. The authorities were causing trouble. They said his application to register the society was incomplete. And one of the leading environment groups, by the name of Brontosaurus, had turned out to be controlled by the Communist Youth Group. Its members were pushing for independence.

Slovak environmentalists, he said, were less tightly

controlled than their Bohemian counterparts and had spoken out against the Danube project. The Czech dam was almost complete, he said, and despite the breakdown in agreement with the Hungarians work continued. His members had sailed through the construction site the previous week. Zdarsky warned that the Czechoslovak government might build a second dam on the Danube if the Hungarians wouldn't. In any case, the single dam could cause considerable environmental destruction on its own.

All this was weeks before the Berlin Wall was breached, before the Ecoglasnost group demonstrated on the streets of Sofia and before protesters besieged Wenceslas Square during the first snowfalls of a Czech winter. But Vargha was already confident of victory. He was certain, he said, that the Prague government would fall. He believed that the Czech dam at Gabcikovo, though largely built, would never be filled. But in that he met early disappointment. The leaders of Czechoslovakia's 'velvet revolution' showed no desire to halt their half of the project. 'Their revolution has changed the leadership, but underneath nothing has changed,' complained Varkonyi in the spring of 1990.

Ecoglasnost

Throughout Eastern Europe during the 1980s environment groups emerged as a major focus for independent activity by intellectuals, students and ordinary citizens. This must have come as a nasty shock to the authorities. Many of the groups had been set up under official auspices during the 1970s in response to the Stockholm Conference on the Human Environment of 1972, and remained formally under the control of the Young Communist Leagues. Initially, they were politically harmless youth groups, a cross between Boy Scout brigades and natural history societies. But some grew up. They began to campaign on politically sensitive issues, such as pollution from steel works, unpopular dams and mines. And during the late 1980s, environmentalism became a magnet for general dissent and finally a crucible for outright opposition to the Communists. As the *Independent* newspaper put it in a review of the momentous events in Eastern Europe in 1989: 'Throughout Eastern Europe, environmental issues were much on people's minds. Because the requirements of five-year plans had taken precedence over the health of the population, there were few environmental controls. Ecological issues provided a focus for opposition and discontent without explicitly challenging the supremacy of the Communist Party itself.' Earlier in the year, Michael Redclift, a sociologist from the University of London, had written in the *Ecologist*: 'In a serious sense, the new green movements of Eastern Europe are the political opposition. What has forged these green movements is the guiding principle that people have a right to decide how their own resources and environment are managed, and the role of the government is to respond to their wishes.' As state-controlled factories poured sulphurous fumes and toxic chemicals into air, rivers and soils, they became a potent symbol of everything that had gone wrong with the Stalinist regimes.

'Coal – the Blood of the Republic', said a sign outside one of Czechoslovakia's dirtiest power stations at Bilana in northern Bohemia. But the foul air resulting from burning the country's sulphurous brown coal also proved the death of the republic, as people shunned bribes of extra wages to stay in the region. Life expectancy fell and doctors, who saw the diseased lungs daily, left in the greatest numbers. As Western television cameras caught the mass demonstrations in Prague's Wenceslas Square in December 1989, the backdrop to the muffled masses was a smog of the kind not seen in Western capitals for 25 years.

Ecology counted in the events of 1989. It triggered events in Hungary; and in Bulgaria, it was ecologists taking to the streets in October 1989 that led within days to the fall of Todor Zhivkov, president for 35 years. Ecoglasnost had been formed to oppose Bulgarian pollution in March 1989. Its co-ordinator, Hristo Smolenov, said then, 'We have no political aspirations. We are seeking a dialogue.' They wanted public discussion of environmental problems, such as the appalling air pollution in the country's capital, Sofia, and pollution of rivers and the Black Sea. By the summer, Ecoglasnost had just 100 members. But as political discontent grew across Eastern Europe, they saw a chance to gather support for the cause during a 35-nation conference on East–West co-operation and security held in Sofia at the end of October. This was one of a series of conferences arising from the Helsinki declaration of 1977. They had a large audience of foreign press and government delegates to the conference, and expected that the Bulgarian authorities would not cause trouble. Ecoglasnost held three public meetings, each attracting more than a thousand people, and collected more than 9,000 signatures on a petition.

Official patience snapped. More than 40 people were arrested, including a Soviet environmentalist attending a separate meeting, and a British journalist was assaulted. The secretary of Ecoglasnost, Alexander Karakachanov, who was also a city councillor, was badly beaten. Many of the beatings took place in full view of delegates to the conference. The delegates suspended proceedings to voice criticisms of the assaults. A Bulgarian minister was forced to admit the use of excess force.

Ecoglasnost ended the conference with a march of 10,000 people to deliver their petition to the national assembly. It was the largest unofficial rally in Bulgaria for 45 years. Journalists reported that many of the chants were for 'Democracy'; and one dissident told them, 'It will be impossible to keep the lid on alternative opinion in Bulgaria any longer. We have crossed a watershed.' Within a week Zhivkov had resigned and within a month his successor had agreed to hold free elections. As the *Independent* observed, 'Bulgaria did not need a quarter of a million people on the streets in order to force a change. A mere 10,000 were enough.' Of course, the environment was not the only or even the major cause of the popular revolts in Bulgaria, or even in Hungary. But in both countries it had proved a catalyst, a symbol of a wider malaise. And there were similar stirrings throughout Eastern Europe.

In Czechoslovakia, the Charter 77 Human Rights organisation had, at its tenth conference in 1987, added environmental issues to its platform. 'When trees are dying, when the water is dirty, when the air is dangerous for little children, that's worse than prison,' said one Czech activist, Lena Mareckova.

In East Germany, groups such as the Arche Ecological Network campaigned in the late 1980s against the chronic winter smogs (reminiscent of the London 'pea-soupers' of the 1950s, which killed hundreds of people). Smogs there are worst in the industrial cauldrons of Bitterfeld and Leipzig, the centre of the first protests in 1989 and of later calls for German reunification. The authorities had clearly realised the danger posed by environmental activities. An official crackdown on dissidents in 1987 chose as a prime target an environmental library set up in the Zion Church in East Berlin.

A thriving network of contacts had developed during the 1980s between environmentalists from East and West. The first stage of the creation of what one might call a 'common environmental house' in Europe happened in the early 1980s, after several Eastern European governments agreed with their Western counterparts to cut sulphur pollution from power plants and factories, the prime causes of acid rain, by 30 per cent. Western environmentalists began to investigate pollution from the East and discovered conditions there that exceeded their worst nightmares. One East German power station was emitting more sulphur dioxide than the whole of Sweden. Visitors to the Erzgebirge mountains on the border between industrial regions of East Germany and Czechoslovakia reported that air pollution had killed the forests that once covered the mountains, leaving a desolate landscape where nothing would grow.

West Germany, which was spending billions of Deutschmarks scrubbing sulphur pollution from its own chimneys, suddenly noticed that most smogs on its land descended when the winds were from the east. (An air pollution inspector in Nurnberg told me about 'the smell of Czechoslovakia – it's like cat's pee.') In 1984 West German Greenpeacers caused a stir in Czechoslovakia when they crossed the border and attempted to hang a poster opposing acid rain to a power station chimney. They were met by a rain of shots and fled into the arms of the police, who released them after official protests from Germany.

Greenpeace was active again in 1988, this time with local collaboration. It sent its mobile laboratory bus round the Baltic coast, working with Polish scientists at Gdansk to sample water pollution and popping into a trade fair in Leningrad. Meanwhile, Italians had forged links in Yugoslavia. Scandinavians became aware that much more air pollution was reaching them from the countries of Eastern Europe (the real 'dirty men of Europe') than from Britain. They made connections in East Germany and Poland, creating the Swedish–Polish Environmental Federation, for example, which held youth training camps in Poland, monitored pollution of one of Poland's filthiest rivers, the Vistula, and organised environmental twinning between cities. Under this scheme the Swedish cities of Gothenburg gave Kracow $1,000 to purchase equipment to monitor air pollution.

Friends of the Earth International enrolled the Polish Ecology Club and the Estonian Green Movement as members of the FoE family, and held its annual meeting for 1988 in Poland. In early 1989, the Dutch-based group, Air Pollution Action Network, set up a three-year East–West project, funded by the Dutch government and FoE. It held its first meeting in Miskolc in northern Hungary, close to that country's borders with Czechoslovakia, Poland, Romania and the Soviet Union, and in the heart of oak forests damaged by acid rain. There were representatives from more than 30 East European organisations. Through these links, greens more than most people in the West became aware that momentous political change was under way in the East.

The very first, swiftly suppressed, signs of rebellion in the East were in Poland. The emergence there in 1980 of Solidarity allowed scientists to speak out against industrial pollution, especially in the south of the country. The metal and stonework of Kracow, Poland's ancient capital and once one of Europe's most beautiful cities, was literally being dissolved and corroded away by acid fall-out from the industrial heartland of Upper Silesia, based on Katowice, to the west. In Upper Silesia, half the area's two million inhabitants suffer air pollution that was officially deemed a hazard to health. They eat garden vegetables heavily contaminated by heavy metals such as lead and cadmium. Further west again are the Isergebirge mountains, probably the most polluted area in the whole of Europe. They are at the epicentre of Eastern Europe's pollution, midway between Upper Silesia, Czechoslovakia's power plants in northern Bohemia and an array of huge power stations burning dirty brown coal lined up along East Germany's eastern border. The East German power stations send more than 2 million tonnes of sulphur dioxide to Poland on the prevailing westerly winds each year. One of the power plants, at Boxberg right by the border, is reportedly the biggest polluter north of the Pyrenees. A reporter for the *New Scientist* returned in 1981 from a trip sponsored by the Polish journalists' Protection of the Environment Club with a long article headlined: 'Poland – the most polluted country in the world?'

In March 1989, on the eve of the changes that brought a resurgent Solidarity to power, a Polish sociologist, Pietr Glinski, estimated that there were 60 national and regional ecological groups. They ranged from the Nature Preserving Guard and the Scout Movement for Environmental Protection to the Polish Green Party, the Silesia Ecological Movement, Ecology for Peace and the splendidly named 'I Prefer to Be'. This last group, a youth movement, was formed by editors of a weekly paper, *Na Przelaj*, in response to a mass of letters following an article it ran on ecological threats in Upper Silesia.

The first and most influential of the new groups was the Polish Ecology Club. It was formed in Kracow in 1980 by Solidarity trade unionists, journalists and academics. It began in a blaze of success, organising a massive campaign of legal actions and local demonstrations against the nearby Skawina aluminium plant, a major source of the town's pollution. It forced the closure of the plant, but after Solidarity's first 16-month honeymoon, when the authorities had clamped down on political activity at the end of 1981, the Club ceased to be a popular mass-based organisation. It became dominated by scientists and intellectuals, who opposed demonstrations and marches by its network of local groups. Many of the

Club's members are also in the Polish Academy of Sciences, whose report on the Polish environment published in 1988 helped sow the seeds of the revival of Solidarity's fortunes the following year. And when Solidarity began its round-table discussions with the ruling Communists in early 1989, the environment was at the top of the agenda, alongside political reform. The resulting joint administration ordered the closure of 18 especially polluting factories.

Radical green activity in Poland today is often centred around Freedom and Peace. Formed in April 1985 with the initial aim of establishing an alternative to national military service, it soon developed an ecological agenda, arguing that 'freedom should also be the possibility to live in non-devastated surroundings.' Usurping the Ecology Club's leading role in popular protest, the group helped persuade the authorities to agree to close Wroclaw's Siechnice steel foundry by 1992. And, Greenpeace-style, four members climbed to the top of a prominent building in Kracow to demonstrate against the state of the city's buildings.

Poland received more radioactive fall-out from the Chernobyl nuclear accident of 1986 than any other country besides the Soviet Union. Afterwards, Freedom and Peace decided to take up anti-nuclear activities, pointing out that proposed new nuclear plants for their country employed Soviet designs. The group held regular demonstrations against the proposed nuclear power complex, Poland's first, at Zarnowiec near Gdansk, and demonstrated against similar plans for the small town of Darlowo on the Baltic coast as well as against a proposed nuclear dump at a power plant at Miedzyrzecz in the far east of the country. In mid-1988 a public meeting to discuss rumours that a nuclear plant was to be built at Darlowo was surrounded by militia and the participants were arrested. Nonetheless, Freedom and Peace's congress in early 1989 launched an 'all-Polish campaign against nuclear power engineering' whose main tactic would be protest marches and demonstrations. The Silesian Ecological Movement has close links with both Freedom and Peace and Greenpeace International. It was formed in 1988 to undertake 'direct ecological actions' against polluting factories in the region.

While the Ecology Club's links with Solidarity placed it within the political mainstream after 1989, Freedom and Peace and its allies seemed set to maintain their radical edge, a thorn in the side of the new orthodoxy as it strove to establish a Western-style economy. In late 1989, one activist said, 'Life was much easier in the old days; we knew what we were doing.' As in Hungary, the political change brought new freedoms, but also new uncertainties. A study by the World Bank, which was eager to invest in the new, democratised Poland, put the cost of cleaning up the worst of Poland's pollution of air, water and land at $25 billion. But it made the country sound clean compared to East Germany where the first estimates put the bill at $72 billion.

The greening of the republics

During 1990, the Soviet Union too showed strong signs of the radicalisation of once-timid environmental groups, with a parallel growth of overtly nationalist green organisations, especially in the Baltic republics. There was plenty to complain about, from Chernobyl and the desiccation of the Aral Sea to air pollution in the Arctic and the loss of the Volga's sturgeon.

Environmental activity of a sort has a long tradition in the Soviet Union, beginning in the 19th century. In the early days of the Bolshevik revolution under Lenin there were strong ecological programmes backed up by the creation of nature reserves, called *zapovedniki*, which at one time covered approaching 30,000 square kilometres of the Soviet Union and were dedicated to scientific research.

All this changed with the advent of Stalin and the first five-year plan of 1928–33. The emphasis was now on rapid industrialisation and the conquest, rather than the study, of nature. Grand projects were pushed ahead at great speed and at almost any cost. There were dams built all along the Dnieper and the Volga, Europe's greatest river, and a canal hacked through ice and rock linking the Baltic and White Seas. The canal cost the lives of a reputed 250,000 prison labourers. The notion, popular even until the 1980s, that pollution was a capitalist notion and inconceivable in centrally planned economies, also dates from this era.

Conservationists, says the environmental historian Douglas Weiner, 'were attacked for their bourgeois social origins, for setting themselves up as a technocratic opposition to economic policies decided upon by the party, for pursuing "science for science's sake", and most crucially for arguing limits to successful human transformation of nature.' Trofim Lysenko, the infamous Soviet biologist, was behind the Stalinist assault on ecological conservation before he moved on to attack genetics.

After Stalin's death in 1953, some nature reserves were reinstated. The All Russian Society for Conservation, formed under Lenin, but virtually disbanded under Stalin, again flourished, eventually being admitted to the International Union for the Conservation of Nature (IUCN) in 1960.

In the 1960s and 1970s, environmental issues were one of the few areas where the sound of something approaching public debate (albeit starved of basic information) could be heard. The most vociferous of these debates concerned the fate of the nation's great lakes, especially Lake Baikal, the oldest and largest body of fresh water on the planet. Baikal is so clear that the bottom can be seen in places through 40 metres of water. The lake contains 1,200 species, including freshwater seals, seen nowhere else on Earth. Weiner says that for Russians it 'symbolised one of the last major natural features of the Soviet Union unmarred by heroic construction projects'. Until, that is, 1957 when it was decided to build a viscose rayon plant and a paper mill on its southern shore.

Anger among writers and scientists, backed by the prestigious Siberian Academy of Sciences, gathered pace in the early 1960s and aroused the support of the new *druzhina*, or student brigades, which had sprung up in the Khrushchev era. Despite being sponsored by the Young Communist League (Komsomol), these groups adopted many sensitive environmental issues, opposing the widespread poaching of furs and illegal felling of trees. And they succeeded in dragging the Komsomol into what amounted to official opposition to industrial development on Lake Baikal.

A group of prominent Russian writers, later called the Village Prose School because of their romanticisation of rustic life, joined the protests. The most famous of these writers was Valentin Rasputin whose book *Farewell to Matyora*, published in 1961, chronicled the lives of remote island communities about to be flooded by a large hydroelectric dam at Bratsk on the Angara River near Baikal. Despite the opposition, the mill kept working. The government's one concession was to build a waste treatment plant to reduce the toxicity of the 100 million tonnes of effluent entering the lake from the plant each year. Because the lake is so large, even this volume of effluent has had virtually no effect on its pristine quality. Nonetheless, the fate of Baikal remained a bone of contention for Russians right through the Brezhnev era, until Gorbachev was again pressed to save the lake from further harm.

In 1987, Rasputin, who had spent some years campaigning for the preservation of the old centres of Siberian towns such as Irkutsk and Omsk, helped to form the Movement for the Protection of Baikal. It won from Gorbachev a promise to close the mill in 1993. The Movement's public meetings became popular events in Irkutsk and Bratsk.

Water engineering projects, which featured strongly in Stalin's plans for subjugating nature, have also excited the passions of the Russian people. The same coalition of intellectuals that had formed to preserve Lake Baikal in the 1960s came together in the 1970s and 1980s to oppose plans to divert north-flowing Siberian rivers south to provide water for the irrigation of cotton fields in the southern republics around the Caspian and Aral Seas. This vastly expensive scheme came close to final approval under Chernenko in 1983, but was finally cancelled by Gorbachev three years later.

This thread of officially tolerated environmental protest appears to have flourished during the Brezhnev era under the mute patronage of the leading Politburo ideologue, Mikhail Suslov. He helped Brezhnev unseat Khrushchev in the Kremlin coup of 1964, and saw environmental concerns as one aspect of his fervent Russian nationalism.

The political dynamite for the Soviet authorities, as for other East European governments, arises when environmental issues become connected to wider political debates. Green campaigners came to see the solutions to their problems in unravelling the centrally planned economy, reducing the role of the Communist Party in the state and giving the republics national autonomy. During late 1989, that challenge was being posed most directly by the Baltic environmentalists.

The Estonian Green Movement, for instance, though admitted to membership of FoE International, was operating in most respects like a political opposition. The Movement began at Tartu University, the same place that formed the first of the Soviet student environmental brigades back in the early 1960s, and was launched officially in May 1988, just a month after the nationalist Estonian Popular Front burst in on the scene. According to Popular Front leader Marju Lauristan, the Green Movement came first and then evolved into the Popular Front.

Late in 1989 I met Olevi Kull, a leader of the Movement. He talked briefly about Soviet indifference to issues such as energy efficiency and global warming, and public opposition to large hydroelectric power schemes. He talked of the possibility of the Soviet Union joining international efforts to curb the greenhouse effect. But, time and again, he returned to the same point: 'In the Soviet Union, where ideology has prevailed over economy and common sense, even international agreements and protocols, signed by the USSR, may not work effectively. In general, the shortest and most exact answer to the question, "What can East Europe do?" is: East Europe must fight against totalitarianism. There is no other way.'

Other leaders of the Movement echo the same theme. Juhan Aare was a delegate to a conference of the Communist Party in Moscow in 1988. He took with him a jar of sea-water taken from the Gulf of Parnu, off the Baltic Sea. 'We in Estonia must be able to begin working in earnest on our own account – independently of Moscow – to solve our most serious ecological problems,' he said. That may mean shutting down local factories in defiance of Moscow. One of the first acts of the Estonian parliament after its declaration of opposition to rule from Moscow in 1988 was to turn down proposals from the capital to expand mining of both oil-shale and phosphorus in the republic.

This overt politicising of the Baltic green groups brought rude words from Greenpeace, after it set up a Moscow office with the help of Yevgeny Velikhov, a leading figure at the Soviet Academy of Sciences and the man Gorbachev sent as his emissary to Chernobyl after the accident in 1987. Greenpeace, the maverick of the international green movement, finds itself allied to an establishment under attack from environmentalists. As one of its spokesmen told the press at the launch of the Moscow office in 1989, 'We won't work with some of the Baltic so-called green organisations, which are really just nationalistic movements.' In the Baltic the distinction was just not understood.

The environment has proved a unifying theme for the separate nationalist movements of the Baltic republics. In September 1988, between 50,000 and 100,000 Latvians, Lithuanians and Estonians linked hands along the shores of the Baltic to call attention to the chronic pollution of the sea. Later that month, some 15,000 Lithuanians formed another human chain, this time round a nuclear plant at Ignalina, which they want shut. The following month, 600,000 people, one in six of the population of the republic, signed a petition opposing the plant. A year later, they won a partial victory when the local authorities agreed to halt work on a third reactor being built at the plant.

In Latvia the formation of an Ecology Club in 1987, when a group carrying a green flag broke away from the traditional May Day parade, acted as a pathfinder for the creation of a political movement, the Popular Front, a year later. The theme there is the same. As Anda Anaspokc of the Latvian Ecology Club told the *Observer* newspaper in 1989, 'Environmental problems can be solved only when the political situation is changed. While the industries remain under the control of the ministries in Moscow, they will only be interested in production.'

In other republics, too, environmentalism goes hand in hand with nationalism. There have been large demonstrations against industrial pollution in the troubled republic of Armenia. In 1986, some 350 intellectuals sent an open letter to Gorbachev claiming that air pollution was causing stomach cancers, heart and lung disease and birth defects in the republic. In 1988 people protested in the streets of Yerevan, the Armenian capital, demanding the closure of a factory producing synthetic rubber. The demonstration triggered the launch of the republic's National Democratic Movement, which campaigned for the return of the disputed territory of Nagorno-Karabakh to Armenia, bringing months of bloody battles with Azerbaijanis. The authorities responded to the angry protests by closing the chemical plant concerned, but had no answer to the nationalist forces that the original protest had unleashed.

Even in republics close to the heart of the union, anger about the environment has been expressed in nationalist terms. Byelorussia was a normally docile republic in the east of the country, sandwiched between Poland and Russia. Local patriotic groups, such as the Byelorussian Popular Front, have successfully resisted plans for a nuclear plant at the republic's capital of Minsk. In 1989, they fanned a tide of anger that details of the full extent of nuclear fall-out on the republic from the Chernobyl accident of 1987 had been kept secret. In fact two-thirds of the fall-out from the accident landed in Byelorussia. The Front produced documents from the Byelorussian Academy of Sciences apparently showing an increase in cases of anaemia and hyperplasia of the thyroid – both signs of radioactive poisoning – in the republic. In 1989, a local physicist was sentenced to two months' 'corrective labour' for organising an anti-nuclear rally in Minsk, which 30,000 people are said to have joined. But a year later, the Popular Front organised a 150,000-strong demonstration in the same city demanding the prosecution of the republic's former Party chief, Nikolai Slyunkov, for hiding the scale of the disaster from Chernobyl fall-out.

In the Ukraine, where the accident occurred, a group called Green World has made similar allegations and brought some 30,000 people on to the streets of the republic's capital, Kiev. In early 1990, Green World became a focus for opposition to the Communist Party in the run-up to local elections and the republic's parliament called for the closure of the Chernobyl complex.

Since the Chernobyl accident, a flurry of protests all across the country has put plans for nuclear expansion in jeopardy. In Gorky, once the closed city where Andrei Sakharov spent his internal exile, 50,000 people signed a petition opposing a nuclear plant for the city. (The Samizdat News Agency reported that one man was fined for displaying placards combining the demand for closure with a call for the town to be given back its old name of Nizhny Novgorod.) And three years of protests against plans for a nuclear plant in the Crimea, organised by the Ecological Association of the Crimea, won cancellation of the project in 1989. There have been protests, too, in the central Siberian town of Krasnoyarsk, headed by the chief of the local Communist Party, who opposes plans for a nuclear dump.

Intellectuals in Russia today vie for leadership in the environmental cause. In early 1989, the weekly *Literaturnaya Gazeta*, which had given over a special issue to the environment, carried an open letter from the Soviet Union of Writers attacking the Soviet Academy of Sciences for past failures to criticise the destruction of the environment. Ukrainian writers led opposition to the Crimea nuclear power plant, it said; Russian writers were first to oppose the diversion of Siberian rivers; and Uzbeki writers were ahead of scientists in leaping to the defence of the Aral Sea, which was drying up because so much water was being diverted to irrigate cotton fields.

When a team of experts left Moscow in 1988 to investigate the state of the Aral Sea and 'arouse public opinion and urge people to come to the defence of the Sea', it was headed by a writer, Grigory Reznichenko of the magazine *Novy Mir*, and partly sponsored by the Soviet Writers Union. (They missed the irony that much of the trouble was caused by an earlier campaign of theirs against plans to divert south waters from Siberian rivers. The water from those rivers had been earmarked to replenish the Aral Basin.)

Despite responding to overwhelming public opposition to particular plants or projects, it was difficult in the first years of Gorbachev's rule to see any sign of government policy changes to preserve the environment. In its first two years the State Committee for the Protection of the Environment had little tangible effect. But if perestroika had failed to deliver, then glasnost was reaping its whirlwind. Even the official news agency, Novosti, was mailing to the foreign press the most damaging news about the Soviet environment. One release described what it called 'the serious ecological havoc wrought in the Volga basin due to lack of forethought, and the efforts now being made by a committee of intellectuals to campaign to save this once splendid river'.

'Mother Volga' has suffered since Stalin began to build industrial complexes, dams and canal systems along the river in the 1930s. Most emotively for Russians, the once-prolific sturgeon, the source of caviar, is now a rarity in the river. Industrial effluent, especially from a vast chemicals complex at Astrakhan, kills the fish, and dams have cut off routes to spawning grounds in the upper reaches. The Moscow-based committee to save the river was set up in early 1989 and headed by Vasily Belov, who in the 1960s was a leading light of the Village Prose group, writing books on the history of Russian village life. The committee wanted reservoirs demolished and pollution reduced so that the sturgeon could revive and Russians could once again dine on caviar. 'However difficult, we have discovered within ourselves the strength to admit that our land is in danger ... Ahead of us is a long, exhausting and probably unequal battle against the technocratic bureaucracy,' wrote Novosti's correspondent.

Such sentiments were certainly a far cry from the official line in the late 1970s when one Soviet official who wrote a tract called *The Destruction of Nature in the Soviet Union*, full of the kind of invective that is common currency in the Soviet press today, had to smuggle his manuscript to West Germany. The official, Ze'ev Vol'fson, published it under a pseudonym, Boris Komarov, which veiled his identity until he left the Soviet Union years later.

The first victory for the Save the Volga campaign came in early 1989 when the Ministry of Land Reclamation and Water Resources agreed to halt construction of a canal to take the river's water for irrigating fields near Stavropol. Ecologists warned that the planned transfer of almost 2 cubic kilometres of water a year would empty the Caspian Sea just as surely as had already happened to the Aral Sea. When the decision was taken, 30 kilometres had been dug at a cost of $100 million. The scheme had originally been a small part of the grand plan to bring Siberian water south. But determined officials from the ministry had proceeded with it regardless of the cancellation of the main project.

Concern about pollution played a prominent part in lighting the flames of rebellion in Eastern Europe in the 1980s. Now, cleaning up the toxic mess is set to be one of the most expensive tasks in repairing the damage caused by 40 years of Communism. In years to come, however, it may become clear that Eastern Europe was the first region in the world where the environment moved to the centre of the political agenda.

6

IN BRAZIL

The warriors gather

Chief Paulinho Paiakan, at 35 the head of the Kayapo Indians
in the Amazon rainforest, left his hospital bed in Belem, where
the wonders of modern surgery had removed his troublesome
appendix. He boarded a plane for the 700-kilometre flight to
Altamira. As he stepped down from the plane in the jungle
boom town, two lines of Kayapo warriors in black and red
body paint and wearing brilliant head-dresses made of parrot
feathers set up a chant. Elders wept. And television crews from
Britain, Japan, West Germany and Brazil set their cameras
whirring in the steamy afternoon air.

Altamira boasts one of the busiest airports in the Amazon
rainforest. The town calls itself the new capital of Amazonia,
taking over from the more famous Manaus, home of past
booms in the Amazon. Its growth is so recent that only
large-scale maps mark it at all. Whereas Manaus has an opera
house, boatloads of tourists and scientists stepping out of the
forest, Altamira is home to tens of thousands of desperately
poor settlers from the cities, many panning for gold in the
river, and the local offices of the rich and right-wing ranchers'
union, the UDR. It is base camp for Brazil's new wild frontier.

Altamira is built on a bend in the River Xingu (pronounced
Shingu), where it is crossed by the Trans-Amazon Highway.
The river and its forested valley are the world of the Kayapo
Indians, who have lived in the forests for some 10,000 years.
The highway and the clearings hacked from the jungle for
miles around on either side are the world of the settlers, mostly
arrived in the 1980s. The uneasy co-existence of the settlers

and the Kayapo, who were finally granted full citizen status within Brazil in late 1988, had been shattered by a plan by the state electricity company, Electronorte, to dam the Xingu at Altamira. Giant pylons would take the hydroelectric power produced by the dam south to feed industry in Sao Paulo. The two dams intended to comprise the Altamira complex would cost $10 billion to build and would together flood at least 7,000 square kilometres, creating the world's largest artificial lake, inundating huge areas of forest and displacing some 70,000 people. Most of the Kayapo people would be flooded from their homes. A small price to pay for progress, said the man from Electronorte. But the Altamira complex was also a small part of a still larger programme of building more than 100 dams elsewhere in Amazonia, including 21 on the Xingu, by the year 2020 as part of the military government's scheme to 'develop' the world's largest surviving rainforest.

Many of the opponents of that plan were in Altamira to welcome chief Paiakan into town. It was February 1989 and Paiakan had recently returned from trips to Capitol Hill, Whitehall and many of the capital cities of Europe, where he had hit the front pages with calls to save the Amazon and its peoples from the dams. Now, building on that success, he had called an extraordinary week-long meeting of tribal chiefs at a community hall in Altamira. Rising from his hospital bed in Belem, he had come to preside over a meeting between a thousand warriors from more than 20 often warring Indian nations and some 500 environmentalists, media folk and assorted stars, all there to focus the world's attention on the crisis in the Amazon.

For five days, the Indians, adorned in feathers and warpaint, held their gathering. And the cameras recorded their greetings with some unlikely supporters from the rich world. Sting, the rock star, was there. He had first met the Kayapo people two years before when he accepted an aerial joyride into the forest from a film-maker during a concert tour of Brazil. 'It changed my life,' he wrote later, and he set up the Rainforest Foundation to help preserve the rainforest and its people. There too was David Suzuki, a well-known Canadian science broad-caster and environmentalist who had fixed up a trip by

Paiakan to Canada and a benefit concert by the folk singer
Gordon Lightfoot. There was even a lone British MP, the
redoubtable Old Etonian rebel, Tam Dalyell, reeling from the
effects of sundry inoculations against tropical diseases. 'It's
one of the most unhealthy places on earth,' his doctor had
warned him.

The gathering was almost certainly the largest convention of
Amazon Indians in modern times. Also offering solidarity
were North American Indians such as the Guujaw and the
Haida from British Columbia in Canada, whose people had
suffered at the North American wild frontier a century before.
And there were messages of support from other beleaguered
rainforest communities round the world such as the Penan
tribe in Sarawak, Malaysia.

The highpoint of the week-long meeting, for the camera
crews at any rate, was a confrontation between Jose Muniz,
chief engineer at Electronorte, and Paiakan's cousin, Tuira.
After a long and hopeless exposition from Muniz on how the
dams would bring 'progress' to the Kayapo, 600 tribespeople
in full battle dress chanted their disapproval, waving clubs and
spears, and Tuira, streaked in warpaint, cut the air with a
machete before ritually slapping both Muniz's cheeks with the
flat of the blade. 'You are a liar,' she said. Even old rainforest
hands were worried at this point. Nicholas Hildyard, a British
campaigner for forest peoples, later wrote in his journal the
Ecologist: 'Around the edge of the hall, the small detachment
of military police fingered their holsters. A few Indian warriors
deftly placed their arrows in their bows. For a moment it
looked as if the worst was about to happen.' But the moment
passed.

Unnoticed, outside the hall most of the settler inhabitants of
Altamira wanted the dam to be built. For the shopkeepers and
traders, it meant business. 'Amazonia is Ours' read a banner
strung across the main street. 'Energy is Progress'. The local
Mercedes dealer was handing out pro-dam T-shirts. Only
Hildyard troubled to report that 6,000 locals turned up for a
rally in support of the dam on the Monday that the Indians
opened their gathering. The settlers are the pioneers in a wild
west show set to run into the 21st century. Unlike the North

American version, however, the Brazilian frontier is in a rainforest – and many of the outside world's sympathies are turning towards the Indians.

With no blood spilt, the Altamira gathering was a dramatic public relations coup for rainforest campaigners from the Xingu valley to the marble halls of Washington – from war-paint to power dressing. It was a set-piece in a concerted campaign during 1989 to make the fate of the Amazon and other rainforests a talking point not just for environmentalists and the people of the forests, but for heads of state and the world's bankers. It had a short-term success. Within three weeks of the gathering, the World Bank, feeling the heat in Washington, its home town, had withdrawn funding from the Xingu dams project. Money was also withheld from dozens of other dams when the World Bank called off plans for a $500 million loan, known as Power Sector II. These rebuffs may, in time, be seen to mark the end of unbridled promotion of huge development projects in the world's wilderness areas, and the gathering at Altamira could mark what one Canadian who went called 'the emergence of native peoples as key players in the worldwide conservation movement'.

During the 1980s, Paiakan had proved himself an effective campaigner, uniting the dozen or so separate Kayapo communities scattered across the southern half of the state of Para to demonstrate against the dumping of radioactive waste and against proposals for damaging restrictions on free speech and travel that were contained in plans for Brazil's new constitution. To face down the latter proposals, his warriors had sat, painted and feathered, inside the parliament buildings of Brasilia for days on end. And in early 1985, they had confronted an invasion on to Kayapo land of 4,000 peasant gold prospectors. Paiakan's leading warriors had captured miners and held them hostage for ten days until the Brazilian government agreed to their demand that prospectors should pay a commission to the Kayapo on gold profits.

Despite these victories, the Kayapo could have had a less sympathetic press. There was the small matter of the hostage taking, which under other circumstances Americans might not have approved of. More worrying for environmentalists, it turns out that several branches of the Kayapo nation not under Paiakan's control are chopping down their own forests for cash. At the time of the Altamira gathering, the current issue of an American journal, *Cultural Survival Quarterly*, reported that five Kayapo settlements – Gorotire, Kikretum, Kubek-rakren, A-ukre and Koraimoro – traded in mahogany, and others would like to join in. One contract signed with a Brazilian timber company in 1984 handed over 10,000 mahogany trees in return for the construction of a 70-kilometre road. Another contract included payment in the form of 15 kilometres of road and a Toyota to drive on it. The journal recorded that one Kayapo chief, Pombo, and his sons moved to a city hotel, where they had a car, alcohol and lived with 'white prostitutes'. Three workers with a lumber company were shot by Kayapo after a dispute over lumber between two Indian groups.

This is not the stuff of green heroes, and the Kayapo are clearly no simple martyrs to the cause of the rainforests. Nor are they immune to the temptations of the Brazilian government's ideas of development. But for both environmentalists and for scientists who have studied the Kayapo, their way of life proves vividly that they are an extraordinary storehouse of knowledge about forest plants and ways of living in the forest. It will all be lost if the Indian nations of the Amazon and their cultures are trampled in the rush to open up the Amazon basin.

One man above all others is responsible for bringing the Kayapo to the attention of the world. He is Darrell Posey, an American ethnobotanist, who has spent more than a decade working in the Gorotire Indian Reserve, heartland of the Kayapo people, investigating the complex systems evolved over thousands of years by the Kayapo to 'manage' the Amazon rainforest – that is, to live in it without destroying it. Scientists such as Posey have discovered that almost everything they learn about the rainforests and surrounding areas of bush is already known to the Indians living there. The average Kayapo child can name and identify 60 different sorts of bee, for instance. The Kayapo classify bushland into 15 distinct types, depending on the mix of vegetation, and they recognise and use 600 species of plants.

The Kayapo practise slash-and-burn farming in the forests, clearing an area for cultivation for a few years before moving on, leaving the land to recover. For many, this sounds primitive, and scientists from Europe and North America until recently frowned on the practice, which is widespread among native peoples throughout the tropical rainforests. They accused the natives of destroying their forests. Yet the crop rotation systems used in their clearings are extremely sophisticated. In their gardens, they plant particular types of bananas that are enjoyed by wasps that would otherwise feed on the crops. Before abandoning plots to the forests, the Kayapo plant groves of brazil nuts and fruit trees along trails hundreds of kilometres long that run through the forest and grasslands.

Herbert Girardet, a British film-maker who has worked extensively in the Amazon forest, describes a trip to a Kayapo forest plot that had not been cultivated for 60 years:

> There we found the palms still growing as evidence that the tribe had had village settlements here until some decades ago. The Indians do not leave stone monuments as they are driven off their ancestral lands, but an enriched forest vegetation is clear evidence of their former presence. But what was a source of food and medicines for the Indians is only judged for how well it burns by the new lords of the land, the cattle ranchers.

Outside the forests, says Posey, the Kayapo create 'forest islands' containing a wide variety of plants that they have learnt to grow better together than apart. This discovery could revolutionise the work of agronomists looking for ways to cultivate the forests. The Kayapo's 'ecological engineering', he says, extends to modifying soils using straw, bark and logs to influence soil moisture and temperature and using many different types of plant ash to nourish different plants. He believes that 'the study of indigenous uses of ground cover, mulch, organic matter and ash could lead to the development of modern agricultural systems in Amazonia that succeed in improving rather than degrading soils . . . Recognition of the value of indigenous knowledge by our civilisation would permit Indians to be seen as major intellectual contributors to humanity, rather than mere exotic footnotes.'

When in January 1988 the Florida Rainforest Alliance, a group of US environmentalists, organised a conference in Miami on ways to manage the rainforest, Posey brought along two Kayapo chiefs, Paiakan and Kube-i Kayapo, to speak about their methods. The two chiefs spoke, too, of their fears for the future of their way of life if the dams on the Xingu were built.

Also at the conference were two campaigners from the Washington environment establishment, Barbara Bramble of the blue-chip National Wildlife Federation and Bruce Rich from the Environmental Defense Fund. Rich and Bramble are well connected, in the tradition of the Washington environ-mentalists, and able to set up events 'on the Hill' (Capitol Hill) at which nationally known senators and congressmen ask questions and the TV networks roll the cameras.

Before the following month was out, the two chiefs, with Posey in attendance, were in Washington and repeating their fears to congressmen, to government officials and finally to the World Bank. Every step of their trip was paid for and organ-ised by Bramble and Rich's organisations.

The chiefs returned home with a bump. They and Posey were all threatened by the Brazilian government with criminal prosecution for 'denigrating Brazil's image abroad'. Brazilian law forbids 'foreigners', who include Indians, from meddling in issues of national interest, and the charges were taken seriously. The three had, by their criticisms in Washington, held up approval of loans for the Xingu projects, and they faced up to three years in gaol.

When Kube-i appeared before the courts in October 1988, he arrived with 400 Kayapo warriors, in ceremonial attire. The hearing was suspended when the judge refused to hear the case unless the chief dressed in 'white man's clothes'. Indian dress was a 'sign of disrespect'. But the charges were abruptly dropped a few days before the Altamira gathering.

Undeterred by the pending court cases, Paiakan had gone ahead with his plans for the Altamira gathering and went off again to North America and Europe in November 1988 to enlist more support. This time the bills were paid by Friends of the Earth, the World Wildlife Fund, Survival International and others. All, for their different reasons, had latched on to the Kayapo's cause. Paiakan explained on the Chicago leg of his tour why he needed them:

> The forest is one big thing: it has people, animals and plants. There is no point saving the animals if the forest is burned down: there is no point saving the forest if the people and animals who live in it are killed or driven away. The groups trying to save the race of animals cannot win if the people trying to save the forest lose. The Indians cannot win without the support of these groups; but the groups cannot win without the help of the Indians, who know the forest and the animals and can tell what is happening to them. No one of us is strong enough to win alone; together we can be strong enough to win.

At the close of the Altamira gathering, the Kayapo conducted their traditional New Corn Ceremony, which ties the productivity of the forests to co-operation and friendship among the people of the forests. The gathering symbolised a new stage of that co-operation, said Paiakan. And as the ceremony reached its height, some normally sober Western journalists claim that a rainbow appeared in the sky.

For the moment, the threat of the dam is past. But the pressures bearing in on the Amazon and the world's other rainforests can only intensify while their governments view development in terms of Western-style giant projects. There were perhaps eight million Indian people in the Amazon rainforest before the Europeans arrived. There are around 200,000 today. In the past 20 years, their numbers have begun slowly to rise again. But much must change if they and the rainforests they understand so intimately are to survive.

The martyrdom of Chico Mendes

Chico Mendes took much the same route to international stardom as Paulinho Paiakan. The leader of the rubber tappers' union in Acre, the westernmost state of Brazil, he was first befriended by an anthropologist, Mary Allegretti – a young Brazilian academic who was attracted by the tappers' non-destructive use of the rainforest. The next stop was a conference in Miami, flight courtesy of Washington environmentalists, who later ferried him to the capital itself. In early attendance, too, was a film-maker, a Briton called Adrian Cowell, who spent much of the 1980s documenting the rape of the Amazon and filmed Mendes's unsuccessful candidacy in the 1986 state elections. In the months before he was assassinated on his back doorstep three days before Christmas 1988, Mendes was far more famous outside Brazil than inside.

Mendes was a second-generation white settler in Acre. His parents, like many other settlers, came from the drought-prone north-east of Brazil. They had been sent to work on revived plantations to cut rubber for the Allied war effort. He worked on the plantation from the age of nine and was taught to read – and to find Radio Moscow on his radio dial – by an intinerant revolutionary who was fleeing the authorities and making for the Bolivian border. Mendes remained a left-winger till his death. He was a candidate for the Workers' Party and flirted with illegal Communist groups.

During the 1960s, cattle ranchers from southern Brazil began to buy up the rubber estates of Acre and clear trees for pasture. Many of the tappers were evicted and retreated into the forest, ever closer to the Peruvian border, to continue their trade. As the ranchers advanced, the rubber tappers and others who made their livings from the forest formed the Xapuri Rural Workers Union, of which Mendes was president by the mid-1970s. They began to invade *en masse* areas of forest about to be cleared by ranchers – a strategy, called *empate*, which saved tens of thousands of hectares from destruction during the 1970s and 1980s. Mendes claimed shortly before his death that of 45 *empate* in Xapua and nearby Brasileia, 'we've saved fifteen and lost thirty, but it was worth it.'

The tappers' union also began to confront the ranchers and their hugely influential union, the UDR, in state and government corridors of power. They argued that rubber tapping and gathering nuts, roots and berries was an economically, socially and environmentally better way to develop the forests than to submit it to the chainsaw and firebrand to create low-grade pasture.

Mary Allegretti 'discovered' Mendes after she had written a thesis on the traditional methods of rubber tappers in Acre – the heart of the 19th-century rubber boom in Brazil. She joined a literacy programme being set up by the tappers in Xapuri, Mendes's home town. And later, taking a more political route to helping them in their battle with encroaching cattle ranchers, she acted in effect as their external liaison officer while at the Institute of Socio-Economic Studies in Brasileia, a small town near the Bolivian border.

With the help of Allegretti, the tappers formed the National Rubber Tappers Council, which held its first congress in 1985. Neither Mendes nor the tappers wanted the forest turned into a giant nature reserve. It was much too important for that. Like the Kayapo on the other side of the forest, they saw it as a resource to be sustained, nurtured and profited from, rather than something to be fenced off or, worse, cleared away to 'open up' the region. It was this case that took Mendes in the late 1980s to Miami, where he met leaders of the Inter-American Development Bank, and to Washington and the World Bank. He argued that their grants and loans for ranches, roads, dams and mines in the forest were destroying rather than developing the region.

The Brazilian press largely ignored Mendes's life and took little notice of his death. But his visits to Washington and elsewhere had attracted a lot of international attention and his assassination was headline news round the world on Christmas Eve. There was a memorial service for him in Washington in January. The service was sponsored by Greenpeace, the National Wildlife Federation and other environmental groups in the capital and included readings from letters he had written shortly before his death. In one, in a strange echo of the language used by Martin Luther King before his own assassination, Mendes wrote:

> My dream is to see this entire forest conserved because we know it can guarantee the future for all the people who live in it. Not only that, I believe that in a few years the Amazon can become an economically viable region not only for us, but for the nation, for all humanity. I don't want flowers at my funeral because I know they would be taken from the forest.

Several other rubber tappers' leaders have also been shot dead in Brazil. One of Mendes's members, Wilson Pinheiro, was gunned down in a union office in July 1980. Mendes, too, expected to be killed. Indeed, in an interview a few weeks before his death he said, 'Our movement's leaders are all on the death list of the UDR's assassination squads. Here in Xapuri, these squads are led by Darli Alves.'

The bloody fate of Chico Mendes may have been sealed by his greatest triumph. In 1987 he had launched a battle to save the Cachoeira rubber estate outside Xapuri, where he had been brought up and tapped trees for 20 years before he took up union work. The estate had been bought by a ranching family who tried to drive 60 tapper families from the land. Mendes convinced the tappers to stay where they were, despite death threats against him from the estate's new owner, the man he named as leader of the local assassination squad, Darli Alves. 'We had pickets of almost 400 people out there in the middle of the forest, every one of them determined not to let a single landowner near the place,' he said later. Mendes wanted the estate at Cachoeira to be taken over by the government as an 'extractive reserve', an area of forest where logging and clearing are banned and where the rubber tappers and collectors of other fruits of the forest could continue their trades undisturbed. He and Allegretti had proposed this idea as an alternative method of economic development in the Amazon at the first National Rubber Tappers Congress in 1985. In the summer of 1988, in an atmosphere of mounting violence in Acre which saw the death in a roadside ambush of another of

Mendes's protégés, the government relented. It turned 6,000 hectares of the estate over to an extractive reserve, the first in Xapuri. In July 1988, five months before his death, Mendes was able to lead environmentalists and journalists from round the world through the Cachoeira estate. It was the scene of a very personal triumph and of a new beginning for Acre, and possibly the whole Amazon. But that December, Mendes was shot as he went for an evening shower, allegedly by Darci, son of Darli Alves.

Since 1988, the idea of extractive reserves has gained enormous political currency. Several more are to be established with the help of money put up both by the World Bank and the Inter-American Development Bank, as well as the World Wide Fund for Nature (formerly the World Wildlife Fund). The International Tropical Timber Organization (a trade club of both the producers and users of tropical timber) has responded to pressure from the WWF by setting aside $4 million to finance 12 more reserves in Acre.

The economic case for the reserves has been bolstered by an American study published late in 1989. It showed that brazil nuts and rubber are only the first of many dozens of natural forest products that could be harvested and marketed profitably, including 72 species of trees and 11 species of fruit. The authors found that in straight economic terms the forests of the Amazon were worth at least twice as much as a permanent living resource as they would be either chopped down for timber or converted to cattle pasture. And they concluded that 'without question, the sustainable exploitation of non-wood forest resources represents the most immediate and profitable method for integrating the use and conservation of Amazonian forests.' They continued:

Why has so little been done to promote the marketing, processing and development of these valuable resources? We believe that the problem lies . . . in the failure of public policy to recognise it. Tropical timber is sold in international markets and generates substantial amounts of foreign exchange. Non-wood resources, on the other hand, are collected and sold in local markets by an incalculable number of subsistence farmers, forest collectors, middlemen and shop-owners. These decentralised trade networks are extremely hard to monitor and easy to ignore in national accounting schemes.

Flaviano Melo, Acre's governor, insists that he wants to save the state's rainforests. 'This is Brazil's last frontier and we intend to ensure there is rational development,' he says. He is an active supporter of extractive reserves and his state's new slogan is 'the green state with new ideas'. But the fate of the state's forests and their inhabitants remains in the balance. The rubber tappers themselves believe that the creation of the reserves is no substitute for the eventual removal of the rubber barons from the area and the return of all the land to the people who live and work on it. Less well publicised than their calls for extractive reserves has been the decision of most of the region's tappers to stop paying rent to their landlords, and to set up their own rubber co-operatives to sell the rubber they produce.

The first such sale, by the River Tejo Association of Rubber Tappers and Farmers, was in July 1989. Tanya Schwartz, a young British volunteer helping to establish the co-operative, called it 'the first time in a hundred years that income from the sale of rubber went to the primary producers themselves'. Now the tappers want to begin to sell other produce such as black beans and rice grown in forest clearings and along river banks, and perhaps forest medicines. Theirs is a political as much as an environmental movement, something that annoys some environmentalists in the US who don't want to be seen dabbling in politics, still less Marxist politics.

Meanwhile, the highway is coming. The asphalting of Highway 364, the road across the Amazon that is heading, apparently inexorably, for Peru and the Pacific Ocean, has reached Acre. In Brazil, roads bring ranchers, homeless settlers, guns – and the fires whose progress fills the world's press each autumn. When the road's builders reached neighbouring Rondonia in the early 1980s, 24 per cent of the state's once-complete blanket of rainforest was destroyed within a decade. In Acre, which has lost 5 per cent of its forests in the past 15 years, the destruction may have barely begun, despite the new, greener noises coming from the state's governor.

As Antonio Macedo, a leading figure in the co-operative movement, told Schwartz, 'Along with the road will come wild capitalism. Rubber estates have already been bought – ready to extract wood. We have seen helicopters above the Tejo river. They are marking suitable logging sites.' But there are many who want the road. The governor of Acre told the *Financial Times* in mid-1989, 'It may sound paradoxical, but this road will help, not hinder, a sensible settlement of the state.' For one thing, he says, it will improve the access of the rubber tappers to export markets in North America or Japan. Juneia Mallas, the Brazilian film-maker and wife of Britain's leading rainforest campaigner of the 1980s, Charles Secrett of Friends of the Earth, agrees. 'Even the tappers want the road,' she told me. 'It will stop them being cut off in the rainy season and is essential if they are to export produce from a sustainably run forest.' The real need, she agrees, is Brazilian land reform that would allow the tappers to use the road without being engulfed by 'wild capitalism' and the landless poor heading down the road from Rondonia.

Few believe that, without such reforms, the machinery of even a green-minded state government in this remote outpost of Brazil, where the gun still rules, could halt the tide that will follow the completion of the asphalting of Highway 364. What has happened to Rondonia since the highway came seems set to happen in Acre. In May 1989, the federal government's chief environmental inspector in Acre, Paulo Beninca, was forced from his car at gunpoint and beaten with clubs after fining a local sawmill owner for felling brazil-nut trees. Beninca had recently been transferred from a previous job – protecting the trees of Rondonia.

Bankrolling disaster

Until 1968, the state of Rondonia, like Acre beyond it, was virtually impossible to reach by land. To penetrate these western recesses of the vast Amazon region, any traveller from Sao Paulo or Rio would first have to travel far to the north, to the River Amazon, and then take a boat upstream. The journey would take several weeks. At that time Rondonia's population of perhaps 70,000 was made up largely of Indian tribes and itinerant rubber tappers. The coming of Highway 364 changed all that. You could drive from Rio to Rondonia in a couple of days, initially only during the dry season, but once the road was paved in 1984, courtesy of a loan from the World Bank, all year round.

Settlers came in their tens of thousands – poor farmers thrown off the large mechanised plantation estates in the south of the country; the destitute from the shanty towns of the big cities and the drought-plagued north-east of the country; and land speculators eager to take a slice of the Amazon basin by the traditional Brazilian method of chopping down the forest and herding on to the charred land a few cattle. For all the talk by Western environmentalists of the Brazilian rainforest being destroyed for hamburgers, the truth is that the cattle are a pretext. As Philip Fearnside of the National Institute for Research in the Amazon puts it, 'Pasture represents the easiest way to occupy an extensive area, thus considerably increasing the impact of a small population on deforestation. Real estate speculation is a major force driving deforestation in the Brazilian Amazon.'

Throughout the 1970s, the forest was hacked and burned at an ever-increasing rate. Then, in 1981, the World Bank agreed to fund a new $1.5 billion development project for the state called Polonoroeste. A major feature of the project was the paving of Highway 364 and the construction of new feeder roads into the jungle. The original aim of the project was to stem the environmental destruction by encouraging farmers to replace cattle with crops such as cocoa, coffee and rubber. 'From an environmental standpoint,' said a joint report by the World Bank and the World Wildlife Fund, 'tree crops are strongly preferred over animals and pasture because of their superior ability to protect fragile soils from erosion.' Crops would also provide more work for migrants who were then being encouraged to move to Rondonia by ambitious state authorities. The paving of the highway was essential so that the new crops could reach markets all year round.

The plan failed totally. As the joint report, published in 1989, admitted: 'The available data indicates that the actions carried out under Polonoroeste have neither slowed the pace of deforestation nor appreciably altered traditional patterns of land use.' Quite the contrary. In 1980, before the plan, 3 per cent of Rondonia's forests had been cleared; by 1988, says the Bank, 24 per cent were gone. 'There has been a rapid conversion of forest into pasture, one of the least desirable forms of land use in Amazonia from the environmental point of view.' Polonoroeste was an environmental disaster with little return, even for the Brazilian economy. The World Bank absolves itself, blaming instead the government's tax policies and other fiscal arrangements, which encouraged ranching and land speculation. And it points to unexpectedly poor soils that could not support the kind of farming the Bank had in mind for the area. Poor farmers, many forced off their fertile farms in southern states such as Parana, moved to Rondonia under the scheme with the intention of planting crops. Now they have had to sell their land at knockdown prices to ranchers.

The scheme has also caused havoc among the 8,000 local Indians. An internal Bank report leaked by environmentalists in 1987 found that 'the security and health of the Indians in the area of influence of Polonoroeste are seriously threatened, since the [government] agency responsible for defending their interests seems ill-equipped to deal with the indigenous reality.' Loggers and gold miners had with impunity invaded Indian reserves and there were 'constant epidemics of tuberculosis, measles and malaria'.

It will take many decades for even the most rapacious industrialists and ranchers to clear the entire Amazon rain-forest. But they are doing their best. The destruction is greatest in the east of the region, especially since the construction of the Belem–Brazilian highway in 1960 and its paving in 1974. The surrounding states of Para and Maranhao have lost 50 per cent of their trees. The plans for dams on the Xinghu River were to mark the latest westward expansion of this development front.

Now they are paving Highway 364, going east through the state of Rondonia to Acre. And the discovery of oil and gas fields in the Jurus and Urucu River valleys in the northwest of the Amazon basin has added to the pressure for road construction in that region.

Foreign environmentalists believe that the best way of halting the destruction is to put pressure on the international banks that fund many of the larger projects in the forests. So far, they have concentrated on the World Bank, which is dependent on donations of taxpayers' money from the rich nations. During the 1980s they succeeded in demonstrating that the Bank frequently disregards the needs of the environment and the native people of the forest when making its loans. The classic case was the Carajas iron ore project in the eastern Amazon basin.

The Carajas scheme began in 1982, when the World Bank gave a loan of $300 million to a government-controlled mining company, the Vale de Rio Doce Company (CVRD), to dig a giant open-cast iron ore mine at Carajas, a 900-kilometre railway to the coast at Sao Luiz and a deep-water port. The Carajas iron deposit contains 18 billion tonnes of high-grade ore. It is much the world's largest known deposit with a value put at $350 billion. It is sufficient to allow mining for 250 years and so large that during the 1970s US Steel, which first found the ore, is said to have refused to develop it for fear that it could produce a glut on world markets and cause a slump in iron prices.

Much of the iron is for export to Japan and Europe, where the European Community gave a loan of $600 million in return for guarantees of an annual 13 million tonnes of cheap iron ore for European steel mills for at least 15 years. Human rights and environment groups in Europe prompted sympathetic MEPs such as the Dutch social democrat, Herman Muntingh, to question why the terms of the loan did not protect either the environment or native peoples. But the deal was approved with little fuss in either Washington or Brussels

Teddy Goldsmith takes a camel on the campaign trail in Eye, Suffolk, at the 1974 general election. A vote for the People Party (later renamed the Green Party) could stop farmers turning Suffolk into a desert, he said. He lost his deposit. *(East Anglian Daily Times)*

Japanese demonstrators protest against the destruction of rainforests outside the office of Marubeni, one of the nation's largest timber companies. *(Michael Cross)*

Greenpeace derring-do against the Russian whaling ship *Vostok* in the early 1970s. *(Greenpeace/Weyler)*

Ark's campaigners were discredited for their claim that Blackpool would become an island as the greenhouse effect caused sea-levels to rise. *(Ark)*

Greenpeace's anti-furs campaigners were forced to resign because angry artwork like this upset Canadian Indian hunters. They set up a new organisation, Lynx, to carry on the work. *(Lynx)*

It takes up to 40 dumb animals to make a fur coat.

But only one to wear it.

If you don't want animals gassed, electrocuted, trapped or strangled, don't buy a fur coat. P O Box 509 Dunmow, Essex Tel: 0371 2016

Fighting the fur trade

Saving animals in the tabloid press: how the WWF was launched in the *Daily Mirror* in 1961. *(Syndication International)*

Copenhagen's mermaid is supposed to protect wild animals. Greenpeace picked her to help protest against Japanese whaling because she is a favourite with Japanese tourists. *(Greenpeace, Denmark/Kristensen)*

Environmentalists successfully turned dioxin into the most feared chemical in the world during the 1980s. Scientists were less certain about how dangerous it really was. *(Peter Armbruster)*

Wangari Maathai, a Kenyan who founded the Green Belt
Movement, an organisation which has encouraged millions of
women to plant and tend trees across her country. *(Runar Malkenes)*

and construction of the iron ore mine was completed in 1987.

The scheme was always destructive to the forest, though World Bank guidelines for the mine itself, including the creation of ecological reserves and green belt buffer zones round the mine, were met. But the project has since been transformed by the Brazilian government into a catastrophe that will probably end up destroying forests covering the 900,000 square kilometres of the Carajas region – an area the size of France and Britain combined. The mine has become the centrepiece for a much broader development strategy by the Brazilian government for the region, which appears to be one of the world's richest storehouses of minerals. The wider plan, known as the Greater Carajas Project, includes a bauxite mine producing 8 million tonnes a year and attendant aluminium smelters. The giant Tucurui dam on the River Tocantins has been built to supply electricity for the smelters. There are also plantations for cash crops that will cover some 50,000 square kilometres and ranches covering a comparable area.

By far the most devastating aspect of the project, however, is the 30 iron and steel mills to be built along the railway from the iron mine to the sea. The first iron ore smelters were in business by early 1988. They will have an eventual output of 2.5 million tonnes of pig iron or steel, much of it again for European markets. All the smelters are to be fuelled with charcoal made from rainforest wood; and therein lies the catastrophe. It takes all the wood from one hectare of forest to produce 30 tonnes of charcoal. The project is likely to eat up some 700 square kilometres of natural forest every year.

The environmentalists' assault on the World Bank for its role in the Greater Carajas Project began in August 1987, when 29 green and native rights groups from round the world signed an angry letter by Bruce Rich of the Environmental Defense Fund in Washington to the Bank's new president, Barber Conable. In response the Bank threw up its hands. Its chief environmental scientist, Robert Goodland, called the smelters a 'potential disaster of gigantic proportions', and admitted that there are 'no feasible plans to plant new trees, such as eucalyptus, to fuel the smelters. It would be uneconomic.'

Nonetheless, the Bank insists, just as it does with the Polonoroeste debacle, that it cannot be blamed. It points out that it funded only the mine, railway and port and had no involvement in the smelters. Yet, say its critics, without the mine, railway and port there would be no smelters. Rich replied, 'The present disastrous situation would not exist without the World Bank's participation.' He adds that the Bank has failed to hold Brazil to conditions attached to the original loan, which required it to protect the wider region of greater Carajas.

The campaign against the Greater Carajas Project is a good example of environmentalists making common cause with groups defending the rights of native peoples in the face of damaging development. Studies by David Treece at Survival International, a London-based organisation, found that among the 12,000 or so Indians from 27 separate territories likely to be pushed aside by the Greater Carajas Project will be the Guaja, the last entirely nomadic hunter-gatherer tribe in the Brazilian rainforest. The Guaja once practised farming, but abandoned it about 300 years ago when they began one of several eastward migrations as successive waves of settlers invaded their territories. Now there are just 250 of them left and two-thirds of their territory has been taken over for cattle ranching, while the charcoal merchants are waiting to move in on the remaining third. The Guaja have nowhere left to go.

Other threatened communities include the Parakana, who Survival International estimates have been moved 11 times for various development projects, the last time to make way for the flooding of the Tocantins valley by the Tucurui dam, which was completed in 1984. Now they are to have a mine, run by Broken Hill G., on their land. 'The Carajas programme is turning the region into a massive agro-industrial park of mines, smelters, dams, railroads, charcoal-burners, ranches and plantations, and is transforming its people into a destitute, landless labour pool,' says Treece.

As dams, railways, roads and power lines extend across the Indian lands – and as the government ignores their requests for protection – the people of the forest are squeezed into camps where they succumb to disease. In one village, according to Survival International which published a joint report on the project with Friends of the Earth, a quarter of the population of one camp died within six months of their arrival. At another, the Guaja population fell from 120 to 29 in eight years.

Western campaigners continue their efforts to halt the Greater Carajas Project. Brazil now provides half the European Community's iron, and the Dutch branch of the IUCN has traced the arrival of specific shiploads of iron ore from Sao Luis, the Carajas port, to Ijmuiden, a port used by the Dutch national iron and steel company, Hoogovens. It wants to use the publicity surrounding such shipments to persuade the company to back a resolution of the European Parliament for a moratorium on the import of pig iron from Carajas blast furnaces that burn local charcoal.

Meanwhile, in 1989, the Brazilian government tried to persuade the world that it had turned over a new leaf. It announced a programme called 'Our Nature', aimed at helping to preserve the rainforest. Some environmental groups rushed to embrace the idea. Others were sceptical. 'Although the rhetoric is now of greening development policies, little or nothing has changed on the ground,' said the *Ecologist*'s Nick Hildyard. 'Repeatedly, we find environmental safeguards being flouted, guidelines being ignored and environmental protection being relegated to mere window-dressing.' He charged the Brazilian government with using its Our Nature programme as yet another weapon against Indian communities. 'Environmental protection has been invoked to justify more than 50 per cent of the Yanomami's traditional territory being designated as a national park or forest reserve, categories that deny the Indians rights over the land and which specifically allow for economic development.'

The road to Gaia Corner

As international pressure, orchestrated by green groups, grew on the Brazilian government to 'stop the burning', so pressure grew inside the country's political heartlands: the cities. In the federal Congress, Fabio Feldman organised an all-party group in defence of the Amazon. He talked realpolitik. In the past, the entire country had seemed to support 'development' of the Amazon basin at all costs – and certainly without much concern for the environment ('We are too poor to worry about that') or the Indians or rubber tappers ('They should not be allowed to hold back progress').

Feldman wanted to change the allegiance of the tens of millions of Brazilians who see little of the rainforests except on plane journeys or from their TV screens. 'Our strategy is to create a confrontation between the people who are getting rich out of rainforest destruction and the rest of Brazilian society,' he said. He was among the first to push the Brazilian government towards negotiating with Western leaders a kind of Marshall Plan to bale it out of its appalling debt crisis. In the late 1980s, Brazil was paying out more interest on foreign debt than any nation in the world. Much of that interest was being paid with foreign exchange earned from cash crops and the export of minerals extracted from the Amazon basin.

Feldman called for some of the debt to be 'swapped' in return for a commitment from the government to rainforest preservation. Brazil has traditionally viewed such ideas as tantamount to giving up sovereignty of the Amazon. Feldman's was far from being a lone voice in the late 1980s. 'Green' floats have begun to appear at the Rio Carnival each year. Friends of the Earth has an active office there. And there was a small Green Party, Partido Verde. Few Western environmentalists who went to visit the Party's leader, Fernando Gabiera, and to swap ritual denunciations of the Brazilian government, realise that he, like Mendes, is a Marxist. Moreover, Gabiera was, during the 1960s, an urban guerrilla, locked up for several years by the military government before being freed in exchange for a German ambassador kidnapped by his band of guerrillas. He fled into exile in Europe, only returning after the accession of a civilian government in 1985. Today he says, 'Marxists were influenced by the optimism of the bourgeoisie; they thought progress was continuous with no physical limits. Now we know better.'

But the key to change may be an enigmatic, fundamentalist green who in 1990 was made Brazil's environmental minister by the country's new president. Jose Lutzenberger – usually known as Lutz – was born in Brazil of German parents and, after studying agricultural engineering and soil sciences, went to work in Germany for the chemicals giant BASF in the mid-1950s. He stayed there until 1972, during the great years of expansion for agricultural chemicals, as fertilisers and pesticides were ruthlessly marketed to eradicate pests and push forward the 'green revolution'. The conventional wisdom of the day was that chemicals were essential to feed the world's population, which grew by more than a billion people during Lutz's 15 years at BASF. But he came to believe that the chemicals were causing as many problems as they solved and he returned to his native Brazil to fight for 'environmental sanity and social justice'.

After almost two decades of speaking his mind, he emerged in the late 1980s as a green celebrity, arguing the case for using organic farming methods both on the prosperous farms of southern Brazil and to regenerate rainforest soils. He established a small farm near Porto Alegre in his home state of Rio Grande do Sul, and an educational centre for his ideas called Fundacao Gaia, or Gaia Corner.

Lutzenberger travelled widely, often courtesy of the more well-heeled green groups in the developed world. Anyone who is anyone on the green circuit spoke knowingly of 'Lutz'. His green canonisation came in 1986, when he delivered the Schumacher Lecture, held in Britain each year to honour the late author of the influential book, *Small is Beautiful*.

A year before his elevation to the Cabinet, Lutz claimed that the Brazilian government 'wants the whole forest to go and a few little dots to be left on the map, representing Indian reserves, rubber-tappers reserves and a few biological reserves. Well, this the forest cannot take, and if we destroy the forest then not even the reserves will survive.' In any case, he later suggested, the fact that we need even think about fencing off nature reserves is 'a recognition that something is wrong with our form of civilisation'.

Lutz favoured a root and branch approach to environmental reform and became by the late 1980s a regular pundit on Brazilian and foreign TV, offering his own version of biological holocaust. He said on a visit to London in 1988:

> Modern industrial society is a Messianic movement. It is a fanatical religion, with a missionary fervour to take over the whole planet, that we follow every minute of our lives. Its force is such that when it touches another culture, that culture is immediately destroyed or totally demoralised. The people want to be converted. When we contact an Indian tribe, the minute they see our technology they lose interest in their own way of life. It is the end of their culture. It means that when Brazilian technocrats look at the Amazon rainforest they see only money: six hundred billion dollars of timber. Everything in this region is a resource waiting to be exploited. It is not just dumb Brazilian politicians. It is all of us. We are destroying the planet. We find it impossible to leave places untouched.

With such an uncompromising vision, Lutzenberger was more surprised than anyone when he was picked by Fernando Collor, the newly elected Brazilian president, early in 1990 to be the country's environment secretary.

Collor was in the mood to make radical gestures to international concern about the fate of the Amazon. In the summer of 1990, Lutzenberger won an end to all tax incentives for clearing the forests, and gained the support of the Brazilian army to prevent illegal burning. He also won a postponement of work on Highway B364 through Acre.

It was inconceivable that Lutzenberger's world view could hold sway even inside Collor's Cabinet. But his appointment clearly reflected the complaints about the destruction of the Amazon rainforests that Collor received from innumerable Western leaders while on a pre-election trip round the world's capitals in the autumn of 1989.

In Lutz, the Amazon Indians had, perhaps for the first time, a champion in the government. 'Lutz is our friend,' said Ailton Krenak, head of the Union of Indian Nations, soon after Lutz's appointment. 'I met him in his office in the first week after his appointment. And he visited our Embassy of Forest Peoples in Sao Paulo. He stayed the whole morning and told us his thinking about how we could work together, about his wish to implement policies inspired by forest peoples.'

Euphoria ran high in the environment movement over his appointment: it was a victory for their campaigns. But there were fears, too. Had Lutzenberger been hired to buy off foreign critics of Brazilian policies in the Amazon? Was the forest effectively being handed over to the army? As this book went to press, it was too early to say.

Among the European disciples of Brazil's green guru are Liz Hosken and Ed Posey. After visiting Brazil in the late 1980s to work with Lutz and meet Chico Mendes, they returned to London to set up their own Gaia Foundation, a counterpart to Lutz's cultural and educational Fundacao.

There, apart from raising money and support for Lutz and the people of the forests, they have set up a 'safe house' for visiting environmentalists from the developing world, a Gaia Corner in the midst of London. The house is a haven of peace, with big windows and high ceilings in Well Walk, a quiet enclave of Hampstead. Besides Lutz, visitors there during 1989 included Paiakan and the man who brought him to the attention of the world, Darrell Posey; Julio Barbosa, Chico Mendes's successor at the head of the Brazilian Rubber Tappers' Council; Ailton Krenak and Martin Hildebrand, the head of Indian affairs for the Colombian government, which is handing back large areas of forest lands to the Indians.

'We marry the scientific with the spiritual,' Hosken told me over tea in Well Walk's verdant back garden. 'We aim for an affectionate alliance with the forest people, with people we love and respect. They tell us what is going on and we offer long-term support and create spaces for their voice.' Such spaces range from press conferences to evening sessions when, after wine and quiche, some of the gentler greens of London gather on cushions to hear words of inspiration from the south. It sounds precious, but it is effective. For many young environmentalists and media folk, saving the rainforests is for the first time about people as much as trees.

Hosken is angry that active forest campaigners such as Friends of the Earth in Britain make few contacts with forest people. 'They raise money from the public to save the forests, but spend it all on going to meetings and lobbying people in the rich world. They rarely ask the people on the front line, in the forests, what they need,' she says. So the Gaia Foundation, through its Forest Peoples' Fund, is raising money to send south to help fund the offices of people like Krenak and to pay for small projects developed by forest people to help them maintain and live on their land.

Some of the contributors to the fund are distinctly unlikely, such as the right-wing financier Jimmy Goldsmith who gave £3,000 which helped to fund a legal centre for Krenak's Union of Indian Nations. More is being spent on sending Indian students to study law and biology at a Brazilian university, bringing to the university what they know as well as returning to their villages with new knowledge. And there is money, too, for an extractive reserve on the Tejo River in west Acre, where both Indians and settlers are attempting to sell their own produce, thereby cutting out middlemen and landowners. They need a boat, timber yards and a small factory unit to refine manioc flour. 'The forest people have their own priorities and rhythms which will determine the funding and development of the Fund,' says Hosken. From the Hampstead refuge, she wants to respond to that and avoid the hectic world of lobbyists and jet-setting campaigners. As Paiakan put it while being ferried around from press conference to TV studio during his visit to Europe:

> You rush me from one meeting to the next as if I am a machine. You are mistreating me, just as you mistreat yourselves and the Earth. You are too busy to stop and listen. You do not hear any more and are endangering all of us.

7
IN MALAYSIA

A boy from the forest

Anybody who think environmentalists are middle-class
dilettantes should talk to Harrison Ngau. Anyone who thinks
concern for the environment is some kind of luxury should
visit Borneo. Ngau is a member of the Kayan community, one
of the largest of the tribal peoples who still live and farm in the
forests of Borneo, reputedly the oldest rainforests in the world.
Ngau was brought up at the Long Kesseh longhouse, a community of some 30 families all housed in separate apartments
under one roof. Long Kesseh is several hundred kilometres
from the coast on the River Baram in the Malaysian part of
Borneo known as Sarawak.

Ngau spent his childhood in the longhouse before the timber
companies began to move into the interior of Sarawak. His
parents cleared small patches of forest to plant crops, such as
rice and sago; they fished in the rivers and hunted for boar and
venison in the forest. There were fruit trees planted by their
ancestors and plenty of other forest produce from mushrooms
to wild bananas.

'We never had famine then,' he says. 'My parents could sell
their produce for cash in the markets.' There was enough
money to allow their brightest son to go to school in Marudi,
half way to the coast.

'The loggers first came to our longhouse in 1977,' says
Ngau. He was 17 at the time. Since then, the men with
chainsaws and bulldozers have destroyed most of the forest for
miles around. The forest will take many decades, probably
centuries, to recover. In many places, where soil has been

destroyed by heavy machinery or eroded by the local rains, the trees may never return. The logging company had a ten-year concession, during which time its chainsaw gangs went through the forests of Long Kesseh several times till most of the mature trees were gone.

Besides taking the wood, the loggers destroyed fruit trees and traditional gardens and frightened away the forest animals. Soils from the denuded hillsides washed into streams, killing fish. Now, says Ngau, 'food is difficult to get. People go hungry. They have to buy food, but they have less produce to sell.' The government says that the foresters are bringing development to a poor and backward region. Ngau says they have provided temporary work for a few but destroyed the forests upon which most people depend for their survival. Surveys have shown increased malnutrition and more disease in the longhouses.

Ecological decline has brought social decline. 'At night now, people get drunk in the longhouses,' says Ngau. 'They always used to drink, of course, but now there are alcoholics, young and old.' Some village elders have taken gifts from the timber companies and are no longer respected. 'At my longhouse, some people were given shares in a timber company. It caused a family split and there is still fighting now,' he says. The story turns out to be a family tragedy. It began with Ngau's grandfather who, he says, had taken an interest in town life since the days of the British colonialists. He had 'always saluted' the British. When the timber companies arrived in the area, he and one of his sons went to the state capital, Kuching, to complain. One day, after several such visits, they returned home with a share in a logging company. 'Overnight that family had so much money,' says Ngau. 'They had cars and bought a house in Miri,' the boom town on the coast that grew prosperous on oil brought ashore by Shell. 'They kept their rooms at the longhouse but spent much of their time on holidays, visiting Taiwan and Hong Kong. There were fights whenever they returned.'

The grandfather 'died a troubled old man,' says Ngau. The son, Ngau's uncle, eventually went back to the longhouse to plant cocoa, while the grandchildren who had taken over the family business activities still spend most of their time away.

Ngau's side of the family did not take the timber company's money. In any case, by then Ngau had finished school and found a job in Miri with a Scottish oil-prospecting firm. From there, he watched the timber companies complete the devastation of the coastal forests and move more of their camps inland. There were protests from the longhouses through the late 1970s. Groups of warriors went to the logging camps demanding cash in compensation for the destruction of their lands. Two Malaysian dollars for each tonne of timber extracted was a typical demand. In 1979, people from Long Niah, the next longhouse upstream from Ngau's home, hit on the idea of erecting barricades on the logging roads. But the aim was still to extort cash rather than to end the logging.

Ngau joined a group of young men from longhouses working in Miri who took the protests to the towns and into the newspapers. He was soon invited to a conference on the destruction of the Malaysian rainforests and was talent-spotted by environmentalists from the mainland of Malaysia. Within months, he was installed in an office in Marudi as the first Sarawak representative for Sahabat Alam Malaysia, the Malaysian branch of Friends of the Earth.

The forests of Borneo, parts of which are 150 million years old, are being destroyed by timber and mining companies, and by agricultural and settlement schemes run by both the Malaysian states of Sarawak and Sabah and the larger Indonesian state of Kalimantan. In Sarawak, the destroyers are almost exclusively the timber companies. The best way to see what they are doing is from the air. During several hours of flying along the coast of Sarawak and inland to Marudi and beyond, I could see clearly why Malaysian biologists predict that before the 1990s are out, the state's 250,000 square kilometres of virgin forest will have been largely reduced to scrub and mire.

For many miles around Miri, the once-forested peat bogs are almost completely treeless. As the plane loses height on its flight from Bintulu, another logging centre, you can see with growing clarity the waste land of felled trees and abandoned bulldozer tracks, of hillsides scraped clean of soils by falling timber. Much of the land is waterlogged. Here and there are shacks and overgrown fields, where farmers have attempted and failed to cultivate the land. You can only hope that they find oil beneath this land, for it seems of little use for anything else.

Inland, much forest does remain. An area of national park between Miri and Marudi shows what virgin forest should look like. Further in, you can spot the areas of forest used by the longhouse people for shifting cultivation. As in the Amazon rainforest, small plots of land have been cleared for the farming of rice and other crops. After a few years, farmers leave the fields fallow and the forest regrows for 30 years or more before they return. In the meantime, the villagers often embellish the forests by planting fruit trees. In some highland areas there is evidence that this form of cultivation has caused the permanent loss of forests. But government claims that shifting cultivators are the villains of the forests here carry little weight among forest scientists. In any case, says a study by scientists for WWF Malaysia, 'All the evidence points to the fact that shifting cultivators make very little use of primary [virgin] rainforest, preferring to return to old plots in rotation.'

The report contrasts this with the activities of the logging companies which 'severely alter the floral and faunal composition of the forest'. And that, too, is all too clear from the air. From time to time you see giant geometric shapes hacked out of the jungle. In these areas, every tree has been removed – a process called clear-felling. In a land of undulating hills and drunkenly meandering rivers, it comes as a shock to see a straight line.

In other, much larger, areas, the logging companies have been engaged in what they call 'selective logging'. In theory this means that they remove six or eight large mature trees from each hectare, leaving the rest intact and returning some decades later to find newly mature trees. In practice, according to a recent study for the International Tropical Timber Organisation, a UN-backed trade body, such 'sustainable forestry' is virtually unknown in the tropics. Indeed, since tropical soils are generally thinner and ecosystems more fragile, mechanised sustainable forestry that preserves the ecology of the forests may be impossible.

One reason is practical. A leading botanist at the University of Malaysia, S. C. Chin, points out that for every tree taken from the forest for timber, many more are felled. Some are damaged as trees plummet to the ground, or are dragged down by the many climbers and creepers that wind their way from tree to tree. Many more are destroyed by the bulldozers and trucks as they carve their way to the trees. One of the more obvious signs of a logged forest in Sarawak, seen from the air, is the network of winding yellow gashes across the land, where logging roads have been gouged from the thin sandstone soils. In many places the tracks, which follow ridges and escarpments, have triggered landslides. In all, says Chin, the 'sustainable' removal of six or eight trees per hectare destroys at least 40 per cent of the forest.

Few timber companies have much interest in sustainable forestry. In Sarawak, their licences to cut down trees last ten or twenty years. In that time they may set up their logging camps in each logging zone three or four times – a rapacious and ugly parody of the traditional shifting cultivators. By the time their licence expires, there is barely a tree left on their patch. You can see these repeatedly logged areas everywhere. They contain perhaps one dead-looking tree every 50 yards or so. Equally remarkable: there is often little sign of undergrowth returning. Logging has been so intense and damage to soils so great that the forest is dead.

The waste of timber is terrifying. Sitting on the bank of the River Baram near Marudi, I watched occasional giant rafts of logs up to 400 metres long being shepherded towards the coast for export by men in dinghies. But I also saw a constant flow of broken timber – often large tree trunks – floating untended to join the jetsam in the South China Sea. And the river, always silty, is now a deep reddish colour from the heavy load of soil lost from the denuded hillsides. This soil, too, is heading for the ocean.

Forest rebellion

Marudi is the meeting place between the jungles of northern Sarawak and the outside world, which wants the state's timber. The town's immaculate little one-man-operated airport is busy with Twin Otter 20-seater aircraft flying in from Miri on the coast. Its jetty on the River Baram is crowded with new steel-hulled longboats, with names like *The Chainsaw*, that show kung-fu videos as they plough upstream towards the larger longhouse settlements of the interior.

Marudi has its own road network, stretching out into the forest for a few miles around, but there are no highways to other towns, or the coast. Everything, including the town's several hundred cars, comes by boat or plane. The local shops do a roaring trade in outboard motors, mostly Yamahas. On the hill behind the town, next to the airport, there are benches overlooking the river, which is roughly twice as wide as the Thames. You can watch the oil slick spreading out from the Shell jetty below. White faces occasionally pass through on their way to the Gunung Mulu National Park upcountry, but they are still a novelty. So too these days are the occasional old men in tribal dress or women with earlobes stretched to their shoulders. While oil prices are low and the timber companies are in town, Marudi has an air of boom-town prosperity.

It is here that Harrison Ngau spent his schooldays and now runs the Sarawak office of Sahabat Alam Malaysia (SAM), the Malaysian arm of Friends of the Earth. It is a kind of front line for the environmental movement. If there is any legitimacy to the high hopes and aspirations of the campaigners sitting in their offices in London, or stalking the committee rooms on Capitol Hill; if their talk of an awakening of international environmentalism has any meaning, then it must manifest itself in places like Marudi, on the edge of the rainforest.

Ngau's office is above a bank and five doors down from a decrepit-looking branch office of Sarawak Plywood, one of the larger timber concession companies, with an annual turnover of more than M$100 million. 'They don't build big offices here,' says Ngau. 'These people come in from Miri, Sibu and Kuching, use Marudi to make their money and take the money out again.' The SAM office contains three cubicle offices, a small reception area, a ceiling fan and a very dusty library. On the wall is an official land-use map of Sarawak, which contrives to avoid all mention of the timber business.

An old man from one of the longhouses sat in reception, wearing two shirts and a straw hat with foot-high feathers, and smoking Marlboro Light. He didn't seem to have much business to do there, and I later saw him in several cafés and even bought him lunch without ever discovering what he was about. The old man apart, Ngau's office was constantly busy. I met Jok Jau Evong, a Kayan and president of the Residents' Association at Uma Bawang, a longhouse village far up in the hills that had been the scene of blockades against logging companies since 1987. He was the plaintiff in a test case to be launched in the High Court at Kuching. The case was designed to test the legality of logging licences handed out for forest land owned, according to land statutes enacted in the 1950s, by the longhouses. It was set to be a long and important battle.

Ngau was one of the first people within Friends of the Earth to insist that the key to the conservation of the rainforests lay in land rights of the forest dwellers. Jok's case is being handled by a couple of lawyers from Miri – the only two out of 30 lawyers in the town whose business is not servicing the timber firms, I was told. When I met Jok, he was on his way back to his longhouse after swearing yet another affidavit.

During my two days in Ngau's office, it constantly filled and refilled with people down from the longhouses for the day and reporting on the latest doings of the timber companies. 'Nothing happens in the forests without Harrison knowing about it pretty quickly,' I had been told. I could believe it. And his sources extend well beyond the longhouses. His parties are attended by local policemen and he has friends inside the state government's forestry service. They are appalled by the destruction of the forests but feel powerless because, as Ngau puts it, 'the politics of Sarawak is the politics of timber.' More than 50 per cent of the state's revenue comes from timber taxes of one sort or another; and that income pales into insignificance beside the fortunes made by many of the politicians and their relatives as beneficiaries of the timber licences.

In 1981, the district officer for Baram, based in˙ offices overlooking the river at Marudi, wrote in his annual report:

> The logging operators bring along tons of their equipment and plant for land and riverine usage, such as giant bull-dozers, trucks, locomotive engines, electric generators, small vehicles, fuel tanks, tug boats, barges and so on. With this equipment, they can work out their concession areas by building criss-cross roads and railways, bulldozing hills, mountains and plains with devastating effect. Sometimes it has to cross over the local peoples' customary land, paddy farms, gardens, cemeteries, pipelines and catchment areas [for water] and other private properties. Extraction of timber has caused extensive and irreparable damage to the natural land surface and vegetation.

But even such official acknowledgment of the abuses inflicted on native peoples brought no response from the governments in Kuching or Kuala Lumpur.

Press clippings at the SAM office reveal that throughout the late 1970s and early 1980s there was a constant stream of complaints about logging from a number of the different tribal communities in the north Sarawak districts of Baram and Limbang. A century ago, in the days of rule by the British adventurers, James and Charles Brooke (known as the White Rajahs), these people were head-hunters. During the early 1980s they invaded loggers' camps and stole a tractor or blocked a logging road, demanding cash in return. (In one unpleasant case, however, Iban warriors entered a camp, took keys to several vehicles and killed a Japanese workman.)

During this period, there was little sign of a co-ordinated response by the natives, certainly nothing to justify later claims by angry state ministers that Ngau was stirring up trouble. From 1986 on, however, when the logging companies began to penetrate deep into Sarawak's interior, into the districts of ulu (meaning upper) Baram and ulu Limbang, the hand of Ngau is evident. He began to catalogue the lengthy, frequently un-answered correspondence from longhouses to ministers and officials complaining about the invasion of their lands. His anonymous barefoot 'runners' began to bear messages into the forests, and a new round of formal letters began, many drafted with the help of SAM's lawyers. The letters argued that land newly declared a 'protected forest' (protected for loggers, that is, not natives) lawfully belonged to the native forest dwellers, and that such declarations were 'improper and may be unconstitutional'. This was the basis for some of the court actions against the government eventually launched in early 1990.

Ngau also began to channel the local anger. They had erected barricades before, but only as weapons in demands for money. From 1986, the barricades were part of a demand that the timber companies keep off longhouse land. Lawyers brought in by SAM had helped to devise this strategy. Even more important, Ngau began to organise meetings at which people from different tribes – the Penan, Punan, Kelabit, Kayan, Iban and so on – discussed their problems and devised strategies. The meetings coincided with the first outward signs of a breakdown in the strict social order of the longhouses in which the elders had once been all-powerful. In December 1986, the press reported that 'youths in ulu Baram have formed a Longhouse Action Committee to defend their rights from further encroachment by logging firms.'

The trigger for this unprecedented move was an agreement signed between the leaders of 12 longhouses occupying a large area of land around the River Baram upstream of Marudi and a logging company called Syarikat Samling Timber. The deal allowed the firm to enter customary land claimed by the longhouses in return for a payment of M$30 per square chain [4400 square feet] of land affected. Under the terms of the deal, the elders had to ensure that their people did not complain about pollution of drinking water from rivers or the loss of wild animals or jungle products such as fruit trees. Among the longhouses affected by the deal was Long Kesseh, Harrison Ngau's family home. The youths, many of them Ngau's friends, said that there had been no consultation within the longhouses about the deal and they pledged to fight it. Ngau's staff at Marudi provided the secretariat for the new committee.

From then on events moved fast. The loggers were encouraged by a growing demand from Japan for timber, as the fall of Marcos cut supplies from the Philippines and Indonesia put curbs on exports of unprocessed logs. They moved their camps further inland. In April 1986, SAM had appealed to Sarawak's chief minister to intervene to halt logging in remote inner areas, and in particular in areas where the Penan people lived. The Penan are hunters and gatherers many of whom depend entirely on the forest's wild resources for their survival. Many communities do not even farm. They had the least contact of all the groups with outsiders and their elders remained uncorrupted by the blandishments of timber firms.

In February 1987, Penan chiefs issued what they said was a final appeal to the state government:

> Stop destroying the forest or we will be forced to protect it. The forest is our livelihood. We lived here before any of you outsiders came. We fished in clean rivers and hunted in the jungle. We made our sago meat and ate fruit off the trees. Now the logging companies turn our rivers into muddy streams and the jungle into devastation. You took advantage of our trusting nature and cheated us into unfair deals. You take away our livelihood and threaten our very lives. We want our ancestral land, the land we live off, back. We can use it in a wiser way. When you come to us, come as guests, with respect.

The plea was ignored. The next month, Penan people living along the Tutoh River of ulu Baram barricaded a logging road. Within days, communities from several different tribal groups all across Baram and Limbang began to put up wooden barricades on the makeshift roads that led into the new logging areas. The barriers were hardly impenetrable, but they were surrounded by dozens of men, women and children all defying the timber lorries to pass. In all about 25 blockades were erected, halting logging from 16 camps for several months. The loss in revenue to the timber companies was put at M$5 million per month. During this time, says Ngau, people noticed that animals began to return to the forests, the rivers became clearer and there were more fish.

At the headquarters of SAM they were hard at work gaining international press coverage for the blockades. SAM's president, Mohammed Idris, believed that the best way of forcing change on the state government of Sarawak was to put pressure on the federal government in Kuala Lumpur. The first step was international publicity about deforestation in Sarawak and the plight of the Penan in particular. Conveniently, Friends of the Earth in London and other groups such as the Rainforest Action Network in the US and the Rainforest Information Centre in Australia had all begun to campaign aggressively for protection of the rainforests. Most of their concern was for the Amazon forests, but Sarawak became a 'second front' in the campaign.

The next step was to bring the issue direct to the Malaysian capital. So in June 1987, 12 representatives from most of the main tribal groups in Sarawak flew to Kuala Lumpur, together with Harrison Ngau, for meetings with ministers and police officials. There was also an international press conference and meetings at the local university and the Bar Council. They demanded a halt to logging and a recognition of their customary land rights. It was a public relations coup. The sight of tribal people 'roaming barefooted and attired in mere loin cloths through the paved streets of Kuala Lumpur brandishing their blowpipes', as one paper put it, excited great attention in Malaysia and around the world. It mattered not at all that tribal gear was not their normal attire. Photographs reveal that by the end of the visit, all but one of the petitioners were wearing Western clothes.

Back in Marudi the following month, SAM organised a workshop where over 100 people put their signatures, or more usually their thumb prints, to resolutions for the return of their land. By this time, SAM's lawyers had drawn up guidelines for how communities should react when loggers entered their land. First, they should 'lodge police report', then 'contact lawyers – apply for injunction', then 'blockade' and 'when police come, explain, show reports/letters, take photographs of police in action'. Finally, in September, SAM hosted another workshop at which the Sarawak Penan Association was formed.

The Penan have proved a PR godsend. They fit the romantic notion of an untainted people of the forest. There are only 9,000 of them, however, so at the same time, SAM is also anxious to emphasise the many hundreds of thousands of other, less 'primitive' people who rely on the forest for at least part of their living. One interesting social change in the Sarawak forests since the beginning of the blockades has been in the social status of the Penan. Once regarded by other groups as backward and primitive, the Penan are now held in high regard for having taken on the logging companies.

The Sarawak timber traders, busy growing rich out of the rainforests, did not enjoy the publicity afforded to the Penan's plight. They decided to fight back. One morning in July 1987, they placed a large advertisement in the national Malaysian paper, the *New Straits Times*. It attacked Ngau personally for stirring up trouble and claimed: 'To the best of the association's knowledge, logging operators have never entered or occupied customary rights land . . . without first compensating.' In October, after more than six months of blockading, police simultaneously visited all the blockades and arrested 42 Kayan villagers from a blockade at Uma Bawang.

At the same time, as part of a national sweep of 'subversives' under the notorious Internal Security Act, Ngau himself was arrested at his office and placed in detention for 60 days. He was released just before Christmas, on condition that he be home each night by 10 p.m. and did not leave Marudi without police permission – conditions that remained in force for 18 months. By the time Ngau was released, the state legislature had passed a law making it an offence to set up any structure on any road constructed by a timber licensee, whether on your own land or not. The offence carried a heavy fine and up to two years in gaol.

King of the jungle

While the forest people had been protesting about the loggers, the political élite of Sarawak had been engaged in an extraordinary exercise in bloodletting which revealed the depths to which local politics had been corrupted by the booming logging business. It came at a time when Sarawak was probably the largest source of unprocessed tropical timber on the international market.

The battle began in April 1987, soon after the barricades had gone up across Baram, when the state's chief minister Patinggi Taib Mahmud froze 25 timber concessions worth M$22.5 billion and covering more than 10,000 square kilometres. He alleged that the licences had been corruptly handed out by his predecessor and uncle, Tun Rahman, during his term of office. Taib claimed, 'The records show that during Tun Rahman's time, forest licences were issued to many of his allies [and to] companies in which his relatives have interests.' A published list revealed that more than half the concessions were held by people with obvious political or personal allegiance to Tun Rahman, including three brothers-in-law and three nephews. Three large concessions were in the name of one of his daughters.

The ageing Rahman denied wrong-doing and defended giving concessions to politicians on the grounds that it 'freed them from being obliged to their sponsors'. One beneficiary of his largesse had been the editor of the *Sarawak Journal*, who days after the original allegations hit back with a list of 'Taib's misdeeds'. The new chief minister, it turned out, had engaged in precisely the same practice as his uncle. And he capped it all by owning the shipping company that controlled the export of logs to Japan, the principal destination.

As the *New Straits Times* pointed out, virtually every assemblyman in the state legislature, and many of their relatives, had become millionaires as a result of this system of political patronage. Far from there being an outcry or investigation by the courts or the federal government, however, the existence of this dirty linen appears to have been accepted as a fact of political life in the state.

The political licence-holders in Sarawak do not chop down forests themselves, nor do their companies, many of which exist only on paper. Logging is normally done, in time-honoured Malaysian fashion, by Chinese subcontractors – an arrangement widely known as the Ali Baba system. One exception, however, is the 'Mr Big' of the Sarawak timber business, James Wong, who has proved a godsend for environmentalists looking for a hate figure. Wong combines being Sarawak's environment and tourism minister with ownership of Limbang Trading, one of the state's largest and most detested timber companies. He denies a conflict of interest, but the environmentalists are unimpressed.

Wong can certainly claim to have been in the Sarawak forestry business for many years and to be a genuine forester, unlike the relations and cronies of the chief ministers past and present. He began in 1949, pioneering the techniques of hill logging which, it is said, he was taught by the Japanese, who also assassinated his father during the Second World War. Until 1987, Limbang Trading was a joint venture with a Japanese trading giant, C. Itoh, one of the 'big nine' combines that control most industry in Japan.

Wong's company has been a prime target for protests by the forest people of Sarawak throughout the 1980s. In 1984, a group of Iban put up blockades on a Limbang logging road at Lubok Lalang in Sungai Medamit. They demanded M$2 million from Wong in compensation for damage to their water supplies caused by the pollution of rivers. Some of the first blockades of logging roads in early 1987 were directed against Wong, whose company has the single largest concession in the Limbang district, covering some 100,000 hectares. People from Long Napir, the nearest longhouse to the main blockade, Long Adang, Long Balau and others walked for days over the mountains to set up a blockade outside Wong's giant Stampin Timber Camp.

Facing them over the barricades were the state's police force, armed on occasions with M16 machine guns. Tama Lawai, a Kelabit headman, told a reporter, 'We have united in this blockade to prevent the company coming in. They've entered our *temuda* [farmland] and flattened it, without compensation. Bulldozers are invading our land; soon there will be nothing left.' One Penan, Rosylin Nyagong, said simply, 'The forest is our source of survival. Without the forest, we are dead.' Wong's retort was that 'logging is my bread and butter', a remark that brought new calls for his resignation from Idris and others.

Wong's men dismantled the barricades in August 1987, but in September they were rebuilt. Meanwhile, Wong brought a court action against some of the protesters for causing a public nuisance by blocking the road. SAM's lawyers in Miri, Mekanda Singh and David Lim, argued in defence that the protesters were defending their customary rights on a private road built against their wishes across their land. They presented to the court a boundary register book, unearthed at the government's district office at Marudi and dating from the days of the British administration. It identified as belonging to the local longhouses a large area of land around and upstream of Long Napir. The area included much of the area later licensed to Wong for logging. Wong subsequently applied for leave to withdraw his action, an application which the Kuching High Court allowed.

This debacle was followed swiftly by the state government's blanket ban on all blockades on logging roads. It also encouraged SAM to increase its emphasis on the Penan's battle with Wong.

When, in early 1988, SAM brought to Sarawak a team of rainforest campaigners – tagged 'international experts' for the benefit of the press – they latched on to Wong. Wong, in return, sank his teeth into them. Wong is repeatedly on record as claiming that a logged forest is indistinguishable from virgin forest after just five years. Regrowth, he insists, is very rapid. And to claims that destruction of the forests could upset rainfall in Borneo, he once famously remarked, 'We get too much rain in Sarawak; it stops me playing golf.' Jenne de Beer from the Dutch branch of the International Union for the Conservation of Nature (IUCN), who is the author of a scientific report on non-timber products of the rainforest, commented: 'James Wong's statements make him the laughing stock of foresters and scientists worldwide.' To which Wong retorts: 'I will not bow to experts. I am the expert. I was here before these experts were born.'

Wong's Limbang operation was again halted by blockades in May 1988. Soon afterwards, Wong, this time with his ministerial hat on, complained in the local press about sympathetic press coverage in Britain of the Penan's case. The Penan, he said, were 'very likeable, simple people' and he offered a poem on their fate which began:

> O Penan – Jungle warriors of the Tree
> What would the future hold for thee?
> Would you choose to carry on with primitive Tradition?
> Or cast that aside and join our Civilisation?

Wong characterised his government as concerned paternalists who had exhibited great patience in trying to persuade these simple nomadic people to settle down. The Penan were being exploited by outsiders, he said, including Friends of the Earth and a Swiss fugitive called Bruno Manser, who was somewhere at large in the jungle. Mohammed Idris in return accused Wong of mounting a 'propaganda campaign against the natives of Sarawak, especially the Penan'. Natives, he said, have a fundamental right to their land and to choose their own path to development.

The battle of the barricades raged again through the summer of 1988, with Long Napir once more at the forefront. In late November, the police moved in and arrests followed. Detainees included Aping Marai, a Penan headman who had been part of the delegation in Kuala Lumpur in June the previous year and had figured in the arrests that autumn. The pattern recurred in 1989, with the arrest in January of 130 more blockaders who were detained for 14 days in what Ngau described as cramped mosquito-infested cells at Labang military barracks. A further 120 people were arrested in the autumn of 1989. Despite the arrests, the protests spread for the first time to southern Sarawak, to Iban communities near Bintulu and along the River Belaga.

There appeared to be total deadlock, but with time on the side of the timber merchants. Logging continued at a record rate, and the timber gangs moved further and further into the hills. In some places, logging roads reached almost to the border with Kalimantan, the Indonesian portion of Borneo. The government hinted at plans to end the export of logs by 1995. By the mid-1990s, said some forest scientists, all the virgin forest would be gone.

The legal battle was going the way of the protesters. At the end of 1989, after more than two years of arrests and detentions, not a single protester had been convicted of any crime. Even the blanket ban on blockades proved ineffective when the courts ruled that a conviction required that the accused be seen erecting the barricades. There were celebrations at Marudi magistrates court in November 1989 when 22 Penan were acquitted of the charge. Another 220 cases seemed likely to be dismissed as a result. By this time the timber companies were working 24 hours a day in all weathers, removing timber under floodlights in their effort to maximise profits. Even so, they would be hard-pressed to actually witness the barricades being put up and to identify the builders.

Meanwhile, SAM is taking its case against the loggers back to the courts, to contest their right to invade forest traditionally owned by forest people. Their test case centres on Uma Bawang, where the old headman was deemed corrupt and in the pay of the logging company. His authority is gone, and in his place the villagers have set up a Residents' Association, with Jok Jau Evong as president.

In the Uma Bawang case, SAM is taking on the timber contractor, the licensee and the state government. SAM claims that the licensing process is corrupt since, it alleges, the licence in Uma Bawang is partly owned by a relation of the chief minister. It argues that the people of Uma Bawang were tricked back in 1951, when a large part of the local native lands was designated by the British administration as forest 'protected' for commercial felling. The local people say today that they thought that they were being given a community forest, under which they and not the loggers had special rights. They thought that a protected forest was one protected for them and had volunteered to map the boundaries and mark boundary trees.

At the heart of the dispute is the conflict between the customary law determining the control of the forests and rights handed out in the era of quick profits from logging licences. Mekanda Singh, SAM's lawyer, is masterminding the test case at Kuching High Court. Singh says that nobody disputes that native customary rights that existed in 1957 are protected under the legislation enacted in that year. The problem is in working out exactly what rights to land were in force on that date. In his researches, he says, 'I spoke to several elders of the native communities in Baram and they have claimed that the boundaries of their communal rights had been settled decades ago during the colonial administration. The legal effect of these agreements has yet to be ascertained.' There are two 'layers' of ownership of land under customary law. The first is known as *temuda* and includes land used by the longhouse communities as fields or gardens for cultivation; the second, much wider, area is taken to include farms and gardens, fallow land, forest planted with fruit trees, old house sites, cemeteries and 'all the surrounding forest to a distance of half a day's journey', including virgin forest. The state government, in theory at least, acknowledges the community's ownership of the *temuda* but not the wider realm. To confuse matters further, customary law does not forbid outsiders from taking timber from within the outer zone of ownership, though it hardly envisages large-scale commercial logging.

The Uma Bawang case is the big test of native land rights. On its outcome may hang the ultimate fate of the Sarawak rainforests and, quite possibly, the fate of other rainforests in other countries. But, as well as being an important lever for change in Sarawak, it has demonstrated SAM's preoccupation with keeping the needs of people at the forefront of its environmental campaigning. This determination has ensured that the outside world's impression of the battle of the Sarawak forests is tied far more closely to the plight of forest peoples such as the Penan than, for example, is concern about the Amazon rainforest.

In November 1987, Mohammed Idris flew to Stockholm to receive on behalf of SAM the Right Livelihood Award, established by a Swedish philanthropist to encourage practical solutions to environmental and social problems. Often called the Alternative Nobel prize, it is awarded the day before the official Nobel prizes. That year, SAM shared the award with Jose Lutzenberger, the 'father' of Brazil's environment movement. The previous year, Janos Vargha from Hungary had been the recipient. The jury praised Ngau, who had spent two of the previous twelve months in detention, for taking 'great personal risks' in inspiring 'the fight against the greed-driven demolition of one of south-east Asia's greatest remaining rainforests'. Ngau, however, under the terms of his release from detention, was not allowed out of Marudi, let alone Malaysia, without police permission. Idris, in his acceptance speech, said that the battles on the logging roads of Sarawak represented 'a clash of different systems, of different civilisations – on one side a powerful modern system motivated by greed; on the other a traditional system that is oriented towards fulfilling human needs . . . Despite the so-called greatness of knowledge of modern science and technology, the modern man is far less knowledgeable, in fact far more stupid, than the indigenous, native man who lives close to nature.'

This was no romantic whimsy. A Western scientist who knows the Sarawak forests better than most is the explorer Robin Hanbury-Tenison. He spent more than a year in the forests of northern Sarawak as head of a major international scientific expedition documenting its wildlife prior to the creation of the Gunung Mulu National Park. There he spent much time with groups of Penan. Afterwards, he noted that while his team contained some of the best biologists and botanists in the world, 'the Penan were our professors.' They, he said, hold 'the key to where the real wealth of the rainforest lies'.

A Muslim Ralph Nader

Mohammed Idris is a strange mixture of the ascetic and the flamboyant. He wears immaculate white robes, eats his food with his fingers and for much of the 1980s was driven round

his home town of Georgetown, Penang, Malaysia, in a large
and ancient Mercedes. He is a local businessman in a town
where such men do rather well. He has unspecified high-level
political contacts in a country where such contacts go a long
way. Yet 20 years ago he became a disciple of the angry
American consumer advocate, Ralph Nader, and has spent
most of the succeeding two decades setting up and nurturing
probably the biggest and most effective consumer and environment pressure group in the Third World. He is president of the
Consumer Association of Penang (CAP) and its offshoot, Sahabat Alam Malaysia (SAM). Between them, the two organisations have a staff of a hundred and a network of influence that
runs right round the world.

Idris launched CAP with a group of friends in 1969, the year
that also saw the beginning of Greenpeace in Canada and
Friends of the Earth in the US. It began, he says, as a narrow
consumer group, testing products and investigating consumers' grouses. Soon, however, it began to question the need
for many of those products and moved on to mount campaigns
against the grosser aspects of the consumer society. Dried baby
milk, the alcohol and cigarette businesses were early targets.
From there Idris began to develop a distrust of the whole
direction of economic development in his country, of industrial projects and plantation farming, and of megalomaniac
development schemes such as the $800 million 14-kilometre
bridge, paid for by a loan from the US, that links the island of
Penang to the Malaysian mainland. 'How many thousands of
badly needed rural bridges could have been built for that
money?' he asked. The environmental arm of CAP grew, so that
in 1978 it was turned into a separate organisation, SAM.

CAP is housed in a medium-sized villa fronting on to one of
Penang's famed but litter-strewn white beaches. Peak View
Villa has table-tennis on the veranda and a no smoking sign on
the front gate. Inside, they save the rainforests by using a bidet
rather than toilet rolls. Otherwise the place is stacked to the
high ceilings with box files, cabinets and mountains of paper
that block the air flow from the ceiling fans.

CAP runs like an exceptionally busy branch of the civil
service. Most pressure groups operate in constant conflict with

their organisational structure: all the office staff want to be top campaigners and all the top campaigners want to be boss. CAP on the other hand is full of people doing their own jobs at fever pitch. There are rooms full of workers pasting up artwork for their monthly newspaper and the constant stream of books. Newspapers in several languages are clipped and filed. There isn't a computer terminal in sight, only dozens of old Olympia typewriters clattering away.

The main upstairs room houses more than 20 people. At one desk I found the Third World Network, which collects and distributes to the media articles and information from three continents. At another I met Evelyn Hong, author of a respected study on the social organisation of Sarawak natives. Through a side-door, there were the two in-house lawyers. Somewhere in the building the World Rainforest Movement plotted. Down a back staircase and along an arcade of filing cabinets marked 'health section', there is an outbuilding where they sell bangles and rattan bags made by the Penan.

A couple of blocks away down a well-to-do leafy suburban street is SAM's office. Here the staff work amid a sea of FoE posters and stickers. The slogans are familiar across five continents: The Earth Needs Friends – Join Us; Bring Back Returnables; No Smoking, Oxygen in Use.

In the First World, the countryside is something that most people go to visit – to marvel at the scenery or complain that it is not as pristine as they would like. People get in the way of the view. Rainforests are the stuff of myths, romance and nightmares. Environmental campaigns in the rich world often reflect such values. In Malaysia and throughout the Third World, the environment is where most people live. Millions of people fish or farm or hunt wild animals. SAM's campaigning begins from this perspective. SAM's first campaigners were often trades union people, frustrated by working within the country's official, right-wing unions. Its first secretary and moving force until he died of cancer in 1986, still only in his 30s, was a man called Rajandendran. He spent several years making grass-roots contacts among plantation workers and fishing communities, encouraging them to protect their own livelihoods along with their environment by opposing polluting factories, commercial plantations and high-tech fishing fleets.

Until Rajandendran's death, SAM did not emulate other environmental groups by organising itself around single-issue campaigns. While Friends of the Earth in London had a toxics campaigner, a wildlife campaigner, a rainforest campaigner and so on, SAM employed field workers who involved themselves in any topic of concern in his or her locality. Today, having switched to a more Western style of campaigning, emphasising international links, those field workers are largely gone. Making the best of both approaches, perhaps, is Harrison Ngau, with the entire state of Sarawak as his domain and the single overarching issue of the rainforests to attend to.

The late 1980s saw some bloodletting inside the Idris empire, with nasty stories circulating about disappearing files and missing invitations to annual meetings. The beneficiaries are Idris's two new young lieutenants. Martin Khor (also known by his original name Khor Kok Peng) is a Cambridge-educated economist, who is research officer for CAP and head of the World Rainforest Movement, set up at a meeting in Penang in 1986. Chee Yoke Ling, a former law lecturer, is secretary of SAM. Both began working for Idris as volunteers while at the University of Penang. Both display the attributes of articulate middle-class Western-educated internationalists, rather than grass-roots organisers; and both are highly effective, intelligent and radical.

I had first met Khor in London where he gave a talk at the Gaia Foundation. In it he warned that the 'greening' of rich nations round the world that year could spell environmental disaster for the poor nations. Companies would export their environmental problems from the backyards of Europe, North America and Japan to the rainforests and urban slums of the Third World. 'Remember last year's scandal of the export of toxic waste from Europe to Latin America and Africa? The trade has been going on for years. It began after the US tightened its domestic regulations on toxic waste and companies soon discovered that Third World nations would take it. The second wave has come recently as the European Community tightens its own rules.'

Companies are also exporting their hazardous industries, he said. CAP had been involved in a campaign against a company called Asian Rare Earth, a subsidiary of the Japanese giant Mitsubishi, which takes tailings from the Malaysian tin industry and processes them to extract yttrium, a chemical needed by the Japanese electronics industry. One by-product is a mildly radioactive waste called thorium hydroxide, which was at one time being dumped in the open outside the company's works at Bukit Marah in the state of Selangor. CAP claimed that children played on the dump for several years. Some waste was thrown into rivers used for drinking water and, the allegations continued, more had been sold to farmers as fertiliser.

Three local children living close to the plant had contracted leukaemia. SAM had been involved in a well-publicised court case in which it attempted to demonstrate that the waste was causing the leukaemia – a scientific issue fraught with uncertainty, as Khor conceded. SAM had unearthed documents showing that Mitsubishi had operated the same process in Japan until 1972. After the notorious Minamata mercury poisoning scandal, and the subsequent public concern about hazardous industrial processes, Mitsubishi had shut down the plant and moved production to Malaysia. 'The leukaemias are happening at Bukit Marah because of the greening of Japan,' claimed Khor. The Third World was being 'developed to death'.

Chee, however, saw hopeful signs. 'The government here is responding to the green talk in other countries and parts of it are beginning to think environmentally,' she said. 'Our contacts in the bureaucracy are now looking to us for ideas.' But nobody is getting too excited. The federal government of Malaysia, like many others in the Third World, keeps strong powers to control and suppress any dissident organisations. Most of the Malaysian powers derive from the 1950s at the time of the 'emergency' when British troops thwarted Communist insurgents gathering in the rainforests of mainland Malaysia. In late 1989, the ageing Communist guerrillas laid down their guns; but the government announced that there were other traitors in the nation's bosom and the Internal

Security Act, under which Harrison Ngau had been detained two years before, would remain in place.

Idris makes little of these matters, even when his own staff are detained. He has a well-attuned nose for keeping out of political trouble while carrying on his aggressive campaigns against the commercialisation of his country. The nation's bookstalls display CAP's books and sell its strident monthly tabloid newspaper in large quantities.

This is all the more surprising considering the state of apparent siege endured in Kuala Lumpur by the Environmental Protection Society of Malaysia, a small, moderate body. Gurmit Singh, its leader for the 15 years of its existence, seeks to co-operate with the government and to engage in low-key consultancy and education work. He avoids public confrontations with the government of the kind which have become Idris's trade mark. One of his quiet successes was to persuade the government to appoint citizens' representatives on its advisory Environmental Quality Council. Singh was the first such representative, and he lobbied for ten years to persuade the government to implement legislation requiring environmental impact assessments on large new development projects.

Singh says that he turned down the idea of becoming the Malaysian branch of Friends of the Earth to avoid charges of foreign subversion. As a result, says Singh, 'we've never been able to attract foreign funding in the way that CAP and SAM have.' For his pains, he is harassed at every turn. When Singh set up a co-ordinating committee of activists to campaign against a dam planned for a national park in the early 1980s, the government decreed the committee to be an illegal organisation. Technically, all organisations have to be registered before they can operate (a process which can take many months). 'The government selectively uses this law. Other groups are not touched,' complains Singh. Native organisations set up by SAM in Sarawak have been left alone.

In 1986, the Malaysian prime minister publicly called Singh a 'crypto-socialist' and soon afterwards a youth group tried to demonstrate outside his house – 'luckily they did not know I had moved down the street,' he says. Most extraordinary of all, the round-up of 'subversives' in 1987 included Singh's young part-time vice-president, Tan Ke Kheng. He was accused of being pro-Communist, since he had attended a meeting organised by a 'Communist front organisation' in Tokyo while on his way home from a trip to the US, says Singh. He was also said to have organised an illegal demonstration of 10,000 people outside the Asian Rare Earth plant, a demonstration actually organised by a committee initiated by Idris's people in Penang. 'Tan was merely one of the participants,' Singh says. While SAM's Harrison Ngau was released after two months, the authorities held Tan for ten months at a detention centre in Kamunting, Parak, largely in solitary confinement and with daily interrogations. He spent his time writing a long article on hazardous waste dumping in Malaysia for Singh's magazine, *Alam Sekitar*. The article's publication was then delayed for many months while Singh awaited the annual renewal of his licence to publish the magazine.

On his release Tan was told to keep away from political meetings for another 14 months. He cut his losses and left for England to study for a PhD in Environmental Studies at Cambridge University – on a Malaysian government scholarship.

Singh, who did not strike me as remotely paranoid, says that since the detention of his deputy, his phone has often been tapped and strange men are often sitting in parked cars outside his house. Most English language newspapers in Kuala Lumpur now refuse to publish news of his group's campaigns. Meanwhile, most of the students who attend courses on environmental law run by Singh's lucrative consultancy business are civil servants whose fees are paid by the government.

8

SAVE THE FOREST

The wasted years?

Perhaps the strangest thing about the international campaign to save the rainforests is that it didn't start sooner. Half the world's tropical forests – the planet's great biological store-houses – had gone before greens took much notice. The problem of the destruction of the largest of them, the Amazon rainforest, has been begging to be addressed since at least the mid-1970s. The World Wildlife Fund began a small campaign about then, a spin-off from its Operation Tiger project in India. But for most environmental groups in those days, the rainforests seemed a long way away. The natives spoke a foreign language and, anyhow, might forest-savers not look like opponents of economic development? Walt Patterson, the doughty Friends of the Earth campaigner against nuclear power, recalls, 'I predicted in the 1970s that rainforests would become a big issue. But nobody thought about it or was greatly interested.' The nearest FoE in Britain got to rainforests in those days was a quixotic boat trip by its erstwhile director, Graham Searle, to save a forest in New Zealand.

The issues were all there waiting to be tapped. You only had to look at the Sunday newspaper magazines. The writer Norman Lewis put together a long article in the *Observer* magazine in 1979 on 'The Rape of Amazonia'. Its images of cattle ranchers and the overflows from shanty towns heading together down new highways and setting fire to the forest, of eroded soils, and altered climates and the greenhouse effect, were mostly still shaping perceptions a decade later – with many of the same scientists being quoted. Lewis even had room for an item on the 'other crisis' of logging in south-east Asia. The *Observer*'s great rival, the *Sunday Times*, ran a similar splash entitled 'The Last Frontier: Brazil was always the country of the future where the future never came. Now it has.'

Several early forest campaigners were film-makers who spotted the visual potential of the burning Amazon rainforest. Among these were Randy Hayes in California, who kick-started the early days of the US rainforest campaigns when he launched the Rainforest Action Network in 1986. And in Britain there was Adrian Cowell, who began filming in the Amazon in the early 1980s and was the first to document the life of Chico Mendes. Later in the decade, Cowell's footage of desperate victims of the World Bank's development policies in the Amazon, coupled with powerful advocacy from Jose Lutzenberger, swayed many a senator on Capitol Hill to stand up for the forests and their inhabitants.

Most of the first rainforest initiatives by environmentalists in the mid-1980s were rather parochial campaigns. Even FoE in London, which could call on FoE offices in Malaysia and Brazil, launched its campaign in 1985 in this way. It was SAM, in Malaysia, that began the first serious effort at an inter-national campaign to save the rainforests. In September 1986, SAM hosted the annual meeting of FoE International in Penang, and organised a simultaneous conference on rainforest de-struction. In retrospect, that month can be seen as the start of the emergence of global environmental campaigning. For, just days before on the other side of the world, another inter-national group of campaigners held the first campaign meeting to coincide with the World Bank's own annual meeting in Washington.

SAM's meeting on the Forest Resources Crisis was studded with what were to be important names in the forthcoming campaign and included representatives from 22 countries. Apart from the Malaysians, there was John Seed, an American 'deep ecologist' now working for the Rainforest Information Centre in Australia; Vandana Shiva, a fiery young Indian academic; Charles Secrett from FoE in London; Jonathan Holliman, the FoE veteran now in Tokyo; Randy Hayes, the

Californian film-maker; and, crucially for the people-centred approach favoured by SAM, Marcus Colchester from Survival International.

The Penang camp knew what they wanted from the meeting and were determined to get it. Anybody who thought they were there just to discuss rainforests had another think coming. Martin Khor began, 'The factors which cause forest depletion are the motive forces of economic expansion, technological capacity, cultural induction, greed and the "growth-today" syndrome in the Third World, and the political systems which put a premium on the immediate present.'

Throughout south-east Asia, the activities of timber companies supplying the Japanese market are the prime cause of forest destruction; and the most important debates at the Penang meeting were about how to influence or shut down that trade. Following classic pressure-group tactics, Charles Secrett and his colleague Chris Rose looked around for some international regulatory body on which pressure could be exerted. The nearest parallel was during the anti-whaling campaigns of the 1970s when green groups had used the International Whaling Commission with great success, turning it from a whalers' club into an instrument for environmental control. Secrett discovered that for some years the UN Council for Trade and Development (UNCTAD) had been pushing for the producers and consumers of tropical timbers to set up a trade club to discuss matters of common interest. This, he decided, was the ideal vehicle. The creation of such an organisation 'provided the opportunity for campaigning organisations to propose sensible solutions [and] directly influence commercial instincts and timber management policies,' Secrett told the Penang meeting. Not only that, groups such as FoE would be in a position to help write the rules under which the International Tropical Timber Organisation would operate. 'With strong conservation-based clauses,' he said, 'such an organisation could become an invaluable forum for global change.' In the back of his mind, too, was the idea that it could help fund experimental projects in sustainable management of the forests. The ITTO was eventually launched in 1987.

Secrett and Rose had persuaded the WWF to join them in targeting the ITTO, and soon Chris Rose had left Britain for WWF International's headquarters in Switzerland to run the Fund's campaign to influence the ITTO. When Rose returned to London another of Secrett's campaigners, Adam Markham, replaced him.

There was one problem in all this. Half the people at the Penang meeting thought the ITTO would be a waste of time. Idris, in his opening address to the meeting, warned that 'the path of previous commodity agreements has not brought hope to the Third World.' Why should this one be different? He feared being drawn into a long technical argument with foresters about definitions of the sustainable use of rainforests. He wanted instead to defend the forests from all commercial forestry and attack the development policies that brought the foresters in.

The conference ended, as Idris had intended, with an agreement to form a World Rainforest Movement. But it also came close to splitting the movement in two almost before it had begun. The majority of people in Penang, representing the radical wing of environmentalism, wanted to pillory timber companies, to campaign for bans on logging in rainforests and to set up boycotts of tropical timber in consumer countries. But a minority, including Charles Secrett and FoE in Britain, which had become the head office for FoE International, was opposed to bans and boycotts. It wanted dialogue on sustainable forestry at the ITTO.

Secrett was backed by most Washington-based groups, who had neither been to the Penang meeting nor joined the World Rainforest Movement. The prospect loomed of a rift between groups from the North, based in Washington, and those from the South, based in Penang. For the next two years, while the world's attention centred on the Amazon rainforest, where logging was a minor issue, the two factions went their own separate ways. But in April 1989, as logging intensified in Malaysia and US groups began to investigate American timber companies, the crisis came to a head at two separate meetings held simultaneously on either side of the world. In the South, in Penang, the World Rainforest Movement spent four days hammering out 'an emergency call for action for the forests, their people and life on Earth'. The petition eventually carried three million signatures and was handed to the UN that autumn by Teddy Goldsmith, one of the movement's strongest backers in the North. The meeting called for a halt to all development projects, including commercial logging, that were contributing to the destruction of the rainforests. It demanded that governments 'ban all imports of tropical timber and tropical wood products from natural forests'. Signing the agreement were the main rainforest campaigners in southeast Asia including SAM, the Haribon Foundation from the Philippines, SKEPHI from Indonesia, as well as Rainforest Action Network (RAN), the Japan Tropical Forest Action Network, Survival International, Australia's Rainforest Information Centre, the Gaia Foundation's Forest Peoples Support Group from London, Probe International from Canada and, alone from Washington, Chad Dobson from the Bank Information Center.

Where was the British branch of FoE, one of the five regional centres for the World Rainforest Movement? Secrett had moved on, but one of his successors, Simon Counsell, was in New York City for a workshop on the US tropical timber trade, which struck a rather different note. Delegates reached a resolution that 'except in specific circumstances, a boycott of tropical timber products would not promote sustainable forestry at this time.' The workshop argued that a boycott would damage firms trying to improve their forestry practices and would lead to more forests being burned to make way for cattle ranches or plantations. A ban would 'send the wrong signal to tropical countries struggling to integrate conservation concerns into their development framework'.

This last point, of course, was the crux. The people gathering in Penang wanted to change the development framework not integrate with it. The resolution, which was subsequently adopted by a US-based coalition of campaigners called the Rainforest Alliance, gave 'tropical countries four years to make their sustainable forestry programs operational'. In four years, warned the people from Penang, half the remaining forests of Sarawak would be gone – and American timber companies were at work there.

The two groups were clearly at loggerheads. Lined up for dialogue and compromise, however, were Washington green luminaries such as Brent Blackwelder of the Environmental Policy Institute (EPI), which had recently merged with FoE US; Barbara Bramble, of the National Wildlife Federation; and Bob Buschbacher from the US branch of the WWF. As a tangible sign of the kind of dialogue that the organisers had in mind to decide the fate of the rainforests, the workshop included only five representatives from developing countries, but nine from the American tropical timber companies.

The waves from the meetings in Penang and New York City could be felt for the rest of the year. You were either for or against a boycott of tropical timber; you either believed in the possibility of sustainable commercial forestry or you did not. Duncan Poore, a respected forestry consultant, had produced a report for the ITTO which concluded that one eighth of 1 per cent of current tropical forestry practices could be regarded as sustainable (the single exception was subsequently shut down by the Australian government for 'environmental reasons'). Yet Poore did not lose faith in the possibility of sustainable forestry and signed the New York City declaration.

The WWF, like FoE, was split. Branches in the US, Malaysia and elsewhere stuck with sustainable forestry; but the WWF in West Germany called for what amounted to a complete ban on trade in tropical timber from virgin forests.

Behind the row over a ban there were two closely linked disputes. One concerned what was meant by the term 'sustainability'. The second concerned the place of people in the conservation equation. The word 'sustainability' means different things to different people. For the timber industry it meant nothing more than a sustainable yield of timber. One way or another the forest should carry on producing timber. To do that you could tear up the rainforests from the Amazon to New Guinea, provided you put in their place plantations of eucalyptus or some other timber crop. More sophisticated, the ITTO accepted, under pressure from the WWF and FoE, that biological diversity also mattered. A forest was only sustainably managed if it could regenerate itself in something like its pristine form. That was the definition used by Duncan Poore in his study. It was theoretically possible even if not seen much in practice.

The Penang declaration, however, included a 'people factor'. For the Penang signatories true sustainable forestry maintained the rights of forest dwellers and protected the plants they gathered and the animals they hunted. No commercial forester could meet this standard, and that was probably why the articles of association of the ITTO make no mention of forest dwellers. The Penang signatories accepted that they were demanding the outlawing of commercial forestry in natural tropical forests and declared that commercial foresters would have to stick to their own plantations well away from existing primary forests. The world, meanwhile, would have to cut back drastically on its consumption of tropical timber, relying much more on the products of temperate forests.

Before the meeting, Koy Thomson, FoE's top rainforest campaigner in London, moved towards the radical position. He signed a joint letter with Mohammed Idris, Nick Hildyard from the *Ecologist*, and others, backing the case for a 'moratorium on commercial timber extraction in primary rainforests'. However, he still favoured dialogue at the ITTO.

Chee Yoke Ling at SAM welcomed Thomson's move but told me: 'We think that the FoE International campaign has wasted years by getting involved with the ITTO.' It was true that the ITTO now devoted a lot of its time to discussing environmental issues, and that its special projects fund, set up at the suggestion of the WWF and FoE, spent most of its money on conservation projects. But, said Chee, by taking part so actively in the ITTO, the green lobbyists had let the timber trade dictate what they did. FoE and the WWF thought they were setting the agenda for the debate inside ITTO. The truth, she said, was that while the talking went on, the destruction of the forests was escalating.

'FoE and the WWF asked the ITTO to conduct a study into sustainable forestry. It produced the answer we wanted and expected, but by agreeing to the study the traders bought themselves eighteen months during which FoE was not campaigning for a logging ban.' In 1989, the WWF persuaded the ITTO to discuss a code of conduct for sustainable forestry. 'We think a code of conduct is useless,' said Chee, 'and by suggesting it, they have shifted the focus once again from calls for a moratorium.' For her, negotiating perpetuates the myth that, in today's world, sustainable forestry in the tropics is a plausible objective. 'There is no management solution. We've wasted too much time.'

This is a powerful criticism. Millions of people round the world have given money to Friends of the Earth and the World Wide Fund for Nature to save the rainforests. Lobbying at the ITTO is a key strategy of both groups. If they are playing into the hands of the timber traders, their supporters should be very angry. I discussed the issue with Chris Rose, who devised rainforest campaigns both at FoE in Britain and the WWF International in Switzerland. He believes that the campaign in the North has taken a wrong tack. 'At the WWF, we agreed that it would probably be necessary to shut down the international tropical timber trade before we could tackle issues, such as land rights, that the Penang people see as central. We saw work at the ITTO as just a part of that strategy. But FoE didn't believe that anything so drastic was necessary.'

In its internal 1989 campaign report, FoE in London saw as its medium-term aim the use of the ITTO to 'completely restructure the timber trade towards sustainable development', and as its long-term aim that there would be 'no further logging in primary rainforest'. The report argued that 'it is still too early to ascertain whether the ITTO can ever meet our long-term aspirations.'

Rose, who helped devise the original ITTO strategy for FoE, sees no chance of the medium-term aim being met without the industry being shaken to its foundations and faced with widespread boycotts of its products. 'Otherwise, they have no economic self-interest in being reformed,' he says.

Rose once tried to persuade Greenpeace to blockade Japanese ships on their way to Sarawak to collect logs. He saw it as a way of drawing worldwide attention to the logging issue, believing that negotiations at the ITTO would only bear fruit if Greenpeace-style direct action turned the issue into a front-page scandal. He envisaged widespread consumer boycotts in Europe, extending to the US. Ultimately, delegates to the ITTO from these countries would have to pressure Japan into joining a major reform of the timber trade. The scenario was a replay of the anti-whaling campaign of a decade before. But by the end of 1989, the whole campaign had been stalled because no effective progress towards exerting pressure from outside the ITTO to boycott tropical timber had been achieved.

Of Thais and teak

Amid the gloom of rainforest campaigning, the guardians of the world's trees were buoyed up in 1989 by one great success. The good news came from Thailand. In January 1989, the government of Thailand issued two royal decrees, cancelling all logging concessions and effectively banning commercial logging throughout the country.

The immediate reason for the ban was a succession of floods and landslides in the south of the country, where destruction of forests on hillsides had caused soil erosion and the accumulation of silt in river beds. Some 400 people died in the floods and the tide of anger swept the government towards the ban a few weeks later. Behind the success was a long campaign which had brought together the interests of poor peasant hill-farmers, from remote border regions, and the students and intellectuals of Bangkok. The story of this success in Thailand, a country straddling the divide between the rich and poor nations of the world, could have lessons for those trying to create alliances to bring action at a global level.

Larry Lohmann, an American environmentalist working for the Project for Ecological Recovery, was in Thailand as the campaign swept to victory. The Project had pioneered links between peasants and the city greens. He points out that the country's economy had been growing at an unprecedented rate in the late 1980s and timber processing companies, taking advantage of new roads carved into the country's remote forested areas, were racing to supply a fast-growing market for paper and wood products. But as the trees were cut down, rivers dried up and irrigation channels became clogged with silt.

Throughout 1988, says Lohmann, 'village after village had been campaigning against logging. They had petitioned government officials, made appointments with politicians, staged rallies and sought alliances and exchanges with villages and organisations outside their locality.' In Chiang Mai province, in the far north, logging operations were blocked by force in a number of districts after farmers' complaints about dwindling water supplies and silt-clogged streams were ignored by officials. In Phayao, hundreds of farmers had taken control of a government office and refused to leave until the agriculture minister agreed to suspend the right of a local company to cut timber pending an investigation of illegal procedures. Elsewhere villagers had seized logs and won promises from logging companies not to cut trees on a particular hillside.

Village campaigners had been encouraged, says Lohmann, by the success early in 1988 of a campaign against plans for a hydroelectric dam at Nam Choan. Then an unexpected judicial decision set off public anger. Courts ruled that loggers should be allowed to cut down trees in old concessions that had since become part of wildlife sanctuaries. The decision granted a *carte blanche* to loggers to move into 22 sanctuaries. Among the concessions released by the ruling was a 1,000-square-kilometre area of dry tropical forest in the Huai Kha Khaeng Wildlife Sanctuary, which had been saved from dismemberment only weeks before when plans for the Nam Choan dam had been halted. 'Even for many who had watched the villagers' protests with indifference, the idea that some of Thailand's most cherished protected areas were now to be treated as ordinary commercial concessions provoked outrage,' says Lohmann.

Newspapers began to campaign on the issue, giving sympathetic coverage to villagers' protests and publishing pictures showing the burned-out stubble left in other logged forests by Thai Plywood, the company with the Huai Kha Khaeng concessions. On 26 November 1988, over a hundred conservationists met in Bangkok to discuss the court decision; during a break, they heard on TV the first news of devastating floods in the south of the country.

Says Lohmann, 'The groups moved quickly to connect the flooding with the issue of logging . . . and called for an overall ban.' Few of them expected to win their demand, but events moved fast. Protests were so great that the government put a temporary ban on logging in the region of the floods. Then, ten days after the flooding, village campaigners from all corners of the country converged on Bangkok and met the prime minister to demand a nationwide logging ban.

Fearing the worst, timber companies quickly stepped up operations. Reports reached Lohmann's office of threats to villagers who had returned home after going to Bangkok to protest. In many areas, sawmill owners and loggers were the largest employers and were widely believed to have police officers, local politicians and forestry staff in their pay. They blamed villagers themselves for forest destruction. One timber magnate said he would demand $100 million in compensation if his concession were cancelled. The prime minister, Chatichai Choonhaven, was unmoved by these threats. Even seven of his cabinet ministers, who were reported to have stakes in logging companies, realised that public pressure was too strong to resist. 'Concessionaires can file all the suits they wish,' said Choonhaven, '[the ban] is what the people asked for.'

It was an inspiring victory. Yet, almost before Thai environmentalists had stopped cheering, they began to receive reports that Thai logging companies were moving across the remote mountain border into Burma and logging the Burmese forests. These forests contain the world's largest reserves of teak and according to some estimates make up 80 per cent of the world's stocks. The move appeared to be part of a deal between the Thai government and the logging firms. The day before the proclamation of the logging ban, the Thai authorities had quietly announced that they were conducting studies into the possibility of importing wood from Burma, Laos and Fiji to keep their thriving timber-processing industry in business.

Three months later Larry Lohmann left Thailand to attend a meeting of the World Rainforest Movement in Penang, where he reported that 'Thailand is already importing logs from

Burma. The environmental problem will simply be shifted to Thailand's neighbours.' While Thailand's forests had shrunk from covering approximately 70 per cent of the country to less than 20 per cent, Burma was still 40 per cent forested. In 1989, the bankrupt military government in Rangoon had auctioned teak worth several million dollars to timber firms from Japan and Europe. But that was just the beginning.

The Thai–Burmese border had become a thriving area for smuggling. One Thai study estimated that goods worth $3 billion – 40 per cent of the Burmese gross national product – were smuggled into Burma across the border in 1985. Now trade was to begin in the other direction. During congressional hearings in Washington in 1989 into trade sanctions against Burma, Senator Daniel Moynihan named 15 Thai timber companies. All, he said, had recently won concessions to take millions of tonnes of timber from the forests of the Burmese interior. One estimate puts the value of the concessions at $100 million.

According to Moynihan, the concession holders included Chaophraya Irrawaddy, a firm in which Lohmann discovered that the Thai army's commander in chief, Chaowalit Yong-chaiyudhand, and his subordinate General Sunthorn Kong-sompong, had direct interests. It seemed that Thailand's military leaders were, both literally and metaphorically, beating a path to the Burmese teak. They knew the border well after their constant forays against rebellious tribes in the area, including the Karen who had fought a 40-year war against rule by Bangkok, and the Hmong, whose opium plantations gave the region its popular title of the Golden Triangle.

Burma's unique teak forests were once subject to a rigorous regime of control by the British, initially to provide a sustainable source of teak for Royal Naval ships. The regime is said to have been without parallel anywhere in the world. But after independence, the Burmese generals swiftly took control of the forests, and by the 1980s any timber that could be shipped or trucked to Rangoon or Mandalay had been cut down. That left large forested areas of the interior that were almost impossible to reach from the Burmese side. The only rivers along which logs could be transported all drained into Thailand. In any case, many of these forests were in the hands of rebel tribes.

Now, in a bid for foreign currency, the Burmese generals were shrugging off their isolationism and offering their remaining forests to the Thais. By late 1989, according to Lohmann, 'the timber cutters were active along the entire Thai–Burmese border from Ranong in the south to Mae Hong Son 700 kilometres away in the north. By all accounts the destruction is immense.' Thailand, with ambitions to join the club of industrialised nations of the Far East, had decided to preserve its own forests and start chopping down other peoples.'

Plant a tree for industry

In November 1989, Margaret Thatcher made one of her rare and well-publicised visits to the United Nations in New York. She made what her aides called a major speech on the environment – designed to match, perhaps, that delivered a year before by Mikhail Gorbachev – full of rhetoric about the need to manage our planet for the benefit of future generations. Thatcher promised £100 million of British aid money to save the rainforests. When they read the small print, most environmentalists reacted with horror. She was giving the money to the Tropical Forestry Action Plan, a system devised by the UN Food and Agriculture Organization for providing international aid for national forestry plans. Many environmentalists are coming to believe that the TFAP is doing far more harm than good to the world's rainforests.

There are, at root, two views about how we should save the rainforests. One approach is to keep out the modern world of roads and banks, development projects and multinational companies. The other is to invite them in. For one, the modern world is part of the problem. The other sees it as part of the solution. The Tropical Forestry Action Plan – drawn up in the mid-1980s – starts from the premise that the poor and ignorant chop and burn down forests because they have no incentive not to, or lack the skills to do otherwise. The solution, it says, is to let the expertise and capital funding of the rich world take charge. The TFAP says, 'Tragically, it is the poor themselves who are the major agents of destruction.' However, 'properly used and managed, the tropical forests constitute a massive potential source of energy, a powerful tool in the fight to end hunger, a strong basis for generating economic wealth and social development, and a storehouse of genetic resources to meet future needs. This is the promise and the challenge.' Nobody could disagree that the forests are a major resource. The nub of the problem is in that initial clause: 'properly used and managed'. It invites such questions as 'by whom?' and 'for whom?'

Since natives such as the Kayapo in the Amazon and the Penan in Borneo are acknowledged by scientists as the best source of knowledge about their forests, and the only people with a record of making a livelihood from the forests without destroying them, it might be assumed that they know best how to develop the forests. But when the TFAP's backers proposed that forestry aid programmes should be doubled, and overall investment in the forests should rise to $8 billion by the early 1990s, they were not proposing to give the money to forest dwellers. Rather, they wanted to encourage governments to draw up their own national forestry plans, based on commercial considerations and Western science. The requests for help on national plans flooded in. But it is clear also that, whatever the rhetoric from Thatcher, conservation will account for only a fraction of the expenditure proposed under the national plans. In the mid-1980s, only around 5 per cent of aid money for forests went on conservation, while more than 30 per cent went on commercial development. That ratio won't change much.

As Teddy Goldsmith, a strident critic of the plan, points out, 'Remember that it is a tropical FORESTRY plan, not a forests plan. The idea is to invest in forestry as an industry.' The UN Development Programme reported in 1988 that of the first 42 national plans submitted under the TFAP, none proposed national strategies for restoring damaged forest ecosystems, and few looked at issues such as wildlife conservation, shifting cultivation, the use of forests by native peoples – or indeed at anything much except timber production. The plan for Brazil will be seen by many as a test of the TFAP. Initial proposals foresee spending $400 million on agroforestry, $325 million on industrial forestry and just $50 millon on conservation of ecosystems. An ambitious plan for Cameroon sees most of the nation's forests being turned over to logging. Natives will be removed from surviving reserves, which will be set aside for 'tourist-based hunting'. There is little here to justify Thatcher's claim that her £100 million will be spent on conserving forests. Her officials concede that, at its best, the TFAP is merely a way of 'managing the forests' decline'.

Environmental groups were slow to criticise the TFAP when it was published in the mid-1980s. Many, especially in the US, asked to be involved in its work – as consultants on national plans, for instance. The first warnings came from India, which for a decade had been using loans from the World Bank to develop an idea called 'social forestry'. It is a model for the kind of 'progressive' forestry that is envisaged by many to take root under the banner of the TFAP.

The World Rainforest Movement commissioned Vandana Shiva, the fiery head of the Research Foundation for Science, Technology and Natural Resource Policy in India, to write a critique of the TFAP. She concluded that 'the "successful" forestry projects cited in the TFAP, including the Indian social forestry scheme, are all World-Bank-financed projects which have been seriously criticised at the local level for increasing the deprivation of the rural poor and increasing the vulnerability of the tropical ecosystems.'

According to the UN Food and Agriculture Organization, the aim of such projects is to 'raise the standard of living of the rural dweller, to involve him in the decision-making process which affects his very existence and to transform him into a dynamic citizen capable of contributing to a wider range of activities than he was used to and of which he will be the direct beneficiary'. In practice, says Shiva, 'It takes forestry away from the control of communities and makes it a capital-intensive, externally-controlled activity. It totally neglects the economics of tribal and peasant life based on natural forests and food production and focuses exclusively on the economics of production of commercial wood.'

India's social forestry programme started with the very best of intentions. By the late 1970s the widespread destruction of forests across India had led to a crisis over firewood, which 90 per cent of Indian households use for fuel. The idea was to use aid money to grow trees on waste land, railway embankments, roadside verges, or spare land on farms. Forestry would be taken out of the hands of the hated state forestry authorities and given back to the people. Villagers would be encouraged to participate. Jobs would be created for landless labourers. What happened, however, was rather different. Rich farmers and plantation companies rushed to take advantage of the grants and tax concessions for tree planting. Suddenly, all over the country plantations of eucalyptus, almost all on private land, began to sprout. Private profit was ruling over social need, and few jobs were created. Eucalyptus, as Shiva pointed out in her study, are 'quick growing, require little care and hence have little demand in terms of labour input. They are therefore a species that survives best in the absence of community participation.'

In some places, tree plantations have displaced fields of staple food crops such as ragi (millet), oil seeds and pulses, bringing fears of a food crisis among the rural poor. From other areas came the cry that seems to follow eucalyptus whenever it strays from its home in Australia. It grows so fast that it sucks moisture and nutrients from the soil, drying up wells and killing other crops. Eucalyptus 'is inimical to other forms of life,' says Thomas Lovejoy at the WWF.

Where eucalyptus has been grown on 'waste land', it has become clear that the land was not so wasted before, after all. Waste land is frequently a euphemism for common land. Tens of millions of villagers in India graze their animals on common land and collect firewood and other produce from such land. But there is nothing to graze in eucalyptus plantations, not even the leaves, which animals hate. Eucalyptus wood is only for sale and it is far too expensive for firewood. Most of it is destined for rayon and pulp mills. Social forestry in India has turned into something distinctly anti-social.

In 1983 in the state of Karnataka in southern India, the World Bank, riding on a wave of enthusiasm for eucalyptus, launched its largest ever social forestry project in consort with the British Overseas Development Administration and the Indian authorities. Within weeks, local farmers had marched to a eucalyptus nursery at Holatalli, ripped up the seedlings and replaced them with tamarind seedlings, a native species. Five days later, the same thing happened at another nursery. If community participation meant anything, this particular social forestry project ought to have been halted on the spot; but it wasn't. When tens of millions of dollars of aid money are involved, it is not that easy.

In 1987, the Supreme Court of India granted to a local citizens' group in Karnataka an order halting the handover, under the social forestry programme, of some 30,000 hectares of common lands in four districts of the state to a company called Karnataka Pulpwood. The company had been set up by the state government and a firm named Harihar Polyfibre to plant trees. Harihar's mills were to turn the trees into synthetic fibres. The company already had a bad local reputation for polluting local rivers and destroying fisheries with waste from its mills. Now, villagers who had depended for generations on the common lands for fodder and fuel were to lose yet more of their common resources.

Both social forestry and now the TFAP are, at least in part, being carried out in the name of the environment. The potential for disputes among environmentalists over the TFAP is great, and several environmental groups are deeply involved in its development. The World Resources Institute was involved in its initiation. Jim Barnes, at the Washington-based Environmental Policy Institute, was a leading consultant for the plan and favours the FoE family working with rather than against it. For him the TFAP is part of the solution to a range of environmental problems, especially the loss of the world's forests. For many environmentalists who have seen social forestry in action, however, the TFAP is part of the problem, the further privatisation and industrialisation of commonly owned resources on which the poor depend. Reforms proposed for the TFAP in 1990 did not change that view.

Never one to duck a dispute with fellow environmentalists, Vandana Shiva wrote in her critique of the TFAP: 'Citizens working at making the World Bank more accountable to its human and environmental responsibility will have to develop a new ability to discriminate between international non-governmental organisations organised by the World Bank . . . and NGOs reflecting the voice of local grass roots movements and struggles.'

The stories from India about the perils of social forestry seem set to be repeated in Thailand. There the decision in 1989 to ban further logging of natural forests has set off a stampede to establish eucalyptus plantations on former forest land. Promoters of such projects include Shell Oil, which wants to replant 200 square kilometres of former forest land in Chanthaburi province near the border with Cambodia. On the surface, says Larry Lohmann from the Project for Ecological Recovery, 'it looks to be impeccably conservationist and in addition helps take reafforestation out of the hands of a government which has been able to plant a mere three hundred square kilometres in seventy years.' But, says Lohmann, eucalyptus plantations will end up evicting many of the one million people now living without formal land titles in the 61,000 square kilometres of National Reserve forests; forests which were once licensed for logging and are now earmarked for replanting. Shell estimates that it will employ about five families for each square kilometre of its own plantation. That leaves perhaps half a million families who may eventually be forced off their land. 'Many of the evicted will inevitably be forced to encroach on natural forests elsewhere,' says Lohmann, 'just as victims of unequal land distribution in Brazil and Indonesia are being settled on the forest frontiers of these countries. Without serious attempts at land reform, commercial reafforestation often only accelerates deforestation.'

Lohmann, who in 1990 took a new job with the World Rainforest Movement, calls the new plantation schemes 'a continuation of deforestation by other means'. Plantations carry on the process of dispossessing native people. Villagers in the remote north-east of Thailand who spent the 1970s and 1980s fighting logging companies are now, like the Indian farmers, fighting the plantation companies. In early 1988, farmers from several villages in the province of Buriram forced planters from the land. But in other regions, reports Lohmann, squatters are accepting money to move off the land needed for plantations, 'then moving on to dwindling forest resources elsewhere'.

Lohmann calls the eucalyptus tree 'an exceptionally efficient device allowing the world economy to annex supposedly marginal areas, smash the patterns of livelihood and nature conservation there, and convert the fragments into "resources" for global exchange. Local villagers will be cut loose to seek niches as producers, consumers or (in the case of prostitutes) commodities in the world economy. Because such niches will not always be available, many people will become simply expendable.'

9
DAMMING THE WORLD BANK

Reservoirs of protest

Giant concrete dams are potent symbols of progress. Since the 1930s, when the US watered the arid west with the Hoover dam and the Russians dammed the Volga, dams have been seen as shining examples of engineering prowess, of the taming of nature and of a certain kind of economic progress. Nehru called them 'the temples of modern India'. The Aswan dam in Egypt was hailed as a new wonder of the world on its completion in the 1960s. It was 17 times heavier than the Great Pyramid and would trap the waters of the Nile – the world's longest river – generating hydroelectric power, irrigating fields and controlling floods. When Sri Lanka embarked on a dash for economic growth in the 1980s, it spent some $3 billion in international aid money on taming the Mahaweli River with a series of dams. The project attracted the largest ever aid loan from the British government and promised to double the country's electricity capacity within a decade, setting it up as a future industrial power.

By 1990, there were more than 100 dams round the world with heights greater than 150 metres. Of these most were in the Third World and almost half had been completed during the 1980s. Dams were taking up an ever larger proportion of international aid programmes. Governments, eager for cheap electricity, saw them as the golden key to economic growth and they were prepared to run up huge debts to buy them. The world's largest hydroelectric complex at Itaipu dam between Paraguay and Brazil cost $16 billion to build. And China spent the late 1980s considering whether to go ahead with what would be the world's largest dam project at Three Gorges on the Yangtze River. One version of the project, so its designers claimed, would cost perhaps $20 billion to build and increase China's electricity generating capacity by almost 40 per cent.

Yet, as the concrete and the dollars poured in, and the first of the new generation of super-reservoirs filled, the doubts were setting in. Engineers and hydrologists began to take stock. One of them, Phil Williams, a professional hydrologist who runs the International Rivers Network from San Francisco, warned in 1984, 'The technology which inspires so much faith and requires such a great sacrifice of resources is a new one and its impacts are largely unknown.' Williams was writing an introduction to a remarkable book edited by Teddy Goldsmith and Nick Hildyard at the *Ecologist*. The book set out to prove that all large dams, without exception, were proving to be expensive and destructive failures. In case after case, the contributors related sagas of environmental destruction affecting the livelihoods of millions of people; of the spread of disease and corruption; and of the unfulfilled promises of engineers. From the James Bay Project in Canada and Tasmania's Franklin River, to the Danube in Hungary and the Cabora Bassa dam in Mozambique the stories in the book were so compelling that even the journals of water engineers were forced to commend it to their readers.

Certainly, electricity was being generated; though usually not as much as promised or as cheaply. Certainly, fields were being irrigated; but often supplies were irregular and inappropriate to the crops being planted. But what of the costs? Upstream of the dams, millions of people had been flooded out of fertile farmland. The Akosombo dam on the River Volta in Ghana forced 80,000 people off their land; the Aswan in Egypt, 120,000; and the Damadur in India, 93,000. Three Gorges in China could dispossess 1.2 million people. Few resettlement schemes worked well. In any case they usually excluded people who have no formal title to the land on which they lived. The Tucurui dam in the Amazon rainforest flooded 2,000 square kilometres of virgin rainforest and displaced 10,000 so-called squatters. Downstream of the dams, the effects are scarcely less severe. Silt that once fertilised fields is now caught uselessly behind dams, reducing the reservoirs' capacity and at the same time depriving downstream fields of their natural fertiliser. River flows are so altered that fisheries disappear.

By and large, governments and their Western advisers have ignored these problems. They regard them as small compared with the promise offered by the dams themselves and the power they could generate. Phil Williams caught the issue well. He said:

> Dams transform the social life of a country, destroying indigenous, traditional cultures and accelerating the change to a cash economy centred on cities. This very power to engineer human lives makes large dams attractive to governments and development agencies alike. The promise of radically changing a country's economy is frequently used to justify the destruction of communities, of ecosystems and of traditional agricultural systems.

As traditional economies suffered, however, the promised economic benefits from dams to the national economies were proving illusory. At the end of the 1980s, the chickens were finally coming home to roost. Prompted in part by Goldsmith and Hildyard's epic review, engineers had been taking a closer look at their creations – and finding a discouraging pattern. Even in the narrowest financial terms, leaving aside environmental damage, and the destruction of national resources such as fisheries and forests, most schemes are a disaster. A study by the Asian Development Bank, one of the biggest funders of dams and irrigation schemes, found that for 40 of its largest schemes, the financial returns were between 15 and 30 per cent of those predicted.

There were even doubts about the great 'success story' of the 1960s: the Aswan dam. It is filling up with soil washed down from the Ethiopian highlands. For thousands of years the soil helped to maintain the fertility of Egyptian fields, and Ethiopia's loss had been the Egyptian farmers' gain. But the most graphic effect of the loss of the silt is the retreat of the Nile delta, which needs constant deposits of silt in order not to be

204 *Green Warriors*

eroded away by the tides of the Mediterranean. Today the delta is retreating, and as it does so, salt water from the sea is permeating the well water of the delta, making it too salty for farmers to use.

In West Africa, too, the giant Akosombo dam in Ghana, once the pride of President Nkruma, has cut off the supply of silt to the coast of Ghana and neighbouring Togo and triggered massive coastal erosion. The homes of 10,000 people living in Keto on the coast of Togo have disappeared beneath the waves. This dislocation has come in addition to the 80,000 people flooded out when the dam's reservoir rose to cover an area of land the size of Lebanon.

For many reservoirs, silt has become the great destroyer. In Asia, it has filled several within a few decades of their completion, and made the economics of the dams, which assumed that they would carry on generating electricity and filling irrigation canals for a century or more, look very foolish. In Pakistan, engineers are constructing expensive new works to protect the $1.4 billion Tarbela dam, built in the late 1970s, from a 45-metre-high wedge of silt moving slowly through the reservoir towards the dam. Latest estimates say that the reservoir will be useless by around 2012.

In India, home to some of the world's largest dams, siltation rates behind dams in the Himalayas are anything between two and ten times those predicted by engineers. At a dam across the Maujira River at Nizamsagar in Andhra Pradesh, the rate is 16 times that predicted and the dam had lost 60 per cent of its capacity within 40 years of construction. The Sriramsagar reservoir lost 36 per cent of its capacity in its first two years. Soon, all that will be left of these follies will be a hard unfarmable mass of baked silt, held up by hundreds of tons of concrete.

Indian geologists have warned that the Tehri dam, a 260-metre monster on the Bhagirathi River in the mid-Himalayas, whose various works have been under construction since the early 1980s, may fill with silt within 35 years – three times faster than the construction engineers claim. If it is finished, the Tehri dam will be the second highest dam in Asia. It is partly financed by the Soviet Union and bears all the hallmarks of an economic and environmental disaster in the making. Construction began in the mid-1970s, but by the late 1980s, work on the main dam had not begun. Opponents, led by a local lawyer, say that the government should abandon the dam and build instead a series of much smaller 'run of the river' dams, which could supply local needs and be controlled by villagers.

The dam will flood one of the most fertile valleys in the region and displace some 100,000 people. Many have already moved on to land carved from the forests around the nearby town of Dehra Dun. The people of Tehri itself are promised a New Tehri Town 1,000 metres up the hillside.

By the late 1980s, opposition to the dam had become a *cause célèbre* in India, as national concern grew about widespread environmental destruction of the Himalayas. The 'struggle committee' launched a court action, partly funded by the World Wildlife Fund India, to fight the dam. Meanwhile the government's advisers were raising doubts. A special committee reported in 1986 that the weight of water in the reservoir when it filled risked setting off an earthquake in an area known to be susceptible to tremors – a large tear fault runs across the valley. The report was kept secret until campaigners obtained a copy and presented it to the Supreme Court. They claim that the downstream holy cities of Devaprayag, Rishikesh and Haridwar would be obliterated if the dam burst, and hundreds of thousands would be killed. Opponents of the dam included Sunderlal Bahuguna, the legendary leader of the Chipko movement of 'tree-huggers' whose campaign is centred in nearby hills. Bahuguna forced the government to call a temporary halt to the project in early 1990 by going on hunger strike; but with the state government and the energy ministry in Delhi both still backing the dam, most observers expected work to resume eventually.

Dams are usually justified on three grounds: they will provide cheap hydroelectric power, water to irrigate fields, and protection against floods. Often they fail on all three counts. Usually flood-prevention is at the bottom of the list of priorities for the operators of dams. Most keep them full to the brim in order to maximise the generation of hydroelectric power. They often cause rather than prevent flooding. That is what happened in West Bengal in 1978, when unexpected rain 'overtopped' a dam, causing extensive floods across the state. It happened again on the Colorado River in the US in 1983 when operators ignored weather warnings, causing more than $100 million worth of damage to property downstream of the dam.

Almost 40 per cent of the World Bank's spending on agriculture in the Third World in the past 40 years has gone on irrigation projects, the vast majority of it during the 1980s. Yet often dams are complete before anybody thinks about the details of the irrigation schemes, and frequently the money runs out before the canals are dug. Technical failures in canal schemes mean that water supplies are insufficient, canals clog with weeds or pumps fail. In a speech to state irrigation ministers in 1986, Prime Minister Rajiv Gandhi revealed that 'since 1951, 246 large surface irrigation projects had been begun in India. Only 65 had been completed. Perhaps we can safely say that no benefit has come to the people from these projects. We have poured money out. The people have got nothing back ... no irrigation, no water, no increase in production, no help in their daily life.' He called on states to give priority to completing existing schemes. Such is the lure of the 'temples of modern India', however, that a year later, his cabinet approved plans for two more giant dams on the River Narmada with the intention of irrigating yet more fields.

The vast amounts of standing water in reservoirs and canals make them an ideal breeding ground for malarial insects and freshwater snails which harbour the parasites that cause schistosomiasis. This is a crippling disease endemic in parts of Africa where fields are irrigated. The incidence of the disease amongst children living near to the Aswan dam rose from 5 per cent before the dam's construction to 90 per cent today. According to the World Health Organization, there are now 200 million sufferers, almost double the number of 40 years ago. Nobody doubts that dams are the main cause, but engineers have so far devoted little attention to finding a solution.

A terrifying consequence of field irrigation in tropical lands is waterlogging and the accumulation of salt. When water on the land evaporates, it leaves behind a residue of minerals in the form of salt, which accumulates in soils until it eventually becomes toxic to plants. The UN Food and Agriculture Organization estimates that half of the world's irrigated fields suffer from salt poisoning; and one study reckons that during the 1980s as many fields were being taken out of production because of salt poisoning as were being brought into production by new irrigation schemes.

Tens of millions of hectares of the Indus Valley in Pakistan and of the Punjab and Haryana, rich alluvial plains in India, have become salt-encrusted 'wet deserts'. Well water in parts of the lower Indus Valley can be as salty as sea-water. A billion-dollar rescue plan is under way in Pakistan to drain the salt from the fields and return them to production. Meanwhile, the Pakistani government, banking on the success of this project, is planning to build yet another dam, with a price-tag of $5 billion, where the Indus descends from the Himalayan foothills at Kalabagh. A fledgling Pakistan Environmental Network, headed by a geography lecturer at the University of Karachi, Nasir Gazdar, is fighting the plan.

Through the 1980s, campaigns to oppose big dams in developing countries began to gain force; and they began to win. Perhaps the first important victory came in 1983 when the Kerala Sastra Sahiktya Parishat, one of India's myriad local organisations involved in environmental and science education, won the abandonment of the Silent Valley project. The scheme, in the southern state of Kerela, would have flooded one of India's few remaining tropical rainforests. The group's campaign won international backing and the prime minister called off the project. Anil Agarwal, one of India's leading environmental campaigners and a close adviser of Rajiv Gandhi before his election defeat in 1989, called the controversy 'the fiercest environmental debate in the country'.

In 1988, the Thai government dropped plans for a dam at Nam Choan in Kanchanaburi province after a spirited local campaign by a coalition of environmentalists. The campaign has been analysed by the American environmentalist then living in Thailand, Larry Lohmann.

The Nam Choan dam on the Khwae Yai River was the first

environmental issue to catch the public imagination in Thailand. It was to be built close to the Burmese border and upstream of two other large dams and the famous bridge over the River Khwae, built by prisoners held by the Japanese during the Second World War. The Japanese wanted to help pay for and build the Nam Choan dam.

The dam proposal, first hatched in the late 1970s, brought storms of protests organised by student environmental clubs in 1982. The students objected to the likely destruction of rainforests and wildlife from flooding, roads and other features of the project. The 200-metre-high dam would create a reservoir 75 kilometres long, flood a large tract of rare riverine forest, and would split into three fragments Huay Kha Khaeng and Thung Yai, two adjoining wildlife sanctuaries which are acknowledged to be among the best in south-east Asia. The splitting of the sanctuaries would cut the migration paths of tigers, tapirs and elephants. It would also inundate villages of the Karen and opium-growing Hmong tribes north of the sanctuaries and dislodge some 5,000 tribal people living, technically illegally, in the reserves themselves.

Equally pressing for the students were fears that the dam could be destroyed by an earthquake. The students' protests in the early 1980s helped to persuade the government to put the plan into cold storage, where it remained until March 1986, when the government revived the project.

Opposition to the dam swiftly re-formed. A grand alliance of university scientists and conservationists was headed by the WWF-affiliated Wildlife Fund of Thailand, which also enjoyed domestic royal patronage. The opposition included more radical critics of large development schemes, including the Project for Ecological Recovery, where Lohmann worked. Tensions arose because the Wildlife Fund of Thailand, backed by the US WWF, argued publicly the need for economic development in western Thailand, while groups such as the Project for Ecological Recovery strongly opposed it. Crucially, Lohmann believes, the opponents managed to keep their disagreements to themselves.

The dam's backers included the military, who wanted to secure a large area of wilderness above the dam site, which had been a seat of Communist activity during the Vietnam War. Proponents of the dam employed dirty tricks, says Lohmann. The Wildlife Fund of Thailand was pilloried as being composed of 'hunters wanting to keep Thung Yai as their private reserve. Anonymous leaflets were circulated in the cabinet and the senate claiming that the opposition was being led by people selling arms to the Karen hill tribes.

The dam's public opponents, who included Prince Philip and Prince Bernhard, hardly fitted such descriptions. Nor did the popular singer Ad Carabao, the governor of Bangkok, or a well-known abbot from a temple in Surat Thani; all of whom had lent their voices to the opposition. Popular protests included a bizarre joint 120-kilometre 'jogging protest' by wildlife campaigners and Karen tribespeople, a mass bicycle ride in Bangkok, and large rallies and concerts in Kanchanaburi province. By early 1988, the press switched sides and a former prime minister warned that the protests could bring down the government.

With government nerves clearly on edge, Nam Choan was officially shelved – probably for ever. Within weeks of that decision, however, news surfaced that the international committee in charge of managing the Lower Mekong River Basin – which includes Laos, Thailand, Vietnam and Cambodia – was being pushed by the Thais to back a plan for a dam to be built at Pamong, on the Thai–Laos border, to supply electricity to Thailand. It was part of a much larger plan to harness the 4,000-kilometre Mekong River. The dam builders were still very much in business.

Many believed that the case against large dams in the tropics was overwhelming. They did not suit an environment where soil erosion was an ever-present danger, and salt problems severe in the hot sun. The economics did not add up for anybody except the Western engineers who designed and largely built them. Most important, they were brutal agents by which city-based governments wrought havoc on rural communities. By the late 1980s, those rural communities were learning how to fight back, and they were gathering friends in the rich world to take up their cause.

The greening of the Bank

It was not, as these things go, a particularly impressive demonstration. Probably because nobody could work out if they were
celebrating a victory or mourning defeat. We began in a small
park, known as Lafayette Park, across the road from the White
House. For a while, we were heavily outnumbered by groups
of tourists. It was misty and seemed set for rain as protesters
sheepishly began to unveil their banners. 'Dam the World
Bank: Not the World's Rivers', said one. 'World Bank =
Death and Destruction', said another. Others were in German,
Russian and Arabic. The tourists looked bemused.

Someone from the palatial offices of the National Wildlife
Federation showed up wearing a blazer and tie and carrying a
fancy flag with a gold-tipped pole. Then a friend appeared. 'Is
this the five-million-member NWF?' he asked with heavy
sarcasm. Well, at least they were there. The even richer World
Wildlife Fund was nowhere to be seen. 'Washington is not
really a demonstrators' town,' said Chad Dobson – a smiling,
balding, glad-handing, jeans-wearing radical who seems to
know everyone in a town of grim-faced, toupeed, suit-and-tied
insiders. Chad had helped organise the show, as head of the
Bank Information Center, an ill-disguised outfit for leaking as
many confidential documents from the World Bank about its
secret dealings round the world to as many of its beneficiaries/
victims as possible. The man with the two police permits
necessary for our small band to march the three blocks to a
patch of muddy grass outside the World Bank's headquarters
was the San Franciscan hydrologist, Phil Williams. He had
spent most of the 1980s being rude about the havoc his fellow
professionals were causing round the world by working on big
dams paid for by the Bank and other organisations with deep
pockets. He confesses to feeling almost as foreign in Washington as the clutch of top environmental campaigners from
Africa, Asia and Latin America trailing behind him.

Our demonstration was a small sideshow to the annual
meeting of the World Bank and its sister organisation the
International Monetary Fund. The Bank is the world's largest
provider of loans for 'development' projects and so bankrolls

most of the biggest and most socially and environmentally disruptive schemes under way in the Third World. It has paid for the iron ore mines, power plants, farm projects and roads that are paving the way for the destruction of the Amazon rainforest. But for the Bank, many of the world's largest dams, irrigation projects, plantations and power stations would never have been built. But for the Bank, say its opponents, millions of shanty-town dwellers and plantation labourers round the world would still be at work on their own farms, and dozens of nations would have avoided debt burdens that are crippling their economies. For them, the Bank does, in the words of the banner, equal death and destruction.

That week, in September 1989, the rich environmental lobbying organisations of Washington had paid for a hundred or so campaigners from Africa, Asia and Latin America to join them and sundry hairy Europeans, Australians and Californians in Washington to lobby the Bank and attend a week-long meeting to discuss tactics for making it more environmentally friendly. It was the nearest thing to a worldwide gathering of international environment campaigners that has yet taken place.

A few of the more obstreperous campaigners (though very few of the hundred or more Washingtonians attending the meeting) made it to the demo. But there seemed barely enough to fill a couple of the 'stretch limos' heading under police escort to the Bank's deliberations at the Sheraton Hotel. There was Girish Patel of the Adhikar Sangh organisation, a swarthy Indian who had no time for the sophisticated lobbyists of the WWF, NWF, and the rest of the Washington green acronyms. 'I have not come here to pressure the World Bank. I have come with a message. The Bank must get out of India. We don't want their money. We don't want their expertise.'

In the state of Gujerat, he said, the World Bank is paying $450 million towards the cost of the Sardar Sarovar dam on the Narmada River. As it took shape in early 1989 some 9,000 people had marched to the construction town of Kevadia to protest at the dam, which will flood out 90,000 people. Others sat down in the road to block the paths of construction vehicles. 'We are arrested for being spies and saboteurs whenever we ask for information. The construction workers are not even allowed to talk to us,' said Patel.

Giselda Castro from Amigos da Terra in Brazil, wielding a shopping bag with dangerous intent, said, 'In Brazil, dams have brought nothing but social, economic and ecological disaster. We don't want them; we don't need them. We have to tell the mighty of the world that without us they are powerless . . . Viva Chico Mendes.'

'The rainforests, the river systems, the tribal peoples are all slipping away,' said Randy Hayes, the Californian film-maker turned organiser of the Rainforest Action Network. 'It's a biological meltdown; engineering gone mad.' Pat Adams, one of the chairpeople for the week's formal deliberations, climbed on to the soapbox. 'We are witnessing the birth of a worldwide movement capable of changing the face of development,' she said. Maybe, but the police wanted us moved on.

Sometimes this worldwide movement seems extraordinarily feeble – unable to organise a decent demonstration in a town with a thousand TV crews on standby. The year before, the Bank had met in West Berlin – most definitely a demonstrators' town. There, tens of thousands of people took to the streets. And they did change hearts and minds, both among World Bank officials and among the many financiers in town. As Yukio Tanaka from Friends of the Earth in Japan remembers it, 'That was the environmental turning point for the Japanese government. The big demo shocked the bureaucrats and bankers. They were surrounded. Their limousines were shaken and they were physically threatened. It made them think. They were macroeconomists; it had never occurred to them before that they did anything special to warrant such attention. After Berlin, the [Japanese] Ministry of Finance started to look at our aid policies. For the first time we got access to officials at the ministry.'

The Berlin demonstrations for the first time brought on to the world's front pages the news that the aid packages handed out by the World Bank might not be good news for the Third World. In Washington a year later, all the talk was of the 'greening of the Bank', espoused at every turn by its new president, a former New York banker, Barber Conable.

The big problem for the lobbyists was: could they believe him?

The World Bank and its sister regional development banks, such as the Asian Development Bank, are known collectively as the Multilateral Development Banks or MDBs. The genesis for organisation among their opponents, who call themselves the MDB campaign, was in Washington. It all began in 1983 with three Washington insiders who remained at the start of the 1990s at the heart of the campaign. Barbara Bramble of the National Wildlife Federation, Bruce Rich, a lawyer with the Environmental Defense Fund, and Brent Blackwelder of the Environmental Policy Institute (now merged with FoE) testified at hearings of the House Banking Committee on Capitol Hill. They told the senators about the damage being done in the Third World by big projects funded by the Bank and its smaller sister banks, and asked that the US, as the biggest source of funds for the banks, should insist on higher environmental standards. Most of their examples, then as now, were of giant dams.

Brent Blackwelder inaugurated an international session at the EPI's annual conference on rivers and dams. The first meeting was held in March 1984. Blackwelder remembers, 'It rapidly became obvious that the worst dams in the US were mild in comparison to the superfund catastrophes created in developing countries.' Many commercial banks and government aid agencies funded such projects, but the World Bank and the other multilaterals were the largest sponsors. There were also practical reasons for campaigning specifically against the MDBs. 'The clear handle for change was on those projects funded with US tax dollars,' says Blackwelder, 'and that led us to look at the role of the development banks.'

At that first meeting in 1984, Bramble, Rich and Blackwelder met Phil Williams from San Francisco and Pat Adams, the head of Probe International in Toronto. Two years into her job, Adams had already built up a fat card index of dam projects, many funded by the Canadian government's development agency, that were bringing misery to remote lands. Williams, a longtime campaigner against expensive water projects in California, was beginning to follow the gaze of

Californian water engineers seeking bigger projects abroad. He wondered what kind of havoc they were wreaking. 'We found we were soul mates,' says Adams. 'We started to share our files and realised that we were staring at a major problem.' They discovered that Teddy Goldsmith and his assistant Nick Hildyard at the *Ecologist* in Britain were already engaged in their ambitious project to document the destruction caused by large dams.

The card indexes were transferred to computer and the dams meeting became an annual event. In 1986, it was shifted to September to coincide with the Bank's own annual meeting and there was a demonstration outside the Bank. It was at this stage that the campaigners began to involve environmental groups from round the world. They were becoming sensitive to the charge that they were a bunch of eco-freaks trying to stop the rest of the world gaining American prosperity through economic development, and they found plenty of anger in Third World countries to sustain their own views.

The campaign broadened in other ways, too, extending its range from dams to rainforests. The key to this was the discovery of vastly ambitious Brazilian plans to dam tributaries of the Amazon, flooding huge tracts of the forests in the process. It became clear that other World-Bank-funded schemes in the Amazon, such as the Polonoroeste resettlement scheme in the state of Rondonia and the Carajas iron ore project, were doing equal damage.

In 1986, at Pat Adams's suggestion, another strand was added to the campaign: human rights. Early on, Adams had met Marcus Colchester from Survival International in London. He had quite separately identified dams and other World Bank projects as the cause of millions of native peoples round the world being expelled from their lands and losing their livelihoods. That same year Bruce Rich invited Colchester to testify before another senate hearing he had set up on development banks and the environment.

The fusing of a rather dry campaign against development banks with more popular issues such as the destruction of the Amazon rainforests and the rights of primitive communities turned the activities of the World Bank into a major international issue. It put the critical spotlight on an institution previously thought by most to be an agent for good. The Bank's press conferences ceased to be the preserve of the financial press. Suddenly, environment reporters and aid specialists were showing up too. At the same time there was an upwelling of isolationism in the US which made it ever more reluctant to contribute to international bodies, from the UN's Food and Agriculture Organization to UNESCO, and the Bank's top officials felt threatened.

In 1987, the lobbyists made some very public noises, handing in a 20,000-strong petition complaining about the Bank's destructive large projects – especially a 'fatal five'. And they touched raw institutional nerves, as when Rich charged that 'what the World Bank needs is a good dose of glasnost to lift the veil of secrecy on its big projects and to let the people who will be affected become part of the decision-making process.'

With their eyes on halting a big loan for new dams in Brazil known as Power Sector II, the campaigners at the 1987 World Bank meeting demanded a moratorium on the funding of new large dams and offered investment in energy efficiency as an alternative. Meanwhile, Randy Hayes and a bunch of West Coast radicals, including Mike Roselle and others from Earth First!, got themselves arrested for blocking the entrance to the Bank.

That year, the Bank began to offer concessions. It issued visitors' passes to some MDB campaigners, allowing them to attend parts of its annual meeting to lobby officials. ('We had the passes,' says Adams, 'but we didn't know what to do once we got inside: how to reach the executive directors and to get into meetings.') The Bank's president, Barber Conable, issued a declaration in a speech to his friends at the conservative World Resources Institute: 'We will strengthen the Bank's long-standing policy of scrutinising development projects for their environmental impact and withholding support for those where safeguards are inadequate,' he said.

It wasn't the first time that such promises had been made. Earlier that year the *Ecologist* had dug out a similar promise from 1970 and asked somewhat rhetorically on its front cover: 'Can We Trust the World Bank?' But this time, at any rate, the

Bank admitted a few past mistakes – over the Greater Carajas Project in Brazil, for instance – and insisted that there was new substance behind its new greenness. Moreover, it promised to back up that commitment by raising the number of staff in its environment department from five to more than 100. Teddy Goldsmith at the *Ecologist* was not easily impressed. He sent an 'Open Letter to Mr Conable: You Can Only Be Judged on Your Record'.

The issue was whether the Bank was serious about reforming itself and genuinely recognised past mistakes, or was merely responding cynically to pressure from passing world headlines and the politicking on Capitol Hill. Was it, as they chanted on the Washington demo, 'greenwash'? Conable began staffing up his environment department, but his critics complained that most of the appointments were retreads of middle-ranking executives with no past enthusiasm for things green. In September 1989, at a big environment conference in Tokyo (another sign of changing times), Conable spoke of the 'finite' environment and how 'today's needs have to be weighed against tomorrow's obligations.' What did he mean by such phrases? He talked also about 'the pollution of poverty' and the bank's 'mission' to reduce poverty and protect the environment. He was, he said, proud of progress so far in 'harmonising the imperatives of development and environmental care'.

But what did that amount to? Earlier that year, the critics had highlighted two planned World Bank projects whose fate they regarded as a litmus test of the Bank's green credentials. The first was a large rag-bag of energy projects that Brazil's government wanted money for. Known as the Power Sector II loan, it was worth $500 million if approved. It included money for several large dams, a small amount for energy conservation and may have been intended by the Brazilians to help pay for nuclear power plants. The second critical project was the Narmada Valley dams scheme in India, probably the largest river-taming scheme in the world. One loan of $450 million for the Sardar Sarovar dam, granted in principle in 1985, was up for reassessment because of growing fears within the Bank itself that resettlement of the 90,000 people to be made homeless by the reservoir was degenerating into farce. The second loan, of $350 million for the equally disruptive Narmada Sagar dam further upstream, was due for approval. While the Bank appeared determined to press ahead at Narmada, public concern about dams in the Amazon rainforests was sufficient to encourage Washington environment groups that they had a real hope of halting Power Sector II.

Lobbying by the EPI, which other Washington groups had agreed should be the lead agency on the Power Sector loan, reached a peak in February 1989. As senators and journalists headed south for the Altamira media circus, Barnes and Blackwelder sent a final plea to the Treasury Secretary, Nicholas Brady, claiming that the loan 'would support an investment plan that includes as many as 79 environmentally-questionable dams' and threatened tribes that 'have had little if any contact with the outside world'. It quoted a study by the top Brazilian physicist, Jose Goldemberg, who was also president of the University of Sao Paulo. He had analysed the Brazilian government's energy plans, which involved spending $38 billion in the coming decade on new electricity-generating capacity, much of it from dams. Goldemberg's conclusion was that two-thirds of the extra energy capacity would be made unnecessary if just $8 billion were spent on energy conservation.

While such sums are much greater than the value of the loan itself, Barnes and Blackwelder knew that Japan intended to match the World Bank loan and that several large loans from commercial banks for energy projects hung on the Bank's decision on Power Sector II. 'The US', the EPI told Brady, 'can play a creative leadership role by putting forward a positive alternative for Brazil.'

The US government, under pressure from the rainforests lobby as well as a right wing that opposed large aid programmes, appears to have responded. At any rate, a month later in March 1989, the Bank called off the Power Sector II loan, demanding more research into Brazil's energy needs.

The Washington lobby proclaimed the decision on the Power Sector II loan as a major victory. Jim Barnes and Brent Blackwelder at the Environmental Policy Institute saw it as a

vindication of their insider approach to campaigning, though
the public relations fireworks of Altamira probably had an
important bearing. The EPI strategy had been to arm-twist the
US delegation to the World Bank, as the largest donor to the
Bank, to stick up for the environment and insist that 'our tax
dollars' are not used to finance damaging projects. This is a
potentially divisive strategy among environmentalists. It is
based on the US delegates using their financial muscle to get
their way in an international agency (the World Bank), an
approach roundly condemned on other occasions. It also
inevitably involves horse-trading behind closed doors and
confirms the sometimes resented power of the Washington-
based groups within the environment movement.

Yet few complained at the manner of the success. The stakes
were too high. The Power Sector I loan, made a few years
before, had helped completion of two notorious dams. One
was the Tucurui, which flooded nearly 2,500 square
kilometres of virgin forest along the Tomatins River in the east
of the Amazon region. It was helping to power the new
industries being built in the forests as part of the Greater
Carajas Project. The second was the Balbina dam, which
flooded some 1,900 square kilometres of rainforest in return
for a modest electrical capacity of 250 megawatts, or a quarter
of a typical large conventional power station. Even the director
of Brazil's special secretariat for the environment had called
the Balbina dam 'a disaster . . . one of the greatest errors
committed in the Amazon'.

A decade's investment of around $2 billion in Brazil by the
World Bank and its sister agency the Inter-American Development Bank had mostly been spent on dams. The programme
had, in the words of one review of the Bank's work, 'become a
byword for inefficiency, staggering environmental destruction
and systematic failure to address the interests of indigenous
peoples'. Just one of the dams likely to have been paid for by
the Power Sector II loan, at Machadinho on the River Uruguai,
threatened to flood out 18,000 people, who after a decade of
negotiation had failed to win compensation or new land.
Money from Power Sector II would also probably have helped
to pay for the dams on the Xingu River near Altamira.

In the week before the 1989 annual meeting of the Bank, Conable announced new long-awaited guidelines on environmental impact assessments. In future, governments wanting World Bank money for large projects would have to provide a detailed study of the likely impacts of the scheme. It sounded good news. However, it appeared that general loans to particular sectors of national economies, such as the ill-fated Power Sector II loan, might not require impact assessments for smaller individual projects financed under the loans. This looked like a loophole big enough to push several large dams through. Also, it turned out that both the assessments and any reviews of them by World Bank staff would be kept secret. The Bank's critics and the people whose lives were to be transformed by such schemes were to be left out once again.

The Bank said that it would be a breach of confidence to publish such reports without the approval of the governments concerned. But the reality of the Bank's environmental commitment was again on the line. Some remained hopeful. There were certainly very many good, intelligent and sympathetic people working there. One stern critic told me, 'If you want to know what these projects mean for the Indian communities in the Amazon, the best people to talk to are the anthropologists employed by the Bank.' Even Teddy Goldsmith, one of its most implacable foes, told me that Robert Goodland, the Bank's top environmental scientist, is 'on our side'. The trouble was that the views of such people never penetrated the rooms where the big decisions were taken.

The greening of the Bank won Conable a good press, and brought leading articles from the American newspapers warning the government against withholding funds from the Bank. But the suspicion was growing among Washington greens that they had for once been outmanoeuvred. Where one might have expected euphoria, there was anticlimax.

The lobbyists remained committed to attempting to reform the Bank. But many were exhausted. 'It's very hard to make real progress with Bush, Thatcher and Kohl around,' said Bruce Rich, one of the MDB campaign's founders and now the international director of the Environmental Defense Fund. 'The campaign began six years ago. It's lasted longer than

World War Two. So far we've had to be content with small gains.'

If the Bank's aim with its green initiative had been to divide its opponents, then there were clear signs of success. Barbara Bramble of the National Wildlife Federation told the World Rivers Review, 'The campaign has come a lot further by now than I expected. The NWF intends to push MDB reforms as far as they can go.' While Randy Hayes said, 'The MDB campaign isn't working. Efforts to reform the World Bank should be abandoned. We should design new institutions to help provide for the needs of people in developing countries.' Pat Adams later told me, 'I don't think there is much hope for a change in the direction of World Bank energy policy – not by their own volition.' Despite the avalanche of information about the economic and environmental advisability of investing in energy efficiency, the Bank continues to lend almost exclusively for energy supply projects.

Two closely connected conflicts among the environmentalists have been opened up by the Bank. The first is between the Washington insiders, who have made careers out of lobbying with the Bank and its staff, and the outsiders who feel excluded from the process. The second is between those who believe the Bank can be reformed and those who do not. Can environmental issues be addressed by technical adjustments to projects and an occasional 'No' to the worst? Is the Bank capable of more fundamental reform? Or is the very existence of an organisation such as the World Bank part of the problem?

Some felt that the Washington environment establishment had gone over to the other side. David Reed, MDB policy co-ordinator at the World Wildlife Fund in Washington, called on environmentalists to become 'partners' with the Bank, 'making resources, opinions and policies available'. The WWF was at work on contracts for the World Bank around the world. When the head of the Bank's environment department, Ken Piddington – a former director-general of conservation in New Zealand – addressed the campaigners, he held out the prospect of environment groups helping dole out the money for a proposed new Bank Environment Fund.

Chee Yoke Ling, from SAM in Malaysia, wanted none of it.

'The danger of lobbying the World Bank', she told her Washington hosts, 'is that it is so comfortable that you lose sight of the basics ... until the bulldozers come.' She, of course, works a great deal closer to the bulldozers than most. Chad Dobson at the Bank Information Center got back to basics. The Bank had spent years presenting itself as an aid agency with a mission to banish the pollution of poverty. Now it had decided that it wanted to play at environmentalism as well. But this was window-dressing. Dobson, who must have seen more internal documents from the Bank than most, concluded, 'Substantial reform ... may be impossible. The Bank does very well what it was set up to do – lend money. Since it is always paid back, its lending practices are reinforced. Last year, the Bank made a billion dollars' profit. With a record like that, why should it change?'

Those lobbyists who felt that the US could lever change were probably mistaken, too, he said. 'It is not in the US government's interest to have the Bank basically modified. The Bank has helped to create an international financial structure that allows the US to continue to consume the resources of the world in a way that is most advantageous to the North.'

That's the kind of talk that makes Dobson friends with Teddy Goldsmith, who has never wavered from his view expressed in his open letter to Conable in 1987. As Conable made his green overtures, Goldsmith said:

> More than half of the inhabitants of the Third World live outside the market system. There is no way in which their lot can be improved by Bank loans ... Such people you cannot and never will be able to help. All you can do is further impoverish them by financing projects that must deprive them of their basic resources such as the natural forests, the fertile land and the uncontaminated water on which their welfare, indeed their survival, depends ...
>
> [From the fertile valleys of India to the Amazon rainforest] the Bank continues to regard tribal people, indeed all people who live outside the orbit of the formal economy, as totally expendable.

Some campaigners see the Bank more as a symbol to be assailed than as an institution to be reformed. Phil Williams at the International Rivers Network told the Washington meeting in 1989, 'We target the Bank because it has an ideology of development that we are challenging. They provide a leadership for ideas worldwide about what development is needed. Sure, some people will benefit from their projects. But it is our experience that you don't have to go much beyond economic grounds to show that big dams are not good. India, for example, is already sliding into a balance of payments problem because of past large dam and other projects which have distorted its economy.'

As he spoke, on the other side of the world, 25,000 people had linked hands and formed a human chain around the town of Harsud in the Narmada Valley in India. The town of 18,000 people, along with the populations of 250 surrounding villages, will be submerged in 1993 as a reservoir fills behind the World-Bank-funded Narmada Sagar dam, the second of the large Narmada dams. It will become the largest reservoir in India. The government intends to build a new Harsud about 20 kilometres away, with an oil refinery to provide work. Despite the fracas over its handling of the refugees from the Sardar Sarovar reservoir downstream on the Narmada, the government is even less precise about what will happen to the tens of thousands of villagers who will lose their land and homes as a result of the Narmada Sagar dam.

Activists such as Baba Amte, a renowned Gandhian social worker, and Sunderlal Bahuguna, father of the Chipko movement of tree-huggers in the Himalayas, addressed the meeting. Smitu Kothari from Delhi, one of the nationwide network of organisers for the demonstration, had spent the beginning of the week in Washington. He had said there that 'the experience of forty years since independence in India is that every big project supported by the World Bank has created similar gross human rights violations and degradation of life-support systems. Twenty million people have been displaced by dams, mines, missile bases and deforestation. We are creating a vast army of internal refugees.' Now he brought messages of support from the Washington meeting, and he read the rally's pledge 'to join hands with all others who think and act as we do'. They wanted an end to the paramilitary dam projects, under which the conditions of a police state had been imposed at Kevadia. There, a 'prohibited area' had been declared within which anybody entering the area 'for a purpose prejudicial to the safety or interests of the State' faced up to 14 years in prison. They pointed to the thousands of small village water schemes – enlarging wells, protecting soils and installing small pumps – that were being starved of funds as a result of the Narmada scheme. None of these schemes evicted people or required the police and army to protect them.

In Harsud, tribal leaders from all over India related their own stories of struggles against eviction. They lit torches and brought with them packets of mud from their land, with which they erected a mud tower, a symbol of their efforts to unite against a common foe: the World Bank's vision of development. Here perhaps, on the plains of India rather than in the corridors of Washington, was the spirit of environmentalism at work. We want development, they said, but our sort, according to our needs.

Mr Kubota's legacy

Behind closed doors at the World Bank, they have a new threat to wave at angry environmentalists: 'If we don't fund the dam/power station/plantation/mine, the Japanese will. And if you think we don't care about the environment, try them.' In 1989, Japan became the world's largest donor of aid, spending a cool $11 billion. The Japanese overall investment in foreign development projects was $23 billion – about the same as the annual spending of the World Bank. That year, Japan was the biggest source of aid in 25 countries, mostly in the Far East, but now it was taking to the world stage.

At a summit meeting in 1988, Japan made commitments to other industrialised nations to recycle some of its huge trade surpluses into aid projects in the Third World. As it tries to offload a lot of money quickly, that could spell a new era of 'megaprojects'. When the MDB campaigners met in Washington in late 1989, Richard Forrest, a young researcher from the US's National Wildlife Federation, reported on an 18-month visit to Japan, looking at the operation of its aid agencies. The quiet American displayed the arrogance of the Washington lobbyists. His conclusion was that 'the Japanese haven't caught up with green concerns. They are five to ten years behind the intellectual trend in the world.' But his case was strong enough.

Japanese aid agencies are understaffed. In 1989 they had 6,000 staff to plan and supervise investment projects, compared to the 13,000 at the World Bank. They tend to take on trust the word of corporations that want their assistance in funding projects abroad. After a row over Japanese aid money being spent on a road into James Wong's logging concession in Sarawak, said Forrest, it transpired that the Japanese aid agency involved, JICA, had taken the word of Wong's Japanese industrial partner that the road would help the local people. 'It didn't occur to them that the road was destroying people's lives. The staff have little understanding of the effects of their aid and less than five per cent of them are based overseas. Also they provide very little information about their activities, so it is hard to influence their decisions.'

One of the few people to investigate the history of Japanese post-war aid, which began as war reparations, is an academic, Professor Kazo Sumi. During the 1980s, Japan's aid budget increased fivefold, and in the late 1980s, Japanese money went into projects such as dams in the Amazon rainforest and the Greater Carajas mining development, which the Japanese International Co-operation Agency had been involved in since the earliest development work. In particular, says Sumi, JICA was behind the disastrous idea that charcoal from trees in the rainforest should be the fuel for iron ore smelters. Japanese banks then funded much of the work; and much of the iron, steel and aluminium from the region will supply Japanese manufacturers. JICA's reports on the scheme 'made no reference to the problems that would be caused to the indigenous Indian groups'. Nor, he says, did they make any provision for the landless farmers who moved into the area. 'As far as the

Japanese aid agencies are concerned, these people do not exist.'

The Japanese government has traditionally had close links with the country's banks, which include the world's ten largest commercial finance houses, and with its giant trading companies, known as *sogo shosha*. So aid is handed out largely in support of Japanese industrial interests. Says Forrest:

Funding has been tied to the purchase of Japanese goods and services, used for large-scale facilities that exploit and process raw materials for export to Japan, and for relocating hazardous and energy-intensive processing facilities from Japan to developing countries. Japanese companies and consultants, rather than law-makers or development professionals, have played the strongest guiding role, and continue to push for large-scale high-technology projects.

A typical example is the Kedung Ombo dam on the Surang River in central Java, Indonesia, which the Japanese Ex-Im Bank funded jointly with the World Bank. Nichimen, one of Japan's largest *sogo shosha*, was contracted to build the dam, and the Ex-Im Bank and another big *sogo shosha*, Hazama-gumi, helped pay Indonesia's bill for the resettlement of more than 20,000 peasant farmers. When the dam gates were shut in January 1989, around 7,000 people remained, living on rafts and moving their belongings to higher ground. They were protesting that the new land that they were being offered was on a waterless plain 5 kilometres from the nearest road.

In India, a $20 million loan from the Overseas Economic Cooperation Fund of Japan, plus roughly ten times that amount put up by Japanese commercial banks, was intended to help pay for the Sardar Sarovar dam on the Narmada River until funding was abruptly withdrawn in June 1990 following a campaign by Japanese environmentalists. Next on Japan's big dams shopping list is the Three Gorges project in China – potentially the world's largest dams project with a price-tag of $20 billion. The Japanese Ministry of Construction spent 1990 considering ideas for 'global superprojects' such as Three Gorges, to be funded by Japanese banks. Other ideas included a second Panama Canal, and a vast scheme to divert water from the River Zaire to the parched lands on the edge of Sahara.

Japan has promised that some of its new loans will be channelled into environmental projects, but Forrest warns that these green schemes are likely to include large forestry plantations. They will be established in parts of south-east Asia denuded by Japan's timber companies and will be designed to maintain the supply of tropical wood to meet the needs of Japanese industry. There will be little monitoring of the impact of the schemes on the environment or people, he said.

A philanthropic gloss is nothing new to the modern Japanese aid business. It began as reparations for the damage inflicted on the nations of south-east Asia during the Second World War. From the first, there was a particular interest in dams, fostered by an engineer called Mr Kubota – the 'father of large dams', according to Sumi – who began with a dam between Korea and Manchuria.

Japanese irrigation schemes have been causing environmental havoc throughout south-east Asia. They include a joint scheme with the World Bank in Laos to generate hydroelectric power on the Mekong River. A major contract for design and supervision of the scheme went to Nippon Koei. Within a decade, Japanese companies were back for a major repair of the dam – funded by Japanese aid moneys.

In Indonesia, Nippon Koei was brought in to carry out surveys for a hydroelectric and flood-control dam on the Brantas River in Java. Again, it was paid for with Japanese reparations money. 'Floods occurred frequently even after the construction,' claims Sumi. 'The Indonesian government complained many times. As a result the Japanese government provided yen loans for engineering services for methods of flood control.' Reparations dams, say critics, have been turned into an agent of Japan's economic invasion of post-war south-east Asia.

Now the stakes are even higher. Japan's efforts to remedy the imbalances in worldwide trading systems by recycling some of its wealth into development projects threaten a new round of environmental destruction.

10

IN THE FAR EAST

Minamata to Mindanao

When it comes to easily identifiable enemies, the Japanese have served the environment movement well, beginning with the scandal at Minamata in the 1960s. Children in the small fishing village began to be born with appalling malformations of the body. It took years of anguished demonstrations and legal actions before the townspeople could wring a confession from the managers of the town's chemical works of what everybody knew. Mercury in factory waste gushing into Minamata Bay had contaminated fish and poisoned the unborn children. Since then, investigative environmentalists have left few stones unturned as they pursue their Japanese quarry.

In the 1970s, Greenpeace and its friends discovered that the Japanese had helped keep afloat a clutch of pirate whaling ships that defied international rules intended to preserve whale stocks. Japan then fought longest and loudest to oppose the moratorium on whaling begun in 1985. Afterwards, it was the only industrial nation to carry on whaling, taking around 300 sperm whales each year from the South Pacific under the guise of research into the population biology of whales. And it bought the whale meat of Iceland which also kept its small fleet afloat under the flag of science.

When Alan Thornton launched a probe into the covert international ivory trade, he had little difficulty in naming Japan as 'the world's largest ivory customer'. Its traders' fingerprints were all over most of the poached ivory shuttling between African truck, Arab dhow and diplomatic bag on its way across the world. Japan had bankrolled the slaughter because around two-thirds of the ivory is turned into Japanese legal seals. Thornton documented how Japanese firms put down a 20 per cent deposit, to allow their agents to go shopping in Zaire and Tanzania. He quoted one legitimate Hong Kong trader, Dominic Ng, as saying that the Japanese 'used Hong Kong traders as frontmen who get the blame when things go wrong. They did not want to know how the ivory got into Japan.'

Japan's taste for the exotic in wildlife is notorious. One speciality is the gall-bladders of North American and Asian black bears, which are ground up in pharmacies to make traditional Japanese medicines. The powder from bears' dried gall-bladders can fetch $10,000 a kilo. Its ingredients include cholesterol and various bile acids which are administered for ailments of the stomach, intestines and kidneys. American game wardens have been conducting an undercover war against networks of hunters and traders in the organs of the North American black bear throughout the 1980s, but without seriously denting the illicit trade.

Greenpeace campaigners identify the Japanese as leading importers of everything from kangaroo skins to turtles. Since 1970, Japan has imported the shells, meat and skins of at least two million sea turtles. It is a prime market for trade in the endangered hawksbill turtle from a British dependency, the Cayman Islands, and the trade has continued in spite of an international ban in force since 1979.

Putting all these into the shade is Japan's insatiable demand for tropical timber from the rainforests. The contrast between Japan's treatment of its own forests and those of other nations is remarkable. Emperor Hirohito, who was buried in 1989 in a box made of Japanese wood, had for the previous 38 years unfailingly led celebrations in an annual national arbour festival, during which he and his people ceremonially planted trees. Japanese forests are revered, especially those planted around village shrines, known as *chinju-no-mori*, where people go to meditate and to hold traditional ceremonies to mark various stages of childhood. Many shrines are built in the hills above rice paddies, and the forests are respected because they help to conserve water resources for the irrigation of those fields. Such good ecological practice is usually forgotten when the Japanese step on to foreign soil.

Across south-east Asia, Japanese bulldozers, paid for with Japanese loans, plough through the ancient burial grounds of Borneo and destroy the hillsides of the Philippines in order to fill Japanese ships, loading at Japanese-financed harbours, to meet the seemingly bottomless Japanese demand for timber.

In 1989, Japan began to feel nervous about its environmental reputation. The government agreed to support a ban on the international ivory trade and called for steps to squeeze the trade in bears' gall-bladders. But on tropical timber there was silence. That may not last. If the government does take steps to curb the trade, it will be due in large part to the efforts of Joichi Kuroda. Kuroda is a graduate in rural sociology and the fiery young co-ordinator of JATAN, the Japan Tropical Forest Action Network, a group set up in 1987 by FoE Japan with financial help from WWF International.

There is only a handful of environmental campaigners in Japan, where social conformity makes life hard for rebels of all sorts. Even the ubiquitous Greenpeace failed to set up shop there, foiled by a chauvinistic hatred of Greenpeace anti-whaling activities which extended even to Japanese environmentalists. Of the small group of Japanese greens, Kuroda, whose dart-shaped beard gives him the look of a Japanese warrior, is the most feared. He won his spurs with a detailed investigation of Japan's position as the biggest importer of tropical timber for the past two decades. But he also staged street stunts and held learned international conferences to bring his findings to the world's attention.

Japan imports around 20 million cubic metres of tropical timber each year – more than a third of the total world trade in raw timber. Around 16 million cubic metres is converted into plywood. Much of this becomes cheap furniture and panelling. 'The life cycle of most goods is designed to be very short,' says Kuroda. 'We move house very often, and when we move we just leave the old furniture on the street.' He calls Japan a 'scrap and build' society. But the largest proportion of Japan's tropical timber ends up as plywood frames into which building contractors pour concrete. After one use, it is thrown away.

Tropical timber is used, says Kuroda, because 'a jungle tree which took hundreds of years to grow is cheaper in Japan than a softwood pine that took only 20 years to grow. A priceless, irreplaceable resource is being rubbished.'

A pervasive myth is that the Japanese turn most of their imported tropical timber into the 20 billion throwaway chopsticks that they discard each year. The idea probably gained currency when, 20 years ago, a group of housewives from the northern island of Hokkaido began refusing to use disposable chopsticks, known as *warabashi*, because they were wasteful. The anti-*warabashi* campaign continues, allowing greens a chance to raise the subject of the rainforests at every meal, but even this example of conspicuous waste is responsible for only about 0.2 per cent of the nation's consumption of wood.

The anti-*warabashi* campaign was worthy, but about as effective as handing piles of old newspapers to Boy Scouts. It was Kuroda who promoted the issue of tropical rainforest destruction from sushi small-talk to the Japanese political agenda. He had begun to crack one of the world's toughest markets for the green message. In 1987, only weeks after the launch of JATAN, he helped to fan the flames of scandal over the discovery that 200 million yen in Japanese aid was being channelled through the Japan International Cooperation Agency to build a logging road in Sarawak. The road was built into the heart of a timber concession owned by Sarawak's environment minister, James Wong. Wong's company, Limbang Trading, was at the time part-owned by C. Itoh, one of Japan's nine largest trading corporations and the biggest importer of south-east Asian timber.

When the scandal broke, the Japanese government told parliament that the road was welcomed by local people, who needed it to develop their land and to provide access for a new school. But Kuroda was swiftly on a plane to Sarawak, where he met Harrison Ngau at SAM's office in Marudi. He returned to tell the real story. Far from wanting the road, the Penan people were in uproar, blocking Wong's road in an effort to halt the destruction of their forest. The road was cut for the convenience of the loggers, not the people, and the 'new school' was, claimed Kuroda, 20 years old. Shortly afterwards,

C. Itoh sold its stake in Limbang Trading. It was an important victory.

Kuroda, like Greenpeace in the Soviet Union, uses the Japanese passion for Western rock music to bring a Western environmental message to the people. He raises funds by organising Rock for the Rainforest concerts, and uses the cash to put on street stunts. In May 1989, the British rock star Sting, with an Amazon Indian leader called Raoni in tow, came to Tokyo at Kuroda's invitation. Earlier in 1989, with a galaxy of foreign rainforest campaigners in town, Kuroda organised a demonstration in the heart of Tokyo's business quarter, Chiyoda-ku, the most expensive stretch of real estate in the world. His demonstrators assembled outside the headquarters of the Marubeni Corporation, one of the 'big nine' *sogo shosha* Japanese trading corporations. They dressed as forest animals and trees, and one wore a three-metre plywood chainsaw with which he ceremonially cut down the trees. Marubeni is a leading importer of tropical timber and Kuroda won headlines for his presentation to the company of JATAN's Rainforest Destruction Award. Marubeni, it seemed, had earned the honour by overtaking C. Itoh through its huge involvement in both Indonesia and Sarawak.

Behind Kuroda the showman is Kuroda the researcher. Earlier in the year, he had broken the story that Marubeni was helping to fund a woodchipping factory that would consume a priceless mangrove forest at Bintuni Bay in Irian Jaya, Indonesia. His talents had attracted campaigners at WWF International who were eager to find Japanese activists. The WWF paid for and published both Japanese and English editions of a book, *Timber from the South Seas*, written by Kuroda and François Nectoux, a French researcher based in London, on the workings of Japan's timber trade and its environmental impact. Nectoux is a veteran of previous studies into the British and then European tentacles in tropical rainforests. The new report was the largest and much the most important, however, involving other top environmentalists in Japan, such as Jonathan Holliman, the British expat, and his colleague at Friends of the Earth Japan, Yukio Tanaka. It pieced together the business interests of vast secretive trading institutions in half a dozen foreign countries. 'Japan is the real enemy,' said Chris Rose, a former rainforest campaigner at the WWF. 'All our work in Europe and the US to clean up their forestry act must, if it is to succeed, lead to us getting action from the Japanese.'

In the 1960s, the Philippines was Japan's largest source of cheap timber. First Mindanao, the country's largest southern island, was denuded, then the Japanese timber firms moved on to Luzon in the north. Logging on these islands was eventually halted as much by the disappearance of the trees as by the accession of Corrie Aquino.

Environmental researchers have tracked the role of Japanese firms in patently corrupt business practices in the Philippines under Marcos's 'crony capitalism'. The files of Japanese environmentalists reveal how Mitsubishi and other Japanese firms became involved with Herminio Disini, a relative of Imelda Marcos, the President's wife, in the operation of Cellophil. The company had secured logging rights to 2,000 square kilometres of Luzon for making paper, cellophane and rayon. Employing a private militia to keep out local hill tribes, the company had operated for more than a decade, clear-felling 450,000 cubic metres of logs a year from the forest until the fall of Marcos in 1986. This, say local environmentalists, has caused landslides, floods, and pollution that killed fish. Disini has since gained new notoriety as the man who, according to *Time* magazine, collected $35 million in 'commissions' from Westinghouse, the American engineering firm, for helping to win the company an overpriced contract to build the Bataan nuclear plant for Marcos.

Perhaps the Luzon tribal people had the last laugh, however. Many of them joined the guerrilla forces of the New People's Army, fighting the Marcos regime in Luzon and elsewhere, hastening his downfall and the expulsion of Disini's men. The new government of Corrie Aquino cancelled Cellophil's concession, which had more than a decade left to run. However, where forests survived, in the large western island of Palawan, logging continued. In 1989, environmentalists headed by the Haribon Foundation were leading a major campaign to halt the chainsaws.

With the Philippines largely logged out, the Japanese companies moved on to Sabah, the small Malaysian state north of Sarawak on the island of Borneo, and to Indonesia. When, in 1985, Indonesia decided that it no longer wanted to export raw logs and preferred to turn them into plywood or pulp first, the Japanese moved on again to Sarawak and Papua New Guinea. At the end of the 1980s, Sabah and Sarawak between them provided 70 per cent of Japan's raw tropical timber. Sometimes, as in Indonesia in the 1970s and Papua New Guinea in the late 1980s, Japanese firms take controlling stakes or part-shares in logging companies; sometimes they merely provide funds; increasingly they invest in processing companies, such as Indonesia's plywood and woodchip factories. Almost always, however, they are the leading customers.

The report by Kuroda and Nectoux remains, in its own right, one of the most impressive pieces of investigation by environmentalists anywhere in the world during the 1980s. It allowed environmental groups in Europe to launch campaigns to boycott the products of Mitsubishi, the best known name among the *sogo shosha* in the Japanese timber business. In the Netherlands in 1989, the local members of the WWF (which is more radical than most national WWF organisations) helped to organise the distribution of anti-logging stickers to be put by campaigners on cars made by Mitsubishi. They organised a mass fax-in to the firm's local office, bombarding it with documents about the destruction of rainforests and calls to 'Ban Japan from the Rainforest'.

The danger, however, is that Japan will eventually be prevented from taking timber from the rainforests not by the endeavours of men such as Kuroda, but by the exhaustion of the remaining forests themselves. The scene seems set in the 1990s for Japan to complete the ransacking of Borneo's forests and to move on to Burma, Laos and perhaps finally Vietnam – all countries with such a yearning for foreign exchange that they will sell timber for whatever price they can get. As we have seen, the Japanese may face increased competition from other internationally minded timber operators, notably the Thais.

The Amazon of the East

The rate of destruction of Indonesia's rainforests is second only to that of Brazil. The World Bank estimates the loss at around 10,000 square kilometres a year. Through the first half of the 1980s, Indonesia was the world's largest source of logs. When the government in 1985 banned the export of raw logs, the purpose was not to save forests but to encourage the local timber processing industry, and especially plywood manufacture. By 1990, the country was the largest exporter of plywood in the world. The Jakarta government had also revealed plans to expand into the pulp and paper market, to challenge the major paper producers of the Far East: Japan, China, South Korea and Taiwan. It planned to build 57 pulp mills before 1995. Leading the field was the most powerful man in Indonesian forestry, the plywood king and head of the Jayanti Group, Bob Hasan.

The focus for this new expansion was to be Irian Jaya, by far the largest surviving source of timber in a country that had chopped down 540,000 square kilometres in the 1970s and 1980s. That is more than a quarter of the country's entire land surface and twice that of the United Kingdom.

Irian Jaya is the western half of New Guinea, the world's second largest island. It was annexed in the 1960s by Indonesia, which then fought a long guerrilla war with the many native peoples living in its remote forested highland regions. Even today, most of the province can be reached only by air, typically aboard the planes of missionaries who, apart from soldiers, are the only people to have penetrated the more remote areas. Taken with neighbouring Papua New Guinea, it is the largest remaining tropical forested area on the planet after the Amazon rainforest and the largely undisturbed Zaire basin.

In the 1990s, the Indonesian government in Jakarta, 2,000 kilometres away, intends to settle some one million poor farmers from its other islands on Irian Jaya. By the middle of the decade, there will be more newcomers than indigenous people there. The government intends to extend mining in the province and take over native forests for plantations to feed the large national plywood and pulp industries. Just as the Amazon basin has been opened up by Brazil in the 1980s, so Indonesia plans to develop Irian Jaya.

The invasion is being masterminded with something like military precision. One of its principal architects will be the Jakarta government's new Minister for Transmigration – the national programme to colonise its outlying islands. He is General Sugiarto, a para commando who specialises in fighting guerrilla wars and saw active service in the bloody destruction of opposition in the small island of East Timor after it was annexed in the 1970s. After his appointment in 1988, Sugiarto announced that 'by promoting economic development in the sparsely populated border regions through the resettlement of transmigrants from Java, Indonesia's territorial defence will be reinforced.' Within months he had announced that migrants would be moved into the Jayawijaya district, the remote highland interior of Irian Jaya. And in 1989, Sugiarto took advantage of an earthquake in the highlands to tell the 40,000 native Dani people – who have lived for many centuries in the wide, fertile Balim valley high up in the mountains – that they must move out of the hills for their own safety.

It was not the first time that the government had attempted to move the Dani, who live a genuinely primitive life and whose menfolk still wear nothing but penis-gourds. The first occasion was in the mid-1970s, when the Dani's part in the tribal rebellion led to them being bombed into submission. Now in 1989, it appeared that the final pacification of both the Dani and of Irian Jaya had begun. But, as in the Amazon, an alliance of environmentalists and defenders of indigenous peoples' rights was determined to call a halt.

Before 1989 was out, the opponents of Indonesia's strategy for Irian Jaya had claimed their first victory. In October 1988, the American multinational Scott Paper Company had won permission from the Indonesian government for a $700-million project to clear rainforest from a concession in the Digul Valley near Merauke in the south of Irian Jaya. The concession covered 9,000 square kilometres, about the size of Cyprus. It was owned by Scott-Astra, a partnership between Scott Paper and a local firm, PT Astra. Scott-Astra intended to plant the cleared forest with eucalyptus trees to turn into tissue paper.

Scott is the largest manufacturer of tissues in the world. Its brand names include Scotties, Handy Andies and Andrex. The company produces 1.5 million rolls of Andrex a day; enough, it says, 'to go one and a half times round the world'. In order to wipe more bottoms with Andrex, the company proposed, in the words of an angry newsletter from Survival International, 'to wreck the lives of 15,000 tribal people living in the concession . . . A complex tropical forest ecosystem, which provides all their needs, will be replaced with a vast mono-culture of eucalyptus trees, from which they will get nothing.' It was to be the single largest foreign investment in Indonesia outside the oil and gas industries – 'man-size destruction', said Friends of the Earth.

The world had been alerted to the plan by a dynamic environment network established in Indonesia during the 1980s. It is headed by WALHI, a coalition of local environment groups that produces a high-quality newsletter called *Environesia*, and SKEPHI, a network established specifically to fight forestry schemes. The two organisations unsuccessfully demanded that the government refuse Scott Paper a licence to operate on its giant concession. Then they appealed to their network of contacts round the world to take up the struggle. By the middle of 1989, a vociferous campaign was under way. Green organisations in dozens of countries were asking their supporters to write angry letters to Scott Paper's head office in Philadelphia. Scott sent all the letters on to the head of Scott-Astra in Jakarta, Barry Kotek. He replied defensively that the company intended to 'leave most of the land in its natural state, to provide for protection of the wetlands, buffers around villages, consideration of sacred grounds of the local people, and other environmental and sociological needs'.

Company plans revealed that planting would cover only a third of the concession area and Kotek promised that some 6,000 jobs would be on offer to local people, both in forestry and at the pulp mill, which would produce 1,000 tonnes of pulp a day. The Indonesian government contradicted this by saying that most jobs would go to migrants from outside the province. But in any case, campaigners for tribes in southern Irian Jaya replied that the local people were hunters and gatherers. 'They do not use money. They live in groups with their own tribes. For those local people, the appearance of this factory will be a phenomenon which they have never experienced before. They will be faced with thousands of newcomers, with new development and a new kind of society and relationships.'

The company responded by agreeing to meet local groups, and by sending a sociologist into the concession area to talk to tribespeople. But the real headway was being made in the US. The screws were being put on Scott Paper. In a series of large newspaper advertisements in the *New York Times* and elsewhere, the Rainforest Action Network, the most radical of the US rainforest campaigns, listed Scott's president as one of the eight men (five of them Americans) who 'share the awesome responsibility of determining the future of much of the remaining rainforest on Earth'. (This piece of hyperbole also added 10,000 to everybody else's estimate of the number of tribespeople in Scott's concession.)

Kotek agreed to meet a delegation of Washington groups headed by Bruce Rich of the Environmental Defense Fund. The delegation did not demand that the project be withdrawn, but instead called for local involvement in every stage of planning, full respect for tribal land law and no go-ahead unless and until impact assessments had shown that the land was suitable for eucalyptus plantations. The campaign also switched to Japan, after the discovery that the Japanese are Scott's largest customers, through a subsidiary called Sanyoko Kosaku. Japanese consumers were invited to boycott its products.

Scott's fightback also hit trouble. The company claimed to have discussed everything with everybody, and to have 'involved Rainforest Action Network and the Environmental Defense Fund in the [impact assessment] process'. Hayes at RAN angrily denied any such discussions and took the opportunity to describe the project as 'a cornerstone in the Indonesian government's campaign to colonise sparsely inhabited Irian Jaya'. Kotek next visited London to talk to Friends of the Earth and Survival International, both of which loudly opposed the scheme.

Meanwhile, the Indonesian forestry industry itself felt under threat of a Western boycott. In the summer of 1989 it declared war on the conservation lobby. Bob Hasan provided $2 million for advertising in the Western press and for lobbying in Brussels and Washington. After RAN's advertisement in the *New York Times*, Hasan retaliated with his own effort, 'Tropical Forests Forever', in which he explained that the forests of Indonesia were safe. 'Indonesia is concerned about the needs of its citizens . . . unlike environmental groups who want Indonesia managed as one big protected park.' At the same time, the Indonesian government had joined forces with Malaysia to lobby in Brussels against environmentalists who had persuaded the European parliament in May 1989 to back an eventual ban on tropical timber imports.

In November, just a year after announcing the project, Scott pulled out. 'The company can meet its needs for pulp from other sources,' said a company press release. 'Pressure [from environmentalists] was the only reason we withdrew,' said Kotek. A government spokesman in Jakarta said that Scott had feared a consumer boycott of its top brand names. PT Astra meanwhile hinted that it had already found a replacement partner – leaving environmentalists to worry whether the new company, probably from South Korea or Taiwan, would prove a greater evil.

The episode demonstrated the growing power of the international environmental lobby to put pressure on Western companies with easily identifiable consumer products – the downside of having a well-known brand name. And it showed reluctant campaigners in the US that merely the threat of a consumer boycott can be a powerful weapon. But Irian Jaya had probably gained little more than a brief breathing space.

When WWF International privately asked a prominent timber trader to produce an estimate of the state of Indonesia's forests, he replied, 'In 5 to 10 years, the forests of Sumatra, in 10 years Kalimantan [the Indonesian portion of Borneo], less than that in Sulawesi, and in 20 to 30 years in Irian Jaya – they will be gone, we will have logged them all and that will be it in south-east Asia.' Irian Jaya is about to be the setting for the last great timber bonanza. According to SKEPHI, at the end of the 1980s, 70 per cent of Irian Jaya's 400,000 square kilometres of forest had been allocated for exploitation: for logging, mining, oil exploration or migrant schemes.

The government had talked of reafforestation programmes and of advanced methods of cutting that would reduce the damage to forests. But official figures reveal that reafforestation in the islands already being logged out remains extremely slow. And a study commissioned from a Finnish timber company reported that much of the land was unsuitable for eucalyptus and acacia plantations. SKEPHI's Hira Jhamtani reported that 'many logging concession holders are former high-ranking military officers who lack expertise or capital to carry out logging operations and sublease their contracts to local or foreign logging companies.' In remote areas, such as most of Irian Jaya, 'operating and reafforestation regulations are rarely, if ever, checked. Various illegal operating conditions go unnoticed.'

Survival International and environment groups in Indonesia have documented dozens of cases of tribal peoples being thrown off their land, prevented from gathering forest produce and so on. One of the first tribal groups to suffer were the Asmat on the south coast of Irian Jaya. The people have a reputation for their superb intricate wood carvings. Today, says Survival International, 'many of the Asmat people have been forcibly relocated to the coast; there they are forced to labour for the timber companies, often being held in a system of debt-slavery and paid only with shag tobacco and cheap clothing. Development has come to mean social and cultural death.'

As if to rub salt in the wounds, the Indonesians sent round Europe an exhibition of Asmat culture. Publicity for the exhibition described the Asmat as 'A primitive tribe, being backwards of all aspects of human life', who due to their 'ignorance of nutrition and hygiene' suffered from 'a lack of mental alertness and concentration, and reduced intelligence'. The Asmat Progress and Development Foundation, which organised the exhibition, proposed a programme to 'upgrade the people's wood-carving skills'.

Hard on the heels of the Scott Paper project came the announcement of an even more ecologically destructive proposal from Marubeni, the Japanese logging giant recently dubbed the world's number one forest destroyer by the Japan Tropical Forest Action Network (JATAN). Marubeni planned to collaborate with a local company to chop down roughly a third of one of the world's largest mangrove forests, at Bintuni Bay on the western peninsula of Irian Jaya. The government had drastically altered the boundaries of a nature reserve in order to allow the project to go ahead. Wood chips would be converted into paper in Japan and JATAN told *Environesia* that one customer would be a 'sister company' of Scott Paper in Japan, Sanyo Kokusaku Pulp.

Mangroves are unique coastal ecosystems of salt-tolerant trees and plants found between high and low tide. They harbour hugely productive fisheries. Throughout south-east Asia mangrove swamps are being logged over and then converted either into rice paddies or fish farms for shrimps.

The announcement of the plan coincided with the completion of a report on Indonesia's wetlands by the Asian Wetlands Bureau, an organisation set up in Kuala Lumpur by a young British biologist, Duncan Parish, initially as an offshoot of WWF Malaysia. 'About sixty per cent of the mangroves in tropical Asia are gone,' he told me. 'They are in the front line for development. Aquaculture is all the rage now and governments are encouraging investment; yet our studies show that none of the schemes are making money. The ponds turn acid and often have to be abandoned.' His study had revealed that more than 11,000 people live in the Bintuni Bay area, taking from the mangroves wood, shrimps, fish and nypa palms, which are used as a roofing material. 'They live a traditional subsistence lifestyle in harmony with their natural environment,' he wrote in a report commissioned by the Indonesian government.

Indonesia's transmigration programme is the largest colonisation scheme attempted anywhere in the world. The

Dutch began moving people from crowded Java in 1905, but the big drive did not begin until 1979. Since then, migrants have been partly funded by the World Bank to the tune of at least $300 million. During the 1980s, the Indonesian government moved four million people from the crowded islands at the centre of the country, Java and Bali, to the fragile forests of the sparsely populated outer islands – first Sulawesi, Sumatra and Kalimantan; now Irian Jaya. The migrants, mostly poor farmers persuaded to seek a new life far from home, faced difficulties as severe as those on whose islands they were taking up residence.

From the early 1980s, the scheme has been fiercely opposed by environmentalists and their friends within the World Bank, several of whom say privately that it is the single most environmentally damaging project in which the Bank is involved.

In 1986, a report on the Bank's worldwide activities, *Financing Ecological Destruction*, by the Environmental Defense Fund, Friends of the Earth UK and others, claimed that 'the project has proven to be ecologically devastating, threatening the destruction of 3.3 million hectares of pristine rainforests and the livelihoods and rights of indigenous peoples living in the forests.' The *Ecologist* put out a special issue that year, edited by Marcus Colchester of Survival International, calling for a halt to international funding of transmigration.

The acid soils on which many of the transmigrants' camps have been set up become infertile after two or three years of cultivation. At exactly the time when aid money for the farmers runs out and they are expected to survive on their own, their soils become useless. Frequently, the farmers have had no choice but to head for the surviving forests to hack out more land for cultivation. Recognising this problem, in 1987 the Bank announced that it would restrict future funding for transmigration to loans intended to prop up existing settlements. This was known euphemistically as 'second stage development'. The Bank also announced plans to spend $145 million on sustaining existing settlements, and an equivalent sum on plantations of palm oil, rubber, and trees such as acacia and eucalyptus. The plantations were to be known as 'nucleus estates' and around them the Bank hoped that smallholders could make better headway, selling their produce to the estate.

Just as with the disastrous Polonoroeste migration programme in Brazil, the Bank found itself investing heavily in an attempt to make good early grave mistakes. But, as at Polonoroeste, the fear was that the new endeavours would make matters even worse. Survival International reported that farmers in the region of one new estate were sometimes being forced by local landowners to join the schemes. In some cases 'their land was seized without compensation and they were offered jobs as casual labourers for the plantation company.'

In one instance, at Lampung in Sumatra, Javanese migrants growing coffee in the forests were evicted, their crops destroyed and some 2,000 houses burned down. Those under 35 were told to join a nucleus estate nearby at Riau. There have been numerous reports of deaths among migrants from poisoning by pesticides. There were 12 deaths in Irian Jaya when wells became contaminated with herbicides.

Life remains tough in the transmigration camps. Lori Udall, Rich's Asia specialist at the Environmental Defense Fund and a regular lobbyist at the World Bank, said that the new phase of the project 'actually succeeds in transforming farmers into helpless labourers who cannot even afford to send their children to school'. WALHI, which had done much to publicise the desperate fate awaiting many migrants on their new land, warned that with world prices for palm oil and rubber depressed, 'the move to turn transmigration sites into monoculture cash-crop production farms could prove to have even worse economic and environmental consequences than transmigration as it was originally conceived.' They would now be at the mercy of world markets as well as their fragile new environment.

While the Bank said that its aim was to help preserve virgin rainforest, critics claimed that the nucleus estate programme was unleashing a new round of rainforest destruction. In April 1988, environmentalists held an International Forum on Indonesia in the Netherlands. From that emerged a new assault on the transmigration programme. Soon afterwards Survival International launched a bimonthly newsletter,

Down To Earth. Described as a 'monitoring service for sustainable development in Indonesia', it set about documenting the huge range of non-sustainable development activities in the country, from the perilous life of transmigrants to the activities of foreign companies such as Scott Paper and Marubeni.

Meanwhile, a flurry of reports and letters to the Bank accused it of flouting its own guidelines on protection both of the environment and of the rights of native peoples in the transmigration schemes that it helped to fund. A revised edition of *Financing Ecological Destruction*, published in late 1988, alleged that 'the last lowland forest in Sumatra, in the Riau province, is being destroyed at a massive rate. Sumatran lowland forests are of critical importance for the conservation of biodiversity [being] the habitat of the endangered Sumatran rhino.'

In parts of Sumatra, the elephants at least were fighting back. The local press reported in 1989 that almost a hundred wild elephants had destroyed several transmigration sites. Migrants had fled for their lives and one had been trampled to death. One report said that 'the frequency of elephant attacks increases in the rainy season when the marshes of southern Sumatra are flooded. The elephants then meet up with herds in North Lampung . . . near the Mesuji transmigration site SP2E.'

While the Bank said that it would not help pay for new transmigration sites, the Indonesian government had no intention of slowing the movement of people, which had a political and military as much as an economic motivation. The inheritors of the empire of the Dutch East Indies were determined to forge the diverse peoples and islands into a single nation – and transmigration was the key to the process. The five-year plan included, for the early 1990s, schemes to resettle 550,000 families – up to three million people – a third of them in Irian Jaya. They would move to more than a hundred timber estates that would require perhaps 40,000 square kilometres of land. Transmigration schemes would absorb more than 5 per cent of the national budget.

Almost unnoticed, in the face of environmental breakdown at the transmigrants' camps, a plan that had begun with the intention of settling independent farmers had turned into one

where migrants would become workers on large estates. It was
not what they had been promised and it held out little hope for
the survival of the last and largest rainforests and wetlands in
south-east Asia. In the 1990s, Indonesia is set to repeat in its
outer domains the mistakes made by Brazil in the Amazon
basin in the 1980s.

WWF *in the Orient*

The only large Western environmental organisation with a
presence 'on the ground' in Indonesia is the World Wildlife
Fund, whose US branch set up an office run by its own Russell
Betts. So what was its line on development? The answer is that
it ducked the development debate entirely, preferring to
concentrate, and to make a virtue of concentrating, on
conservation issues inside reserves and parks.

A long review of WWF Indonesia's activities in Irian Jaya,
published in the US in 1989, began, 'Dense unbroken rainforest, thriving coral reefs, and crystal waters still define Irian
Jaya. Here the Indonesian government and the WWF have a
chance to plan conservation in advance of the inevitable
upcoming burst of economic activity.' It revealed that advisers
from the WWF had helped government officials to design a
'comprehensive conservation programme'. The tone of the
review, by Roger Stone, a WWF fellow, seemed from another
age. It spoke of 'all the fascinating tribespeople' with their
'beguiling assortment of beliefs and superstitions'. The transmigration programme was merely 'ambitious' and the job of
conservationists was to 'brace the region for the burst of
development that, many people believe, lies just ahead'.

Conservation planning in Irian Jaya began in 1980 when an
American wildlife biologist, Ronald Petocz, was sent there by
the WWF and the IUCN. His report to the Indonesian government in 1983 proposed turning 20 per cent of the country over
to nature reserves. Since then, the WWF staff there have
worked hard to persuade natives to leave the reserves alone.
Around the Mount Cyclops Nature Reserve they have worked

with the Ford Foundation to set up 'social forestry' projects on the boundaries of the reserve.

'Eventually', says Stone, 'the trees will generate enough income for the villagers to dampen their interest in leap-frogging [the buffer land] and invading the reserve to open new areas for traditional slash-and-burn agriculture.' It is hard to believe that in Irian Jaya today slash-and-burn is the main threat to the forests. But it would be harder for the WWF to criticise publicly the annexation of part of the Bintuni Bay mangrove reserve for eucalyptus plantations without jeopardising its relationship with the government. Reading between the lines, the signs for the success of the Mount Cyclops buffer zone do not look good. Stone notes that 'insects, shortages of seedlings and other delays have all impeded progress towards long-term goals. Early achievements are so fragmented that the program's overall performance is difficult to measure.'

Elsewhere in the province, the WWF is attempting to convert to conservation the Hatam people near the Arfak Mountain Nature Conservation Area. The Hatam people were ejected from the forests by the government after their involvement in the rebellion against the Indonesian take-over in 1969. Now the WWF wants them to take up butterfly ranching. This is not as crazy as it sounds. There is a growing international market to stock 'butterfly houses' in Europe, which need replenishing every few weeks. It would help the survival of butterflies if they could be ranched sustainably rather than simply captured from the forests. It might also be quite lucrative. The WWF's local manager, Stephen Nash, is quoted as saying that 'butterfly ranching will soon become common-place throughout Irian Jaya.'

He could be right, but the language that Stone uses in his description of how the 'carefully wrought WWF plan' is being introduced hardly inspires confidence. 'A group of Hatam sat on their heels, listening patiently while the details of the program were explained to them,' Stone says. And he quoted the young biologist behind the project as saying, 'Once *we* complete our planning *they* will start work right away. The hope and the expectation is that the Hatam will put as much time into butterfly ranching as they have put into cutting the forest in recent years.' [*author's italics*] Perhaps Bob Hasan, the Indonesian plywood king, should be encouraged to take up butterfly ranching too.

The WWF has more irons in the fire to ease the path to economic development in Indonesia. It is promoting tourism; though again Stone strikes an odd note when he moans that the area earmarked for tourists is 'still virtually devoid of hotels and restaurants'. And it hopes to get more nature reserves declared, including part of the small nearby island of Biak. It could be on to a loser here, however. Late in 1989, the Indonesian government revealed that it is discussing with a US consortium the prospect of turning Biak into a launch site for space satellites.

Perhaps the conservation movement needs people prepared to compromise at every point in order to keep a voice within the inner sanctums of even the most destructive governments. But the approach in Indonesia and elsewhere has created serious tensions within the WWF. As other environmental groups renewed their campaign against transmigration in 1986, memos flew inside WWF International warning that it risked being left out on an embarrassing limb. Policy-makers wondered aloud how far they were being compromised by the WWF's official contacts in Jakarta. Some environmentalists critical of the WWF position claim that Indonesia's own environment minister, the respected but beleaguered Emil Salim, had been more critical of his government's policies towards forests than the WWF.

Within Indonesia, groups such as SKEPHI have little time for conservationists who retreat with their wildlife to safe havens within nature reserves. The creation of reserves generally alienates indigenous people and the reserves are, in any case, perpetually whittled away when the land becomes of use to industry, says SKEPHI. The loss of part of the mangrove reserve in Bintuni Bay made that clear.

Most WWF conservation programmes were essentially bogus, says SKEPHI. Top of its list for myth-blowing was the Dumoga Bone National Park in the north of the Indonesian island of Sulawesi. The park was a joint initiative of the WWF, the World Bank and the Indonesian government. It is often cited as an environmental success story, but in truth it illustrates how conservation can become an instrument of repression.

The story began with the arrival of migrants, partly paid for by the World Bank, into the Dumoga Valley, which was traditionally the home of the Mongondow people, who practice shifting cultivation. The migrants took over the valley for rice cultivation and many of the 10,000 Mongondow were forced into the surrounding hills. Meanwhile, the Bank had helped to fund two dams in the hills to feed new irrigation canals in the valley. In order to prevent any risk of the dams silting up, the Bank promoted the idea of a national park to protect the dams' catchment area.

Initially the park covered only the higher hillsides. But later, says SKEPHI, 'the park boundary was relocated towards downhill due to pressure from the World Bank, World Wildlife Fund, the Indonesian Forestry Service and the local district chief. Today it covers 3,000 square kilometres. In 1982, says the local campaigner George Aditjonro, 'the WWF started identifying farmers who cleared land now included in the park as "encroachers". Forest guards were sent in to confiscate hunted game and all clearing of land for shifting cultivation was banned.' Meanwhile, a buffer zone of fast-growing commercial trees was created at the edge of the park and the whole scheme was promoted afresh as a success for the Tropical Forestry Action Plan.

SKEPHI concludes:

The concept of national parks decrees that they should be free of settlements. This concept that came from the West is actually the main problem since communities in tropical forest areas traditionally depend on the resources. National parks deprive communities of their own resources. Instead of ensuring conservation, such ventures have led to increased conflicts of interest. The Bank should be sensitive to this and try to develop indigenous concepts of conservation instead.

One of the greatest surprises in researching this book was the discovery of so much antagonism towards the WWF and, within WWF, the rows between the old guard and the Young Turks, who are anxious to enter debates on the economics of conservation and on development priorities. A conspicuous example of the old guard in action is WWF Malaysia, established in 1972 and one of the earliest national WWF organisations. Despite increasingly hiring Malaysian scientists, the office retains an expat image. The director, Ken Scrivens, is British enough to have flown home for Sir Peter Scott's funeral. And Mikhail Kavanagh, the conservation officer, came from Cambridge University in 1981 and stayed on. Its office neighbours in Kuala Lumpur are, appropriately enough, two British firms: Saatchi and Saatchi and Blue Circle Cement.

'I have a commitment to the country now,' says Kavanagh. But his idea of campaigning conservation is a world away from that of other conservation groups I met in Malaysia, and increasingly from WWF International. 'We see ourselves as a professional and scientific organisation,' said Kavanagh. 'We are trying to employ career scientists.' The role of the Fund is primarily, he says, 'to draw the attention of governments to conservation issues. As far as possible, WWF tries to do this in a quiet way, eschewing the high profile route of newspaper headlines. We are not a pressure group; we are insiders.'

His policy has been to forge close links with both federal and state governments; with results that can be misconstru~d when the backdrop is some of the fastest and most corrupt destruction of tropical forests anywhere in the world. In Sarawak, Kavanagh regrets the 'hostile stance of foreign environmental groups' because it destabilises his evidently difficult relationship with the state government. Kavanagh worked in Sarawak with the local authorities himself for a while. Today, the WWF has two education officers there working for the government. 'We hope they'll eventually be absorbed into the government payroll,' he says. After the bad publicity for Sarawak forestry in the late 1980s, his work with the state government, advising on conservation, 'could go either way,' he says. 'We hope that our having been good boys will make the difference.' In neighbouring Sabah, there is an equally unsavoury local administration, and some observers, Kavanagh included, believe that forest destruction may be as fast and as indiscriminate as in Sarawak. Unabashed, he aims to 'expand our intimate relationship with the state government'. One of his staff has been working with the department of wildlife there for some years.

Confidentiality is a prerequisite of Kavanagh's work. In 1988, no fewer than seven of the fourteen reports completed by WWF Malaysia were confidential and not published. Several concerned forestry in Sarawak and Sabah, including two assessments of WWF Malaysia's own conservation action in each state since 1972. This secrecy angers staff at WWF International. One source there told me, 'The Malaysian WWF is very conservative. They get all their data from the Malaysian Forestry Department. None of their reports ever cite another NGO. It stinks.'

Other groups are extremely suspicious of such relationships. SAM's Chee Yoke Ling harboured resentment about a criticism of her organisation by WWF Malaysia made two years before. Gurmit Singh, who runs the Environmental Protection Society of Malaysia – an organisation that, like WWF Malaysia, wants to build bridges with government – remembers campaigns on protecting national parks that the WWF dropped out of when the general issue of logging policy came to the fore. 'It happened when we opposed the granting to the Sultan of Pahan of a licence to log in a proposed national park area. The WWF always claim to operate at a higher level. I think they get too embarrassed when we start to criticise people that they meet at social functions.'

The growing influence and money-raising potential of organisations such as Friends of the Earth and Greenpeace is forcing the World Wide Fund for Nature to rethink its role worldwide. During the 1970s its initial concentration on saving individual species – whether elephant, rhino, tiger, or the unique species of the Galapagos Islands – gave way to a greater interest in saving habitats. The WWF had launched its first tentative Tropical Rainforest Campaign in the mid-1970s.

A key moment came in 1980 when, with the IUCN and UN Environment Programme, it published a large document called the *World Conservation Strategy*. This grand overview incorporated the idea that conservation could no longer be kept separate from strategies for the economic development of Third World countries. The report was largely written by Robert Prescott-Allen, one of Teddy Goldsmith's protégés at the *Ecologist* and joint-author with Goldsmith of *Blueprint for Survival* in 1972.

The strategy was the first document to adopt the phrase 'sustainable development'. The WWF yearbook that year recognised that its publication 'represents the start of a new phase in conservation'. The problem, said many inside the organisation, was that even at the end of the 1980s, the rhetoric of matching conservation to development was rarely put into practice. It was all too often attempting to accommodate in its strategies with many governments economic development plans that were most definitely not good for the environment.

One internal study in the late 1980s concluded that despite the constant assertion that conservation and development were being tackled together, perhaps 95 per cent of the WWF's expenditure did no such thing. Key issues at the boundary between environment and development, such as the causes of soil erosion and the economic pressures behind the destruction of rainforests, went unaddressed. The WWF had failed to make links with development and aid organisations such as Oxfam. It had avoided difficult issues, preferring the safe haven of the nature reserve, about which the Duke of Edinburgh could safely prognosticate without offending host governments. (The Duke travelled to Indonesia wearing his WWF hat in 1989 and announced that the country was 'doing pretty well' in conserving rainforests.)

At the end of the 1980s, the WWF remained extraordinarily well known round the world; ranking, as one insider put it, with Coca-Cola, Mickey Mouse and the Queen of England. But it was no longer universally recognised as the ecological brand leader. Having partially dropped its 'save the elephant/rhino/tiger' approach to conservation, its new 'save the planet' strategy lacked both popular appeal and intellectual or political credibility.

Two-thirds of the organisation wanted to spend its time raising money for ill-defined campaigns to save elephants or rhinos; the other third wanted to lobby the ITTO or the World Bank. Meanwhile in Indonesia, the once numerous Sumatran rhino, with just 50 animals left, faced extinction as the rainforest gave way to eucalyptus plantations and transmigrants without the WWF raising its voice in protest.

11

BEING POSITIVE

Neither left nor right

They call the German Green Party the 'water-melon party' – green on the outside but red on the inside. Certainly one strand of the party comes from the student protest movement of the late 1960s. Two decades on, the greens' leader in Frankfurt was Daniel Cohn-Bendit, 'Danny the Red' from 1968. Another strand includes the anarchists and others experimenting with alternative urban lifestyles; many of them squatting in old buildings in Hamburg, Frankfurt and West Berlin, forming rock bands, running alternative newspapers and smoking pot. But there is a third, less radical, strand emerging from the *Burgerinitiativen* – a network of 'citizens' initiative' groups formed in towns and villages all over the country in the 1960s. They had no grand visions for a new way, but objected to the nuclear power plants, airports and highways being visited upon them at the height of the German post-war 'economic miracle'.

The origins of the greens in Germany lie in the alienation from mainstream politics felt by large numbers of young Germans during the 1960s and 1970s. But it was not until the late 1970s, several years after a number of other European green parties had formed, that Die Grunen came into existence. Sara Parkin, co-secretary of the European Greens and author of a definitive guide to the growth of the continents' green parties, argues that factionalism held up the emergence of the greens in German politics for several years. During the late 1970s, the nation was full of anti-nuclear and environment movements. But, says Parkin, at first they 'looked on with deep suspicion' the various local and regional political parties forming around their causes. 'On the whole they felt that these attempts to give voice to their concerns through a political party smacked more of opportunism than anything else,' she says.

The seeds of a national party were sown in Lower Saxony, a conservative and prosperous farming region of northern Germany where one of the main environmental issues is the disruption caused by manoeuvres of British soldiers during NATO exercises each autumn. Activists from nature protection groups gathered under the banner of the GLU, or Green List party, and began to promote the formation of GLU parties in other states from radical urban Hamburg to Baden-Wurttemberg, the Black Forest state in the south of the country. Another more overtly national party, Green Action Future, was formed in 1978, not by a closet socialist but by Herbert Gruhl, author of *A Planet is Plundered* and a former member of the right-wing Christian Democrats. He invented the phrase adopted by green parties throughout Europe who claimed to be 'neither left nor right, but in front'.

In 1979, these two groups established a grand alliance, SPV-Die Grunen, to fight European Parliamentary elections. The new grouping attracted two of the moving forces of Die Grunen through the 1980s, Petra Kelly, who had left the Social Democrats in 1978, and Roland Vogt, as well as another former student radical, Rudi Dutschke. It campaigned for a nuclear-free Europe and regional government. Under German electoral rules, it banked DM4.5 million after winning 3.2 per cent of the vote.

The money set up a national organisation and the success attracted the interest of two radical left groupings, both under the influence of the Communist League that had previously ostracised Die Grunen. They were the Multicoloured List from Hamburg and the Alternative List for Democracy and Environmental Protection from Berlin.

All these groups came together at a congress in Offenbach later that year to thrash out a programme. Parkin quotes one participant:

There were 3,000 people screaming their own positions in the convention hall. Although agreement seemed impossible, I took a piece of paper and wrote four words on it: ecology, social responsibility, grassroots democracy and non-violence. Then I called Gruhl and Reents [the leader on the left] into the rooms where the journalists were and said 'Sign'. We then went back into the convention hall and announced: We have a programme.

The four words became the 'four pillars' under which the Die Grunen alliance (which was more 'left and right' than 'neither left nor right') went into the state and general elections in 1983.

In practice, peace and ecology, the two ideas whose fusion created Greenpeace a decade before, were the touchstone of Die Grunen in the public mind. The new party was quickly able to establish its popular credentials. First there was the groundswell of public anger at the siting of Cruise and Pershing missiles on German soil. And second, there was the discovery by German scientists that the nation's trees were sick. From the Black Forest to the Alps, to the Harz Mountains of Lower Saxony, the forest canopies were turning a sickly yellow, and on exposed hilltops trees were dying. Foresters blamed air pollution.

Almost a third of West Germany is covered in forests, which play a prominent part in German folklore. The sickness, known as *waldsterben*, was considered a national disaster and its diagnosis a few months before the 1983 elections brought a wave of public concern for the state of the nation's environment. Cruise and *waldersterben* made Die Grunen front-page news and secured it 28 seats in the Bundestag, with more than 5 per cent of the vote. Nothing like it had been seen before in Europe, or anywhere else for that matter. If it did nothing else, it persuaded the government that it had to act on acid rain and in the following five years several billion Deutschmarks were spent by German electricity utilities removing sulphur emissions from their chimneys. After much haggling, in particular from Britain, the rest of the European Community agreed that they would fall into line during the early 1990s.

Life in the mainstream proved fractious. Die Grunen's more radical members had only agreed to join in elections because it entitled them to federal funds. Now they found themselves elected. Infighting, always a feature of the party, intensified and two factions formed: the Fundis and the Realos. The Realos saw themselves as political realists, willing to form coalitions with the Social Democrats, as they had done in several states during the 1980s. The Fundis, drawing on the more radical ideas of Petra Kelly and hardliners in Berlin and Hamburg, held out for basic principles and saw parliament as only a small part of their work. Under leaders such as Joaschka Fischer and Otto Schily, the Realos slowly gained the upper hand, trouncing the Fundis at internal elections in 1988.

Today, environmentalists round the world use the tags of Realo and Fundi to frame their own disputes. Among campaigners against the World Bank, Realos play the closed-door lobbying game, build bridges and maintain lines of communication, while the Fundis head for the barricades. Realos lobby the ITTO; Fundis don't.

Through the remainder of the 1980s, amid factional fighting and global *détente*, Die Grunen maintained an 8 to 10 per cent share of the national vote in Germany. It was enough to lead them into coalitions with the Social Democrats in Frankfurt and Berlin and to give them a realistic prospect of making a similar arrangement nationally after elections at the end of 1990. But something else was happening to them. They were getting older.

There was talk of the need to set up a youth section; and even the Fundis were starting to talk of compromise and to see the attractions of power. In 1989, it was the former leftists from Berlin – who still campaigned under their old name of the Alternative List and who included among their number defenders of the urban terrorists of the 1970s – who agreed to enter a local coalition with the Social Democrats to run the city council after a hung election left nobody in charge.

Typical of the reformed Berlin leftists, perhaps, is Frieder Otto Wolf, a former green member of the European Parliament from Berlin. When I met him in 1989, he was wearing jeans, brown sneakers and a flowered shirt. He had a pigtail

and a small pink bow in his hair, a widening midriff and a
hint of a double chin. He described himself as a 'non-
fundamentalist left eco-socialist'. Nobody, he said, was a
fundamentalist any more. The Fundis, outnumbered and out-
flanked, were disbanded in 1988 and replaced by a softer
grouping known as the Left Forum. 'The number of left greens
active at federal level is now down to a hundred or so out of a
total of between three and five hundred national activists,' he
said. The eleven-strong party board contained just four from
the left.

'The Realos and us are both realists,' Wolf said. 'The
difference is that they want piecemeal reform, while we think
they underestimate the problems of creating real change. We
want struggle and we have no illusions.' He said that the Social
Democrats had invited the greens to join them in governing
West Berlin only after a poll found fewer people objected to a
deal with them than with the Christian Democrats. 'They
believe that a successful coalition in Berlin will help them in
the national elections.' Wolf said that greens had won some
ecological measures in the city, fighting for speed limits to
reduce pollution from cars, for instance. But there was little
progress on the 'class issues', which he sees at the heart of
many ecological issues.

The alliance with the Social Democrats 'tends to avoid
conflict with capitalist organisations,' he said. 'For instance,
the city council owns the public electricity company. The
electricity company wants the city council to approve plans for
a new power line to connect us to other companies in West
Germany. This is contrary to the policy of Die Grunen, which
stresses investment in energy conservation. The power line
would also bring nuclear-generated electricity to West Berlin
for the first time. We have the power to replace the electricity
company's directors but there is reluctance because it would
create a conflict with Berlin's industrialists who want more
electricity.'

What would a national coalition with the Social Democrats
look like? Top of Wolf's green shopping list would be the
phase-out of nuclear power and investment in local power
plants, including city power stations that recycle waste heat

into ducts to heat buildings. And he wanted tough new laws against cars, the prime source of acid rain now that power stations have been cleaned up, and also of greenhouse gases. Green partners in a coalition would insist on laws to protect food and water supplies from pesticides, to clean up toxic dumps and control factory farming. But his green agenda contained at least as much on civil liberties and social measures as ecology. He wanted major reform of the prisons, new data-protection laws, an end to limits on abortion and a shorter working day.

For the Third World he backed the cancellation of debt and the opening of markets in the rich world to Third World goods. He opposed the industrialisation of agriculture – the green revolution – and backed a return to 'peasant farming that combines modern ecological knowledge with traditional skills'. He wanted that approach adopted by the European Community, too.

Across the border in the Netherlands, where for decades Germans have sent much of their pollution mixed with the waters of the Rhine, the local Green Party, known as the Radical Party, remains tiny. But that is because the mainstream parties have gone far further than those in Germany in adopting green policies. Galvanised by Rhine pollution and, more recently, by the knowledge that any rise in sea-levels caused by the greenhouse effect would threaten them first, Dutch ministers pride themselves on being the greenest government in Europe. They insist on green issues being taught in schools, and they lavishly fund environment groups. The Dutch government offered Greenpeace International a dockside warehouse if it would move its headquarters from Britain to the Netherlands. It unveiled a 20-year National Environment Plan designed to cut pollution of all sorts by between 70 and 90 per cent, and subsequently fought an election on the issue. The plan puts farm chemicals and car exhausts in the front line.

The contrasting fates of the Dutch and German Green Parties suggest that in Europe the strength of a national Green Party reflects the gap between the greenness of public concern for the environment and the greenness of its main parties. In

that sense, it is a protest vote. This explains the sudden
upwelling of public support for the Green Party in Britain in
1989. The party had existed for almost 20 years, but had
previously polled very badly. Then it took 14 per cent of the
British vote during elections for the European Parliament. As
the main parties rushed to the green barricades, however, the
voters returned to their former loyalties – at any rate, while
they assessed what the new rhetoric from the reds and the blues
added up to.

The British greens will have a hard struggle, not least
because of the British electoral system, which offers none of
the help to smaller parties embedded in the German system, for
instance. But they face a tough time from the electorate, too.
Few people who voted for the Green Party in Britain in 1989
knew of its root-and-branch opposition to economic growth
and the consumer society – still less that it wanted drastic cuts
in the British population. Most Green voters, when polled,
appeared confused about the difference between the Green
Party and Greenpeace. However, it is unwise to be too cynical.
People voted Green because that summer they felt green. For
the country that brought the world the industrial revolution, it
was an interesting moment.

A green belt for Africa

Africa is a desert for environmental groups. The unhealthy
domination of governments over every aspect of the lives
of their citizens leaves little room for genuinely non-
governmental organisations. One partial exception has been
Nairobi, the capital of Kenya. The safari centre of East Africa,
it became the focus for conservation of wildlife in Africa after
the establishment of the World Wildlife Fund in the early
1960s. In the mid-1970s the new UN Environment Programme
set up its headquarters there. Attached to it are groups such as
the Environmental Liaison Centre, the remnant of an ill-fated

attempt after the 1972 Stockholm UN Conference on the Human Environment to set up an umbrella organisation to co-ordinate environmental groups round the world. There is also the head office of the African NGO Environmental Network. All these organisations, like Africa itself, tend to suffer from a surfeit of bureaucracy, coupled with a dearth of popular support and enthusiasm.

Breaking the mould with genuine grass-roots environmentalism is the Green Belt Movement, based in Nairobi. It has planted ten million native trees across Kenya and, arguably, has done more to stall the expansion of deserts and the destruction of soils in Africa than its big brother international body down the road, the UNEP, with its grand but largely unsuccessful anti-desertification programmes.

The Green Belt Movement is the product of one woman's determination. Wangari Maathai had a privileged middle-class Kenyan childhood, followed by college in Kansas in the US and then veterinary studies at the University of Nairobi. She married a young Kenyan politician. Her first trees were planted in an effort to fulfil extravagant campaign promises made to the electorate in the slums of Langata in Nairobi in 1974. 'Something new needed to be done for the needy who had supported us,' she says, and she hit on the idea of what amounted to a private parks and gardens service.

She set up a company called Envirocare to sell services in planting trees, trimming hedges, tending gardens and sweeping streets – hiring the poor to do the work. This seemed at odds with the local political ethos, where election promises were made for breaking. 'The clean-up programme', she later wrote, 'was initiated against much opposition, especially from political hangers-on who enjoyed more confidence and hearing from my husband than I did.' A friendly forester provided 6,000 seedlings, which mostly died during an unusually dry 1976, when the city council banned Envirocare from watering them.

After that, she separated from her husband and Envirocare would have died but for her friendship with people at the UNEP who arranged for her to attend a UN Conference on Human Settlement Habitat in Vancouver. There she met women such as Barbara Ward, one of the conference's organisers, Margaret Mead and Mother Teresa. On returning home, she joined the National Council for Women of Kenya, swiftly became a member of its executive, and pushed through the idea of setting up community tree-planting projects to improve cities and halt the destruction of soils.

The first seven trees were planted at a ceremony in Nairobi on World Environment Day in 1977. The next 60 trees were donated by Mobil Oil, which continued to support the project for several years. In particular, it backed the publicity-grabbing ceremony at which delegates to a UNEP desertification conference in Nairobi later that year planted 800 trees in the Rift Valley. The aftermaths to the first two events taught Maathai an important lesson. The first seven trees were handed into the care of Nairobi city council and all but two were dead by the mid-1980s. But the small wood in the Rift Valley, in the middle of grassland owned by a women's farming co-operative near Mount Margaret, survived. Moral: leave the trees in charge of the people, not officials.

Maathai's acute political sense was getting her activities noticed. She invited national figures to attend tree-planting ceremonies, though, interestingly, and despite her avowedly feminist approach, photographs of these occasions show that virtually all the celebrities were men. This was pure pragmatism. She wrote later in a booklet on how to set up green belt movements:

> Politicians and decision-makers in the developing world are the rich, the élite and the powerful. Their lifestyle is expensive and in many instances the plundering of the environment is being done either by them or for them. Many pay only lip service to conservation. However, it is impossible to effectively take the message of conservation to the rural communities without the support of the decision-makers. They must realise that it is to their benefit if the masses do work to prevent desertification. The message should be taken to the powerful and the communities almost simultaneously.

She always highlighted the practical benefits of trees, such as windbreaks. 'We had read of many schools whose roofs had been blown off by the wind.' The idea caught on. 'The hunger for trees was so great that at every tree planting function where public green belts were to be established extra tree seedlings were issued ... people scrambled for these seedlings and appealed to us for more.' But the planting was always in the countryside. Despite her initial motives to improve the lives of the urban poor, the demand for trees in urban areas was slight.

Maathai took to the international circuit to raise more funds for seedlings and to pay for the rigorous regime of inspections and follow-up care. She was determined to make sure that the green belt trees sprouting across the country survived better than those planted each year on Kenya's National Tree Planting Day, most of which died for want of attention. So she employed teams of children and the poor and handicapped to work as rangers checking up on the trees. Green or not, she had no scruples in recommending the use of pesticides to kill white ants and moles that attacked her trees.

In 1981, she established a permanent nursery with money from a fund set up by the UN Decade for Women. After that there was money from the Norwegian Forestry Society, the Danish Voluntary Fund for Developing Countries and the Spirit of Stockholm Foundation. The Green Belt Movement pays poor women farmers about 50 Kenyan cents (2 English pence) for every tree they plant that survives for three months. For many poor women subsistence farmers, says Maathai, this is their only source of cash.

Her pragmatic approach to the Kenyan élite ensured official support for her work in a country where such support is essential. In 1989, however, rather than sticking to planting trees in the countryside, she spoke out against government plans to chop down trees in Uhuru Park in the capital – one of the few green places available to people from slums such as Langata, where her work began 15 years before. The government wanted to take over a large part of the park to build a 60-storey office block, to be the tallest building in Africa. She took legal action against the government and fired off angry letters of protest. 'If I didn't react to their interference with this central park, I may as well not have planted another tree,' she said.

In late 1989, her international standing was reaching new levels as she flew to London to be named Woman of the World by the Princess of Wales. But at home President Daniel Arap Moi said in exasperation at her opposition to his tower that she must have insects in her head – a bizarre quote that ensured the story's place in newspapers round the world. More seriously, the government evicted the Green Belt Movement from its offices in Nairobi and MPs demanded that the Movement be banned for attempting to destabilise the government. For a government whose park rangers had recently shot dozens of poachers in the name of the environment, it was a bewildering move.

A green lifeline for the Amazon

Martin Hildebrand has a German father and Irish mother, who emigrated to Brazil. Educated at Trinity College, Dublin, and the Sorbonne, he returned to South America to work as an anthropologist before deciding, instead, to devote his life to helping the Colombian Indians. Today, he is head of indigenous affairs for the Colombian government and in charge of a pioneering approach to saving the rainforests – by giving them back to the Indians. In 1988, the Colombian president took a journey deep into the forest to announce that 60,000 square kilometres of the forested headwaters of the Amazon basin, in the south-west corner of Colombia, would be handed back. So far, 180,000 square kilometres in total, belonging to 70,000 Indians, have been returned. For people-oriented greens it is a stunning breakthrough. If Colombia can do it, they say, why cannot the Brazilians do the same?

Hildebrand is less wide-eyed than that. 'In Colombia, we are not being pushed to exploit the rainforest, unlike Brazil,' he says. 'The government says that the best thing to do for the moment is to leave it and study it with the Indians.' Like the Canadians, who have handed over large parts of the Canadian

Arctic to be controlled by the local Inuit, the Colombian government has not ceded all control. 'These territories are not independent,' says Hildebrand. 'The government has not closed the door of access.' While it has handed over much of the Colombian sector of the Amazon rainforest to its Indian people, the rule applies only to the surface of the land. 'The subsoil belongs to the nation,' says Hildebrand, 'and companies could, with the permission of the government, go in to mine'.

Nonetheless, in the face of economic 'progress', the Colombian case seems set to become an important test of the green argument that the Indian communities of the forests should be left alone to run their own affairs.

Colombia's Indians do not pay taxes or do military service, and they run many of their own schools. 'Some teach their children that the sun revolves round the earth,' he says. Should they really be taught such nonsense? Here the anthropologist speaks: 'What matters more than the facts themselves are the values and harmony that go with them. There are dangers when we try to separate facts from their social contexts. We want to strengthen Indian culture.' It's a moot point. It could make their dealings with the outside world harder; but Hildebrand is certain that retaining traditional values and social structures is ultimately essential to maintaining the rainforest.

He first settled in the forest in 1972 after a long canoe-trip through the region. 'I discovered to my surprise that the Indians had been thinking for centuries about how to deal with the outside world. It shouldn't have come as a surprise, but it did,' he says. The communities of the forest need the outside world for metal tools, flashlights and medicines to combat Western diseases. They used to depend for these goods on the rubber barons, who exchanged them for resin. But during the 1970s, many of the barons were forced out when the Indians formed co-operatives to sell their produce and refused to pay old debts. Hildebrand helped them to organise the expulsion of the rubber barons. 'I was accused of trying to start an independent republic,' he remembers. 'The army came to investigate. Then they accused me of wanting to keep the Indians primitive.'

Early attempts to run the co-operative, which sold rubber
and bought in goods from outside for sale, failed, he says. 'The
problem was that the head man in that community maintains
his social status by distributing spare food to the young
unmarried men, who then go hunting for him. The top person
is a distributor, not an accumulator. So the head man gave
away the shop's stock.' The Indians' social structure is more or
less the exact opposite of the Western model, which rewards
the wealthy. In the Amazon, the accumulators are looked
down on as people who have nobody with whom to share. The
community that Hildebrand was living with found a solution
to their problem, however. They decided that the head man
should not run the shop. The job was given to a social outsider
who was happy to accumulate.

The accumulator/distributor relationship had an interesting
effect when coca dealers came, looking for supplies of coca
leaves for the American market. 'The young men sold them
leaves and bought tape recorders, outboard motors et cetera.
But that made them accumulators and did not buy them social
status. So they tried to get back in by using their tape recorders
to record and learn traditional songs from the elders.' This
community is not quite so primed to self-destruction on the
arrival of Westerners as Lutzenberger and others fear.

Just as social status works as a mirror-image of Western
structures, says Hildebrand, so does the local economy. The
emphasis on sharing extends both to social relations and to the
community's relationship with the environment. Central to
this is the role of the shaman. Western dictionaries normally
define the shaman as a medicine man or even witch doctor. But
their leading role in Indian communities is more that of an
ecologist. He is the man with the most intimate knowledge of
the plants and animals of the forest. He decides what animals
can be hunted and when; what fruit trees should be planted
and when clearings should be abandoned.

Indian communities, says Hildebrand, are now combining
the worlds of the tape recorder and the shaman. 'They are now
mapping their environment and the meaning of individual
areas. The shamans are describing how they manage the
ecosystems of the forest and it is being written up in their own

language. Now they want to compare their own systems with those of other communities and with the white man's systems.'

Within the lands now set aside for them, Indian cultures may revive and develop. If so, their knowledge will not then be something that has to be extracted from them before they disappear – a kind of lifeline between the emerging commercialisation of the forests and the disappearing past. It will be a living resource. For the one certainty is that, whether or not they believe the sun revolves round the earth, the Amazon Indians will know far more than Western scientists about the way that the rainforests work for a long while yet.

Tree-huggers for the Himalayas

Mirabehn began life as Madeleine Slade, the socialite daughter of a British admiral. After reading a book about Mahatma Gandhi, she left Europe in 1925 and sailed for India to become his disciple. She spent most of the next 20 years with Gandhi, visiting England with him in 1931 and being arrested with him in 1942 by the British authorities. After independence, she established an ashram in the hills above Tehri, a town to be flooded in the 1990s to make way for a giant hydroelectric dam. There she set to work with many other young idealists to fulfil Gandhi's vision of village self-sufficiency. The foothills of the Himalayas became the heartland for this movement. She also began to study the forests of the Himalayas, which had been taken over by the state forestry departments for licensing to commercial timber companies. Villagers, angry at ecological changes in the hills and at the theft of their forests by the state, had taken to indiscriminate destruction of trees. Meanwhile foresters were moving into the hills with new species of quick-growing trees such as the chir pine.

In 1958, after much thought, Mirabehn published a long and prophetic article called 'Something Wrong in the Himalaya'. In it she wrote:

Year after year the floods in the north of India seem to be getting worse, and this year they have been absolutely devastating. This means that there is something radically wrong with the Himalaya and that 'something' is, without doubt, connected with the forests. It is not, I believe, just a matter of deforestation as some people think, but largely a matter of change of species. This deadly change-over is from banj [Himalayan oak] to chir pine.

While the banj creates a rich undergrowth and soil to absorb rainwater, she wrote, the chir pine being planted by foresters destroys both soil and undergrowth. 'Often the ground in a chir pine forest is as bare as a desert. When torrential rains of the monsoon beat down on these southern slopes of the Himalaya . . . erosion invariably takes place.'

Saralabehn was Gandhi's second constant European companion during the 1930s and 1940s. She was born Catherine Heilman in London and joined him as a teacher in 1936. She was a feminist, campaigned for prohibition, and increasingly took up ecological concerns. She, like Mirabehn, settled in the Himalayas in the late 1940s, where she ran a school for girls and, shortly before her death in 1982, set up a Hill Environment Protection Society. She too had allied a deep conviction that the independent India should follow a Gandhian path to self-sufficiency with a growing concern for the forests, and especially the replacement of walnut and oak trees with chir pine and eucalyptus.

One of Saralabehn's disciples married a young politician, Sunderlal Bahuguna, who was general secretary of the Tehri branch of the Congress Party. Bahuguna had met Mirabehn and, under her influence, had renounced politics in 1956 to work with the rural poor. Through the 1960s, he and his lieutenant, a former booking clerk, Chadi Prasad Bhatt, devoted themselves to establishing a co-operative organisation. It would set up small village craft factories according to the Gandhian ideal, based on timber and other local forest resources, such as natural medicines. But their activities were constantly undermined by large commercial competitors, often with the backing of the state forestry department.

By 1971, with their factories shut down for want of contracts, villagers began demonstrations at the village of Gopeshwar, close to the Chinese border, demanding the restoration of ancient rights to the forests, and Bahuguna began to tour the countryside gathering support. The following year, a demonstration was held on the site of a famous massacre that took place in 1930 at Tilari, when the Tehri Garhwal state army opened fire on villagers protesting against forest policies, killing 17. Bahuguna was tapping into a strong vein of local anger against outsiders, including entrepreneurs from elsewhere in India, taking over the forests of the Himalayas, and he had the support of both the strong network of Gandhian social workers in the villages and of the powerful local Communist Party.

In early 1973, the authorities gave a manufacturer of tennis rackets from Allahabad, a city 800 kilometres away, access to a grove of ash trees in the Mandal Forest, overlooking the valley of the Alaknanda River. The concession was given in preference to a competing claim from a village co-operative. Anger boiled over. Villagers confronted the axe-men and protected the trees by hugging them. The Chipko movement was born.

The protests on this occasion eventually won the villagers the right to the trees, but by now their wider demands for local control of the forests had taken flight. Bahuguna began his first padayatra, a two-month march through the hills, moving from village to village spreading the message that the forests must be saved. India has a long tradition of pilgrimages, and modern padayatras had been pioneered by both Gandhi and, later, his disciple, Vinoba Bhave, who had walked the country asking for gifts of land for the poor. Over the following two years, Bahuguna walked more than 4,000 kilometres, often accompanied by groups of students, musicians or village women. His walks continued periodically right through the 1970s and 1980s, including a 5,000-kilometre march in 1978 the length of the Himalayas from Kashmir to Bhutan. The walks did a great deal to build Chipko both as a potent local people's movement and as a national and then international focus for growing concern about the forests.

An early campaign was to save the forests above the village of Reni, in the headwaters of the Alaknanda River, from being auctioned. The valley had been hit by floods and landslides in 1970 that had killed 200 people and marooned 100 villages. The fear was that treeless hillsides would be even more vulnerable. A four-day vigil in the early 1970s prevented foresters from entering the forest and brought victory. At one point loggers with guns had threatened 30 women and children defending the trees. In response, Gawra Devi, a woman in her 50s, repulsed them by baring her breast, declaring 'the forest is my mother' and challenging them to kill her in order to take the trees. Such stories travelled the countryside with Bahuguna, building the reputation of Chipko as a populist people's movement.

Soon, villagers were planting trees in the hills, often on their own common grazing land. They were prepared even to protect pine trees against the overexploitation of their resin. They did this by removing the blades inserted into the trees to bleed the resin. But tensions were growing within Chipko. Bahuguna was growing unhappy at the movement's support for the rights of villagers to chop down trees. He pointed to the destruction to forests caused by some small local factories, such as those using fuel-wood to boil up resin to make turpentine. Serious flooding in 1978 reaffirmed his belief that all felling of the forests should halt. While Bahuguna pledged himself to saving the ecosystem of the Himalayas, Chadi Prasad Bhatt said, 'Saving trees is only the first step in the Chipko movement. Saving ourselves is the real goal.'

The split was later exploited by the government which took to quoting Bhatt when it wished to denigrate Bahuguna as an enemy of the people. It has also tended to polarise environmentalists in India ever since. The philosophical and personal rivalry began to reveal itself in the numerous articles about Chipko being written by both foreigners and Indians. Many referred either to Bahuguna or to Bhatt, but never to both.

In 1977, Bahuguna met Richard St Barbe Baker, the son of a British clergyman who took up forestry and became one of the earliest crusaders for tree planting. Baker had become known round the world as the 'man of the trees'. He had successfully proposed massive civil works to reafforest the US during the New Deal in the 1930s; and he persuaded Kikuyu natives in Kenya to become 'men of the trees', or *Wattu wa Miti*. He incorporated the idea into tribal custom by promoting a 'dance of the trees', which later became the basis for Chipko rituals in India. Baker twice travelled into the Himalayas with Bahuguna. As a forester, Baker enhanced Bahuguna's scientific credibility within India and brought his story to a worldwide audience. Soon Bahuguna was being invited to forestry as well as to environmental conferences.

Shrewdly, too, the two men publicised the stories of the two Devis: Gawra Devi whose bare-breasted defiance at Reni makes a good modern tale, and the much more startling story, dating from 1731, of Amrita Devi, a member of the ancient Bishnois sect, the original tree-huggers. The sect worshipped its trees and refused to budge when the local maharaja sent workers to chop down their trees to make him a palace. Amrita Devi hugged the first tree marked for felling, and was hacked in two. Her three daughters replaced her and were also killed. Others took their place and by the end of the day 359 people lay dead.

Through the 1980s, the two wings of the Chipko movement continued to grow. Under the leadership of Bhatt it has planted more than a million trees. Under Bahuguna it has captured imaginations. In the words of one visitor to the region in 1989, 'Sunderlal Bahuguna dominates between two and three hundred villages. It's amazing. The schoolchildren all sing Chipko songs about the forests and soils and the World Bank.' In the early 1980s Chipko volunteers led opposition to plans for massive limestone quarries in the Doon Valley and galvanised opposition to the Tehri dam. Chipko has spawned several similar organisations, including the Appiko movement in the southern state of Karnataka, which has campaigned against social forestry projects set up to feed pulp mills in the state.

Bahuguna's ideas have fostered a new strain of radical environmental thought in India. Its most voluble exponent is Vandana Shiva, director of an organisation grandly called the Research Foundation for Science, Technology and Natural Resource Policy, which operates from her house in Dehra Dun, the nearest large city to the Chipko heartland. A physicist, Shiva abandoned a career in India's nuclear power programme to devote herself to a life of radical environmentalism based on feminism. In her analysis, the catalysts for the Chipko movement were all women, most notably Mirabehn and Saralabehn. 'The men of the movement . . . have been their students and followers,' she says. 'Bahuguna has been an effective messenger of the women's concern . . . largely through listening to the quiet voices of the women during his padayatras.' She points to the number of padayatras organised by women and the continuing role of Saralabehn through the 1970s. Frequently, too, it was women who confronted the foresters, placing their bodies between them and the trees. Forest officials accused women protesters at Adwani in 1977 with the words, 'Do you know what forests bear? They produce profit and resin and timber.' The women shouted back, 'What do the forests bear? Soil, water and pure air.' The riposte has become one of the main campaign songs of the movement.

Shiva sees concern for the forests' survival as a female preoccupation and that of forest industry as a male concern. Throughout history, she says, men have been the hunters and women the gatherers and domesticators of plants and animals, and they remain the workers of the land in many subsistence farming communities round the world. Men take over when cash crops are introduced.

Shiva was the first environmentalist to develop a clear critique of the Tropical Forestry Action Plan. Only later did conservative environment groups such as the WWF admit its many flaws. Shiva's uncompromising opposition to Asia's green revolution of high-tech, high-yield farming, and her refutation of the claims of its backers, has likewise gone a long way to undermining a general belief that it must be a 'good thing'.

She characterises the green revolution as 'the worldwide destruction of the feminine knowledge of agriculture, evolved over four or five thousand years, by a handful of white male scientists in less than two decades'. The destruction 'has gone hand in hand with the ecological destruction of nature's processes and the economic destruction of the poorer people in rural areas'. The male world, she says, is technocratic, and based on the cash economy. It is the world of large dams, the taming of nature, industrial forestry and the World Bank. The female world is the world of natural resources, harmony with nature, holistic science, 'small is beautiful', the forests – and definitely not of the World Bank. It is a broad critique that invites contradiction; but it is powerful and also invites adulation. Teddy Goldsmith calls Shiva 'just brilliant'. He sees her as one of three key environmentalists in Asia. (The other two are Idris and Khor in Penang, who share most of her analysis, though without some of the feminist labelling.)

Many Indian environmental groups are involved in ecological regeneration of one sort or another: planting trees, reviving soils or ancient water systems. One such project began, says Shiva, 'in the sunrise of February 28, 1968, when five thousand people from all over the earth gathered on a sandy plateau along the coast of South India, to inaugurate Auroville'. There a project called Greenwork is trying to restore farmland which erosion by monsoon rains and sandstorms threatens to turn into desert. Twenty years ago, the idea was to turn the 20 square kilometres of dust and gullies into 'the city the world needs'. Today, there is no city, just some 600 volunteers brought there mostly by Auroville International, which attracts Western idealists from its offices in the Netherlands and France.

The volunteers have planted about a million trees, dug earthworks to contain rainwater and soils, tended cattle and picked fruit at communities with names such as Success, Discipline, Gaia and Fertile. They all do yoga and hang on the words of someone called 'Mother', whose mysterious messages appear in all Auroville's literature.

Practical in a more political sense is the work of Anil Agarwal, a former science correspondent for the *New Delhi Express* who spent the 1980s building the Centre for Science and the Environment, the most influential and the largest of the many environmental organisations in New Delhi. By 1990, it had a staff of 35. Agarwal's prodigious journalistic contacts allowed him to produce a large report entitled *The State of India's Environment* in 1982, within months of launching the organisation and to provide lobbying in the capital for count-less green causes from round the country. In the late 1980s, Agarwal was appointed as a special adviser to Prime Minister Rajiv Gandhi, which gave him unique access to government until Gandhi's election defeat amid a welter of accusations about corruption at the end of 1989.

Agarwal rejects the fundamentalist ecological position of Bahuguna and Shiva, and his aggressive personality has alien-ated him from other Indian green luminaries, but he too reaches back to the traditions of Mahatma Gandhi in searching for solutions to India's growing environmental problems. He sees the reinvigoration of the villages as the key to both economic development and environmental survival, and he searches for practical answers to the challenge of sustainable development. While Shiva rails against science, Agarwal believes that science can offer solutions to environ-mental problems. He wants people's science. One of the legacies of the marches through India during the 1950s by Gandhi's disciple Vinoba Bhave, asking for land for the poor, was the creation of thousands of Gramdan villages. The residents of these villages communally hold complete power over their own land. Agarwal urges that such villages should develop land-use plans to protect their common lands. He sees such plans as a model for the development of larger national plans based on sound ecology.

'India's planning systems must devolve down to the level of India's ecosystems,' Agarwal says. Separate guidelines can be produced for forest land, deserts or wetlands, but the detailed planning and implementation must be controlled by the villages themselves. 'Why should action be at the settlement level?' he asks. 'Indian villages are highly integrated land-livestock-vegetation systems. Each village has its own crop-land, grazing land and tree or forest land, and all of these components interact with each other. Indian peasants have always understood these interrelationships and it is not sur-prising to find that Indian farmers are not just simply practi-tioners of agriculture, but a mix of agriculture, animal care and silviculture. And, as a community, Indian villages have been great water harvesters – possibly the best in the world.' Every village, he says, is different and must be treated as an entity. Who else can do that except the villagers themselves?

The great issue for rural India, Agarwal says, is the use to be made of common land such as pastures and forests. As we have seen in discussing the TFAP, the Indian government has labelled many commons as waste lands and brought in the World Bank to fund 'social forestry' projects that convert them to productive, that is cash-generating, use. The result has been to deprive the rural poor of firewood and land on which to graze their cattle. Agarwal gave his support to the campaign in the state of Karnataka to prevent forest plantations on common land. But he warns that plantations will sometimes be necessary. At present, 'any attempt to enclose a patch of degraded land will be strongly resented by the people, however under-productive it may be at the moment, for fear of loss of whatever little grass and twigs they may get. Programmes have to be such that people willingly keep their animals away.' Again his message is the need for direct local involvement. His plea is that social forestry should be genuinely social.

Agarwal says that village communities should be given control over government lands and that decision-taking within the villages must be democratic. Today, he says, 'nearly one-third of India's land and most of its water resources are owned by the government. The result is that village communities have lost all interest in their management.' Even the smallest project to harvest water from streams, of the kind developed by local groups in the water-starved state of Rajasthan, runs up against the government's claim that all rivers are its property. Rather than backing such village-based schemes, the government is instead damming the Narmada in neighbouring Gujarat and sending some of the water from the Sardar Sarovar dam down a canal, 450 kilometres long and no less than 750 metres wide, to Rajasthan.

Agarwal wants such megalomaniac schemes abandoned and the resources of land and water returned to the people. He calls for a massive training programme to produce what he calls Barefoot Village Ecosystem Planners 'so that every village has a few such people [to] give advice on small water harvesting schemes, soil and water conservation, afforestation, grassland development, renewable energy and various other such areas.' Modern science, he says, must not seek to drive out traditional methods of living, such as nomadism, shifting cultivation or water harvesting. Instead, 'it must help to increase productivity by building upon the social and ecological foundations of traditional knowledge.'

Debt and a change of direction

Nobody can resist the chance to get something for nothing. In the 1980s, as junk bond dealers and leverage buyout merchants made billions, American environmentalists spotted a chance to make a buck or two for the environment. The plan was called debt-for-nature swaps. Thomas Lovejoy, then a senior biologist at the WWF in the US, is usually credited with having had the idea.

In the early 1980s, Western bankers realised that much of the trillion dollars in loans that they had given to the Third World, especially Latin America, during the 1970s would never be repaid. A few banks wrote the loans off; many more began to unload the debts at heavy discounts to people prepared to gamble on the chance of eventual repayment, or to use them as a tax break. Lovejoy hit on the idea of setting up deals whereby rich conservation groups such as the WWF could buy some of these discounted loans and redeem them in the form of conservation projects in the debtor nation.

It was a clever idea. After all, many of these nations were destroying their environment – chopping down forests and converting fields to cash crops – in a desperate attempt to raise the foreign currency to pay the interest on the debts. The Third World was plunging into a vicious cycle of economic and ecological bankruptcy. Under Lovejoy's plan, they could ease up on the environment, and, crucially, pay off the debt in local currency. There were hopes, too, that the idea might snowball into giant international deals. Brazil, say, would be relieved of its debts, the world's largest; and in return it might agree to leave untouched parts of the Amazon rainforest.

The first deal was done by Conservation International, a Washington-based group. In 1987, it purchased $650,000 of Bolivian debt from a subsidiary of Citibank, one of the most reckless of the 1970s investors. It bought the debt for just $100,000, a spanking 85 per cent discount. Bolivia redeemed that debt by agreeing to set up a local fund worth $250,000 to pay for the operation of the Beni Biosphere Reserve in northeast Bolivia and to develop 'sustainable forestry' in an adjoining area. The deal was not a great success. Within a couple of years, it was clear that the logging was far from sustainable and a road built into the region was attracting colonists. In August 1990, 6,000 local Indians, who had been left out of the deal, began a long well-publicised march to the Bolivian capital, La Paz, complaining that the swap had polluted their rivers, driven away animals, and undermined their claim to land rights in the region.

The WWF was soon doing its own larger swaps. First came Costa Rica. Here the aim was not so much to protect a forest as to re-create it. On the Pacific coast of Costa Rica, a dry tropical forest – a type even more endangered than the better-known tropical rainforests – had been reduced to a few fragments. Costa Rica, a country with ambitious plans to regenerate its environment, planned to replant 1,000 square kilometres of the forest, re-creating as exactly as possible the existing ecology as represented by the surviving forest at its core. The result would be the new Guanacaste National Park.

One irony was that, though much of the forest had been cleared for cattle-grazing, one of the first tasks was to re-introduce some cattle to eat the rampant grasses that had taken over the area. With the grass reduced, wood vegetation began to appear.

What the country's national park service needed was money to buy land for the park from farmers. So the WWF bought up $9 million of the nation's debt for just over $2 million and swapped it with the Costa Rican government for the issue of government bonds with a value of $7 million. Interest earned by the bonds would yield income to be spent in the park, which was decreed in July 1989. Everybody, it seems, was happy, not least the WWF which had tripled its investment. Other deals followed, including a $9 million deal to help preserve the rainforests of western Ecuador, one of the richest regions for biological diversity in the world, and to help with conservation of unique species on the Galapagos Islands. The WWF in the US employed a team of international lawyers to draw up a worldwide list of possible swaps. By late 1989, ten deals had been completed, converting almost $100 million of debt.

There were critics. Was this naked green imperialism a threat to national sovereignty? 'No more than the threat posed by the debt itself,' said David Reed at the WWF. 'The local governments gave up sovereignty when they signed the debts.' In any case, he pointed out, the deals were designed to meet existing national conservation priorities and, where possible, much of the money landed up in the pockets of local environmental groups, who helped to implement the conservation programmes.

In Ecuador, a local group called Fundacion Natura had helped to set up the deal. In the Philippines, scene of the first swap in Asia, the innovative campaigners at the Haribon Foundation received money to help design a conservation strategy for the country. And in Madagascar, the local WWF organisation planned to hire 400 local people, train them and employ them as rangers, according to the WWF's Barbara Hoskinson, who organised the nuts and bolts of the swap.

In Washington in September 1989, critics gathered to have their say. The arguments were as much about the WWF's style of conservation as about the swaps themselves. Ron Rote, of the Forum on Debt and Development in the Netherlands, argued that swaps perpetuated the trend epitomised by the WWF itself to isolate the rainforests from society. 'You depoliticise them, when that is the opposite of what needs to happen. [The debt swaps] detract attention from the real issues behind the destruction of the forests. I dream', he went on, 'of the day that the Duke of Edinburgh calls for a restructuring of the economies of the rich world to help save the rainforests.'

There was some envy at all the money the WWF was dispensing. But there was also a feeling among the critics that, having been attracted by the double-your-money aspects of the deal, the WWF had lost a sense of where its money would be best spent. 'Couldn't we ask the WWF to use its money more radically?' asked Rote. 'Rather than putting money into swaps in Africa, it should put money into helping establish environmental groups there. These groups are what provide hope for the future there, not debt swaps. The cash that could support them is nothing to the WWF.' But this was a criticism that applied equally to most traditional WWF activities.

At a wider level, critics thought that the deals were helping to bail out both the commercial banks that made the loans and the governments that had secured them. In that way, debt-for-nature swaps could actually help to perpetuate the forces that were responsible for the environmental destruction. David Reed disagreed:

Our experience is that the swaps provide an opportunity to make linkages between debt and environmental degradation, influencing the thinking of policy-makers at the highest level. We intend to fund case studies to emphasise these points further. There is a tremendous education opportunity here.

Many environment groups in the Third World opposed debt swaps because they legitimised debts which, they argued, had been fraudulently perpetrated on their nations by a conspiracy of commercial banks and national (frequently unelected) governments. The deal with the Philippines, they claimed, helped to legitimise a debt incurred to build a nuclear power plant ordered, amid tens of millions of dollars in dubious commissions, by the former dictator, President Marcos.

However, even some radical environmentalists saw little point in this stance and were more interested in the potential value of swaps in saving the environment. Among those were Teddy Goldsmith and Nick Hildyard of the *Ecologist*. In 1987, Hildyard had written that 'debt swaps undoubtedly have a role to play as part of a holding action' to save the rainforests. But, he warned, 'At the moment debt-for-nature swaps are too small to challenge the development process.

They shore it up by rescuing Third World economic systems that are damaging the environment.' Larger deals, he said, could trigger more far-reaching changes. Rather than financing a national park here or there, they could be the engines for fundamental change to the operation of national economies, to take them down an ecologically more sustainable road.

'The key is that swaps must be big and systematic,' said Hildyard. 'There must be an international organisation set up to buy up debt and freeze it. Countries would then pay a rent in the form of action in their rainforests.' The deal would be rather like European governments paying farmers to leave their land fallow in the interests of the environment. But 'it would have to involve $30 or $40 billion in order not to refuel the development process.'

Such grand designs had surprisingly wide support among both bankers, desperate to cut their losses on hundreds of billions of dollars in loans, and environmentalists. Several similar schemes were being bandied around and unlikely alliances being forged. One prominent advocate of 'mega-swaps' was Carl Ziegler, a financial consultant and former director of the First National Bank of Chicago, who had played a large part in doling out loans to both African and Latin American governments in the 1970s. 'There is blood on my hands,' he told the *Sunday Times*. In the late 1980s, he was commissioned by the WWF to look at large swaps. He suggested that Brazil might choose to exchange half its debt, $50 billion, in return for agreeing to save, say, 2 million square kilometres of rainforest. Roughly speaking, that would be all the western half of the forest – everything west of Manaus. It put a value on the forest of $250 per hectare – about ten times the valuation in the current generation of WWF swaps.

Other nations could benefit. In Africa, he suggested that Kenya might employ urban youths to work on soil conservation programmes in the north of the country, and it might still have money left over to fight poachers in its national parks. Ziegler believed that the deals should be initiated by the debtor countries themselves but, to get the ball rolling, he lobbied the Inter-American Development Bank to 'advise indebted nations of the desirability of such programmes'. And he told the UN Environment Programme's director, Mustafa Tolba, that the costs of setting up such a global deal 'are immeasurably smaller than the costs of sniping away at the problems today and paying for such inaction in future years'.

Debt swaps provided an interesting meeting of minds for Teddy and Jimmy Goldsmith. When Jimmy attended a one-day environment seminar organised by Margaret Thatcher at Downing Street in early 1989, he submitted a paper proposing a deal similar to Ziegler's. 'The developed nations should recognise that the [tropical rainforest] nations are maintaining a natural and vital resource for the good of all,' he wrote. 'Rightly or wrongly, they believe that they are sacrificing development opportunities by protecting these assets, and that they need to be compensated to do so.' He called for the appointment of an international body, which he called Forestco, to buy up debt at market rates and do deals with the debtor nations. Drawing, no doubt, on his brother's advice, he stressed such matters as the potential effect of the destruction of the Amazon rainforest on Europe's climate and the need to promote 'non-destructive exploitation of the forest by indigenous peoples who, for thousands of years, have been its guardians'.

Thus far, Teddy and Jimmy agreed on the plan. But their conclusions about the economic consequences differed fundamentally. Jimmy believed that the huge scale of the deals would 'help float the economies of the host nations off the rocks and reintroduce them into the world economy'. Business, he believed, could then continue as usual. Teddy believed the opposite: small swaps would perpetuate the system, while a big global deal would force a fundamental shift towards a new green world order. In any case, Thatcher's public green 'conversion' appeared not to extend to such plans, and the Goldsmiths' idea failed to make an appearance in her subsequent green outings.

By the late 1980s, the debt crisis was undoubtedly a major scandal, hopelessly distorting the world economy. Third World debt stood at more than $1.3 trillion. Somalia's debt was 20 times its annual export earnings. Two-thirds of the federal taxes paid by Mexicans during the 1980s went to service the national debt. As countries struggled to pay the interest on their debts, there was a strong flow of cash from the poor nations towards the rich nations. While the total aid budget from rich to poor nations was $60 billion a year, the actual flow of money after the payment of interest on past loans was $60 billion in the other direction. Aid donors and commercial banks appeared increasingly like racketeering money-lenders. Some development lobbyists joined with environmentalists to decry the World Bank's role in the shambles: handing out loans for disastrous 'development' projects such as large dams, and now giving new loans to bail out the Western commercial banks. As Richard Sandbrook of the International Institute for Environment and Development put it to me, 'This is the greatest moral issue of our day.' The poor nations had to be given relief from their debt – not a new round of loans to help them meet the interest payments.

Yet a few campaigners, taking their courage in both hands, warn that debt is a double-edged issue for environmentalists. One is Pat Adams at Probe International. Certainly, she says, Third World governments are chopping down rainforests to pay the interest on their debts. But if they weren't pinned down by debt, they might be investing yet more money in yet more damaging schemes. New plantations, power plants and mines are all being shelved by governments because they cannot afford them. In many places, 'the debt crisis is coming to the rescue of the environment. It has emerged as the best check on reckless lending by international aid agencies and commercial banks to unaccountable Third World regimes.'

Unaccountable is a key word here, she says. 'Given what amounted to a blank cheque, some of these governments borrowed billions in the name of citizens who have little or no say in the investment decisions, but who are held responsible for paying the loans when investments turn sour.' Often the main beneficiaries were the politicians, officials and engineers behind the projects, who received large commissions and kickbacks from contractors. In India, a leading campaigner, Smitu Kothari, claimed to have been told by a former state finance secretary that 'twenty to thirty per cent of the money for the giant Narmada River Project would end up in the pockets of a few politicians and engineers'.

While the world debates how to unscramble the loans, the lessons of how and why they were made are forgotten. 'Brazil, the world's largest debtor, piled up thirty billion dollars in foreign debt on a building binge of unneeded electricity projects, such as the Tucurui and Itaipu hydroelectric dams, that left its creditors dizzy and its environment in tatters,' says Adams. It was a 'kilowatt carnival'. Itaipu cost $16 billion and 1,500 square kilometres of forest, Tucurui $4 billion and 2,400 square kilometres. Brazil's environment and the world's financial system would be a lot better off if the international financiers had kept their money. Anything, even debt, can be good if it stops more loans, she says.

Yet the juggernaut is almost impossible to stop. Brazil's Power Sector II loan, thrown out by the World Bank in early 1989 at the height of concern for the fate of the Amazon rainforest, had been essentially a loan to bail out the debt-ridden Brazilian electricity industry. It was a debt-relief strategy. Its replacement might turn out not to be so different. Soon after the Power Sector II loan was turned down, two of the most heavily indebted and most environmentally ravaged nations were also offered more money to bail them out. Mexico won money from the IMF and the World Bank, much of it to be spent on new hydroelectric dams; and the Philippines obtained new aid from the IMF and promises of up to $10 billion from the World Bank. Electricity transmission was top of the list of investment projects awaiting the new money.

Says Adams, 'Environmentalists throughout the Third World fear that, in the absence of democratic reforms needed to ensure prudent borrowing, this new money will only feed government megaplans.' Certainly the bail-outs for the Philippines and Mexico contained none of the strictures on improved energy efficiency that bathed the World Bank in a green glow for its dealings with Brazil. Away from the public glare and the international conferences, it appeared to be business as usual. As the reformed governments of Eastern Europe began in early 1990 to look to the World Bank and other Western institutions to help them restructure their economies, environmentalists began to worry that here too, they could be jumping from the environmental frying pan into the fire.

Adams joined Carl Ziegler, the reformed financier, in his disappointment at these events. Ziegler wrote to the *International Herald Tribune*, 'As a former banker, I am sorry to learn that environmental factors have not received . . . attention in the negotiations regarding Mexican debt. A proportion, say 20 to 25 per cent, of relieved debt servicing costs should be committed by the Mexican government to environmental concerns.' He listed reafforestation, waste-land reclamation, soil conservation, water and air pollution abatement and energy efficiency. It is urgent, he said, 'that political and financial leaders of all countries take the opportunity to make the problems of Third World debt and environmental degradation converge creatively in building a better world for present and future generations'. Otherwise, says Adams, 'the bankers had better stay home.'

12
FUTURES

Throwing stones in the greenhouse

The conversation over dinner in Toronto before the big conference went something like this. Rafe Pomerance, lobbyist for the World Resources Institute in Washington, put the opening question to Michael Oppenheimer, a fellow lobbyist at the Environmental Defense Fund: 'OK, this week we have a chance to set the agenda for international discussion about the greenhouse effect. The US drought has turned the issue into a big story and there's a media circus in town to hear what the scientists think the world should do. But the scientists don't know. Environmental groups have left themselves out of the greenhouse debate so far. But we can make up for lost time. Let's get the scientists to tell it our way.'

'Well,' said Oppenheimer, 'we should offer a target. To stabilise greenhouse warming would require a 50 per cent cut in emissions of carbon dioxide from burning fossil fuel. That number has scientific credibility, so let's propose that.'

Pomerance frowned, 'You may be right but it sounds too much. They'll never buy it. How about 20 per cent by the end of the century and 50 per cent eventually?'

The deal was done. The two men pushed through their proposal at the meeting of environmentalists running in parallel to the main conference of scientists and politicians. And, with a slight modification allowing an extra five years to reach the 20 per cent target, they got it adopted by the main meeting. The conclusion of the Toronto conference on 'Our Changing Atmosphere' made headlines around the world. A cut of 20 per cent by the year 2005 became the benchmark for the debate on how the world should go about tackling the greenhouse effect. It has had world leaders like Margaret Thatcher and George Bush on the defensive ever since, working hard to justify the delay and their own refusal to endorse any target to reduce the pollution that is warming the planet.

The story is a revealing one. Most environment groups were very late to wake up to the greenhouse threat. For 30 years some scientists had been warning that carbon dioxide was building up in the atmosphere and could be expected, within a few decades, to start warming the planet. A major conference of scientists in 1985 at Villach in Austria concluded that very soon the greenhouse effect would start to change weather patterns, cause storms and droughts, melt ice-caps and raise sea-levels, even destroy national parks. Maybe in Africa the climate was already changing. Surely any friend of the earth would be worried?

Yet somehow none of the thrusting campaigners felt confident enough either about the science or the public's interest to take up the issue. Then in June 1988, at the height of an unprecedented drought across the US, an American scientist working for NASA, Jim Hansen, got the greenhouse effect on to the front pages by telling a committee on Capitol Hill that the effect was the cause of the drought. Suddenly, the scientific abstraction became real. There were photographs of it in the papers.

Once alerted, and with journalists calling for their views, the greens were full of warnings, admonitions and quotations. Some spoke as if they had been in this greenhouse business for years. A year later, as Europeans flocked to join FoE and Greenpeace and to vote for green parties, most voters had come to believe that it was these groups that had alerted the world to the danger; but it wasn't so. Rather as they had let the issue of the thinning ozone layer slip past them in the mid-1980s, so they had missed the greenhouse effect until it was already on the front pages.

Some greens had been very sceptical. Klaus Meyer-Abich, a German philosopher who later became a parliamentarian for the German Green Party, wrote an article for *Climatic Change*, a journal run by Stephen Schneider, an energetic American climate modeller who had decided as early as the 1970s that the greenhouse effect would probably be his life's work. In his article Meyer-Abich argued that global warming would be of no consequence, 'like chalk on a white wall'. As late as 1989, Greenpeace International was being advised by its scientists to stay away from the issue because the science was too uncertain.

There had been a few exceptions, working away in quiet corners. Pomerance had been active since the early 1980s. Rob Peters of the Conservation Foundation in Washington, which is part of the US branch of the WWF, had warned in 1985 that most of the national parks so carefully drawn up by the WWF to enclose particular ecosystems would be wiped out as climate zones shifted. But nobody in his organisation was interested until 1988, after which he was able to organise a conference. Even so, it was not until 1989 that the WWF decided that it ought to take an interest in the wider issues of how the world should meet the greenhouse threat. As Stewart Boyle, who failed to persuade his bosses at FoE in London to launch a greenhouse campaign in early 1988, put it, 'Most environmental groups concentrate on single issues with sharply focused campaigns. The greenhouse effect was just too big and too all-embracing for this approach to work. In campaigning terms, it was very difficult to handle.'

The World Resources Institute had shown the most consistent interest prior to 1988. While Pomerance was the WRI's greenhouse lobbyist, their most important figure in the debate during the late 1980s was Irving Mintzer, who had been with the scientists at the landmark Villach meeting in 1985. It was concluded at Villach that 'scientists and policy-makers should begin an active collaboration to explore the effectiveness of alternative policies and adjustments.' Since few others seemed eager for the job, Mintzer set about trying to knit together the various predictions of future world energy consumption with the climatologists' computer predictions of the impact of rising carbon dioxide levels on global warming. His report on that research was published in early 1987 and was called *A Matter of Degrees: The Potential for Controlling the Greenhouse*

Effect. It sought to undermine the sense of inevitability among scientists about the global-warming debate.

Since Villach, scientists had come up with a range of predictions based on what would happen if carbon dioxide levels in the air doubled, which they expected to have happened by some time between 2030 and 2050. This exercise was useful for them since it gave their various computer models something to argue about. But it was hopeless for policy-makers since it gave them no sense of what their options were.

Mintzer broke through that. He concluded, for instance, that, 'depending on which [energy] policies are adopted, the year when we are irreversibly committed to a warming of 1.5 to 4.5 degrees C . . . varies by approximately six decades.' He sketched out a series of possible futures for the world, each depending on which scientist you believe about the speed of warming, and how seriously the world would take finding technologies to reduce emissions of greenhouse gases.

In one version, which assumed that the world took no such steps and carried on as before, Mintzer's models produced a global warming of an unimaginable 16 degrees centigrade, more than the difference between mid-winter and mid-summer in Britain. And, he said, it could happen by the year 2075, which I calculated could probably be in my children's lifetime. On the other hand, if the world chose a different tack, then we could with luck keep the warming down to less than 2 degrees. This more hopeful scenario assumed big investments in the more efficient use of energy in factories, offices and so on, and in switching from burning coal and oil to gas (which produces less carbon dioxide) and, later, solar energy. It also anticipated an end to the destruction of tropical forests and a major global reafforestation programme to suck up excess carbon dioxide from the air.

The planet, Mintzer said, is far from being 'locked in' to a hot-house future. We have choices to make. His scenarios were not hard and fast predictions: too much of the science of the greenhouse effect was uncertain for that. But he poured scorn on the politicians' claim that the world must wait for the scientists to be certain before acting. Mintzer concluded from his array of graphs and computer runs that if the world waited, say, 30 years for that certainty, it 'would be committed to a warming 0.25–0.8 degrees C higher than that which would occur if the policies were implemented today'.

While groups such as Friends of the Earth are open to criticism for not grasping the greenhouse issue earlier, they get full marks for having argued consistently, since the early 1970s, for energy efficiency. This, Mintzer and others have all concluded, is the swiftest and most cost-effective way of meeting the greenhouse threat. Those stickers left over from the 1970s admonishing people to 'Save It', now applied not only to oil and fuel bills but also to the planet itself.

More troublesome was the issue of nuclear power. By the late 1980s, many energy campaigners in environmental groups were getting bored and looking for new challenges. Most had been appointed to oppose nuclear power; but as the economic and safety cases for nuclear power had collapsed, few countries were building nuclear any more. So the energy campaigners latched on to the greenhouse effect – and were immediately faced with their old foes, the nuclear companies, desperate for orders, arguing that nuclear power would save us from the greenhouse horrors.

In both Britain and the US, groups such as FoE spent much of their time during 1989 countering this claim. It seemed myopic, but many politicians appeared to be doing the same thing from the other side. It was as if both sides felt happiest refighting this old war. FoE in Britain headed up a cul-de-sac, commissioning research to shatter the 'myth' that nuclear power produces no carbon dioxide. All it meant by this was that some carbon dioxide is used in building power stations and in mining uranium. It was hardly an exciting finding. Slightly more promisingly, however, Greenpeace assembled a long list of distinguished scientists, including the Nobel-prize-winning chemist Dorothy Hodgkin, to declare on the eve of a British nuclear conference that nuclear power was 'irrelevant' to combating the greenhouse effect.

The essence of the argument was that measures to improve national efficiency in energy use were up to seven times more cost-effective than nuclear power in reducing carbon dioxide emissions. That is, a pound spent on promoting energy efficiency will prevent seven times more carbon dioxide being produced than a pound spent on building nuclear power stations.

The source of this claim was a study published in 1988 by the Rocky Mountain Institute, a research outfit in Colorado run by one of FoE's original anti-nuclear campaigners in Britain, a physicist called Amory Lovens. As a centre for research into energy saving, the Institute was grinding its own axe, though its figures have not been seriously contested. However, their use in Britain was a little tendentious. Anybody who read the original report would have discovered that the 'seven times more cost-effective' figure applied specifically to the US, which is a grossly energy-inefficient nation. For Europe the report gave a figure of around three times. None of the British campaigners mentioned this point.

Just as the nuclear industry attempted to get in on the greenhouse act, so too, with more credibility, did the energy-efficiency lobby. The British Association for the Conservation of Energy, set up by manufacturers of lagging and the like, pulled off a smart coup when it recruited Stewart Boyle, a frustrated energy campaigner at Friends of the Earth. Soon, to grumbles from purists, the Association was passing itself off as a green pressure group in the press, with ploys such as taking journalists round the Palace of Westminster to show them how energy was being wasted, and unearthing old government forecasts of increased energy use. At least it was campaigning.

At that time, apart from the nuclear sideshow, the only serious initiative from British greens had come from Ark, run by the former head of Greenpeace UK, Bryn Jones. His idea was to cast Ark as the saviour of a flooded Britain. Jones had persuaded a British academic to write a report on how melting ice-caps would raise sea-levels. It suggested that there could be a five-metre rise within 60 years. Jones drew up expensive maps showing how much of Britain would be covered by water, and issued postcards advertising the 'holiday isle' of Blackpool, and sea-horse racing at Doncaster. Then he sat back and waited for the publicity. He got it.

'Prediction of huge sea-rise attacked' and 'Scientists pour cold water on floods warning' were typical headlines. Sen-

sationalist claims have to be pushing at an open door in order
to survive, and Jones's prediction was running counter to new
scientific evidence that the then best estimate of up to a
one-metre rise was too high. Moreover, the tame scientist had
been embarrassed by the wayward interpretation put on his
study and made himself incommunicado. It was a well-
illustrated fiasco, and there were plenty of fellow environmentalists around to twist the knife. Ark's campaigning wing never
recovered.

In grappling with the greenhouse issue, environmentalists
had a tough problem on their hands. While mugging up on the
science, they had to decide what they wanted the politicians to
do and where to direct their lobbying. It wasn't like stopping a
motorway or even saving a rainforest. There were so many
potential targets and so many diverse threats that it was hard
to know where to start.

The Washington groups sank their teeth into an evident split
within Bush's cabinet between his chief of staff John Sonunu,
who thought the greenhouse effect was hogwash, and his
secretary of state, James Baker, who backed proposals for
action made by the head of the Environmental Protection
Agency, William Reilly. But they could not stop Sonunu
winning the battles through 1989 and 1990.

Most of the environment groups sent people to watch
sessions of working groups of the Intergovernmental Panel on
Climate Change, set up to report in late 1990 on the state of
scientific knowledge, and on what the world should do. But the
IPCC proved impossible to lobby. Greenpeace decided to
publish its own 'alternative' IPCC report in August 1990.

Some European greens set out their stalls at a series of
top-level ministerial meetings organised by the French, Germans and Dutch to drum up support for international action.
The meetings started brightly, coming close to backing the
Toronto proposals, but became bogged down in November
1989, when the governments of Britain, the US and Japan
decided to join in and put the brakes on.

Before that November meeting, campaigners from round
the world came together for a strategy meeting to discuss their
approach to the world's most pressing environmental

problem. The most cogent speaker was Irving Mintzer, who had left the WRI to return to academia. 'Our challenge is to use energy without threatening the processes that underpin our civilisation,' he said.

He attacked those fundamentalist greens who want to choke off industrial development. 'There is no choice to the industrialisation of Third World economies,' he said. 'The issue is what we can do in the rich world to minimise the rate of their rise and to ensure that the development there uses the best technology.'

The US is the largest emitter of carbon dioxide in the world. Leaving aside Canada and the odd East European environmental nightmare, it produces more than twice as much per head of population than other industrial nations. In mid-1990, the Bush administration began to claim that it would cost several trillion dollars to reduce their carbon dioxide emissions, and it quoted obscure science foundations who insisted that the greenhouse effect was a scientific mirage. In despair, environment groups in the US accused Bush of 'scientific Stalinism' – putting ideology before the truth – and they reiterated the results of several scientific studies showing that the first actions to stem greenhouse emissions would save money as well as the atmosphere.

One official American study found that Canada would save C$150 billion on its first 20 per cent cut. And Boyle estimates that Britain's first 20 per cent would break even. Nonetheless, no successful international action could go ahead without the US taking the lion's share. In a land where approaching half the carbon dioxide emissions come from vehicle exhausts, 'gasoline prices are lower than at any time since the Korean War,' said Mintzer. 'In the US we must tax heavily the energy-inefficient car and use the money to reindustrialise America using energy-efficient technology. Wall Street should be investing in energy efficiency rather than junk bonds.'

The US government, he said, should set standards for the efficiency of all electrical devices from refrigerators to aluminium plants. Instead of building new power plants, electricity utilities should follow the example of one utility in Maine which bought 70,000 energy-efficient bulbs and gave them away to customers in order to reduce demand for electricity. Twenty per cent of American electricity is spent on lighting – a fact that will not surprise anybody who has ever flown across the US at night.

No green would disagree with much of that. The differences at the meeting in Rotterdam arose over what the role of non-governmental organisations should be in the run-up to an international convention on global warming. Lawyers, who are especially thick on the ground in American environment groups, were keen to draw up their own blueprints for an international convention. In 1989, Michael Oppenheimer at the Environmental Defense Fund was mugging up on international law. Chris Flavin, from the Worldwatch Institute, was devising a worldwide strategy which would bring a 60 per cent cut in North American carbon dioxide emissions, but allow rises in some Third World countries.

The consensus at Rotterdam, however, was that environmentalists would be best occupied fanning public calls for action. 'We need to inject vigour into the debate. We shouldn't be side-tracked into discussions about what should be in a convention,' said Tom Stoel from the Natural Resources Defense Council in Washington. Stewart Boyle of the Association for the Conservation of Energy agreed: 'Don't let's try to turn ourselves into governments in exile. There are loads of global scenarios. Irving Mintzer can give you a boxful. The important thing is how we get to work in our own countries to put pressure on our own governments.' By that measure, very little was happening.

As talk of an international convention to save the world's climate turns into concrete proposals, one central issue will become national sovereignty. Exactly what international duties can a body such as the UN impose on others in so great a cause? And how should the costs be shared? Can the poor nations insist on being allowed to take the 'cheap and dirty' route to industrialisation adopted by the rich world in decades past? Should the rich world pay the poor to take a different route for the good of the planet? And if so, what strings can it legitimately attach? What does the international community do about the nation that puts up two fingers to the entire process? What if the Soviet Union's scientists conclude that global warming would be good for their agriculture?

There is a clash of perceptions, too. The rich nations have been galvanised by the potential horrors of a greenhouse world. Much of the poor world sees such horrors – from flooding and hurricanes to droughts, failed crops and mass migrations – as the everyday reality of life. For all the talk that the poor nations will be least able to cope with climatic change, they have more pressing problems.

Trees, as ever, may become the touchstone for this debate. Forests are a major storehouse for the planet's carbon dioxide. Their destruction – whether in Europe in past centuries, North America in the past 150 years, or the tropical forests in the past 40 – have made a substantial contribution to the build-up of greenhouse gases. Both British and US governments have put preservation of the rainforests, rather than limits on their own industrial pollution, at the top of the international agenda for countering the greenhouse effect. Many greens, fed on apocalyptic visions of having to wear gas masks when the trees run out, take a similar view. But forest destruction is contributing a fast-declining proportion of the greenhouse gases emitted by human activity. Even the appalling destruction of the late 1980s made up only about 20 per cent of the total.

Many US greens back the idea of a global programme of reafforestation, a kind of super-TFAP, to soak up the excess carbon dioxide. The World Bank regards itself as the logical organisation to lead any such programme; and its friends at the World Resources Institute have drawn up an action plan. But why should the Third World be planted with trees to soak up gas put into the air by the First and Second Worlds? It sounds like an example of what Khor at the World Rainforest Movement in Penang sees as the rich North going green and exporting its environmental problems to the tropics. 'Scientists in the North now see forests and so-called waste lands in the tropics as a space for a solution to greenhouse warming,' Herman Verhagen from FoE in Amsterdam told the Rotterdam meeting. 'The people of the Third World may become the first victims of the greenhouse strategy.'

In fact, there is no reason why the new global plantations should be in the tropics at all. With the US and Western Europe planning to take large areas of surplus farmland out of cultivation in the 1990s, the priority should be to replant the ancient forests of Germany, France and the American Midwest.

Any world strategy to damp down the greenhouse effect will require that energy-efficient technologies are quickly handed over to the developing nations. Here again the World Resources Institute's impeccable research department has been ploughing an important furrow. In 1987, it published two reports by Jose Goldemberg, the Brazilian Friend of the Earth and President of Sao Paulo University, who in 1990 joined the Brazilian government as science and technology secretary. He made the case for energy efficiency in the First, Second and Third Worlds. Using existing technologies for energy efficiency, 'per capita energy use in industrialised countries can be cut in half by 2020 while economic growth continues,' he wrote. Moreover, 'in developing countries, the standard of living of Western Europe in the mid-1970s could be reached with only a modest 30 per cent increase in per capita energy consumption.'

For some, the greenhouse effect is the ultimate sign that the world's present industrial road is a dead end. But Goldemberg, whose environmental credentials have wide support throughout the political spectrum, suggests merely that we have got into the current mess through hopelessly profligate management of energy resources. A touch of sanity will see us right. Optimists can breathe again. Whether countries are planning to flood rainforests for hydroelectric power schemes, take World Bank money for coal-fired power plants, or buy nuclear, the message is: Stop, spend your money on energy efficiency. Thus, Goldemberg concluded, his home country, Brazil, could, 'with a total investment of $10 billion for more efficient refrigerators, street lighting, lighting in commercial buildings and motors, defer the construction of $44 billion worth of new generation facilities to the year 2000'. Such statistics helped halt the World Bank's proposed Power Sector II loan to Brazil.

At the beginning of 1990, the World Bank still backed away

from the full implications of energy conservation. David Wirth at the Natural Resources Defense Council in Washington in August 1989 leaked an internal Bank document which soft-pedalled on energy conservation, apparently on the grounds that it would be too expensive for developing nations to adopt.

Environment groups were incredulous. Goldemberg's analysis tells a very different story, and the Bank had done its own research which backed up Goldemberg's findings. A programme of energy efficiency would not penalise poor nations, it would help them to prosper; and it would limit the environmental damage resulting from that prosperity. Energy efficiency offers the poor world, as much as the rich world, the chance to break free from the environmental penalties of economic growth. But it also requires investment in modern technologies. One of the most difficult challenges for green groups in the 1990s is to stress the need for energy-efficient technologies to be made available to developing nations – without creating the erroneous impression that those nations are currently responsible for more than a small fraction of the problem.

Fight for the seeds of life

Biodiversity is a buzz-word for the 1990s. Preservation of the variety of our planet's life forms stands beside halting the greenhouse effect and the survival of the rainforests as one of the great global environmental issues for the coming decade. All three issues are tightly linked. Half the world's species live in rainforests. Rainforest destruction contributes to the greenhouse effect, which in turn will wipe out more species.

Scientists have no real idea how many species of plants, animals and insects there are on the planet. The estimate was around 3 million until Terry Irwin from the Smithsonian Institution in Washington sprayed insecticides into trees in the Panamanian rainforest and waited for the fall-out. He found so many beetles, most of them living on only one type of tree, that ecologists swiftly revised their global species estimate to

30 million. Nor do we know how many species we are destroying each year. One estimate is 15,000, but it could be many more or many less. Most species disappear from the forests without ever having been discovered.

Occasionaly, extraordinary efforts are made to save a single species. The US is spending $15 million on trying to preserve in the wild the California condor. But mostly the world just gawps at the statistics. A one-hectare plot of Peruvian rainforest contains 300 species of trees. In Costa Rica an area half the size of a tennis court contains a sixth as many plant species as there are in the whole of the British Isles. And we shake our heads at particular acts of folly, like the Californian town called Palos Verdes that destroyed the last known habitat for a blue butterfly named after the town – to make way for a baseball field.

Scientists collect and catalogue and revise their global 'guesstimates'. Environmentalists reach for apocalyptic phrases. It is a biological meltdown, the worst extinction since a meteorite hit the earth and wiped out the dinosaurs 65 million years ago. 'Man is bringing down the curtain on evolution,' announced the WWF. A third of all species are under threat, it says, and maybe 15 per cent are doomed to extinction by the year 2000.

In 1989 the WWF launched an appeal for $50 million to help fund nature conservation projects aimed specifically at preserving areas of great biological diversity; and it has earmarked biodiversity as its central theme for the 1990s. As before, this effort will be concentrated on national parks and other biological reserves.

Just as almost three decades ago the WWF and its friends made the case for preserving the African wildlands by pointing to their potential commercial value – for tourism, trophy hunting etc. – so today it points to the hidden commercial value in the rainforests, wetlands and other hot spots of biological diversity. Peter Raven, director of the Missouri Botanical Gardens and a WWF luminary, puts the 'conservation in the service of man' argument like this: 'Only about 150 kinds of food plants are used extensively today. However, there may be tens of thousands of additional plants that could provide human food if their properties were fully explored and brought into cultivation.' One tribe of Brazilian Indians cultivates 140 different types of manioc, for instance. And food is only the beginning. Raven records that 'oral contraceptives for many years were produced from Mexican yams; muscle relaxants used in surgery come from an Amazonian vine traditionally used to poison darts; and the gene pool of corn has recently been enriched by the discovery, in a small part of the mountains of Mexico, of a wild perennial relative.' Furthermore, genetic engineering will increase the demand for and potential value of wild organisms. Scientists will search for genes that protect crops against frost, salt or extra heat from the greenhouse effect, for instance.

The WWF case, then, is that the rainforests, as the world's centres for biological diversity, are a valuable economic resource worth preserving. As the WWF publicity puts it, 'When we destroy tropical forests we could be sending an Aids cure up in flames. We are destroying volume after volume from the natural library before it has even been read.' Here interesting questions arise. How should we preserve this biodiversity, for whom and for what purpose?

There are several aspects to the value of the forests. Most obviously, forest destruction is uprooting the existing, mostly benign, economic exploitation of the forests by native peoples. Even if the ranchers and loggers leave the native people in peace, they frighten away animals that the natives hunt, and destroy fruit, nut and rubber trees, and medicinal plants. Local economies are ruined.

Secondly, there are all manner of little-known forest products that could have an international market in the future. One big hope for extractive reserves of the kind being set up in Brazil since the death of Chico Mendes is that they will tap these markets. Governments may then see the case for creating and protecting more reserves. Ghillean Prance, the director of Kew Gardens in London, believes that Brazil's former trade in crops such as tonka beans and many tree resins, which lost markets to synthetic substitutes, could be revived. Some of the rubber tappers yearn for a big contract with Firestone or Goodyear.

Futures
297

A pioneer in this field is Jason Clay, director of research at Cultural Survival in the US, a body rather like Survival International, which works to improve the lot of indigenous peoples. It has set up a Rainforest Marketing Project under Clay, which is looking for rainforest products to incorporate in cosmetics, sweets and ice-cream, and for companies willing to try them. He works for the Body Shop, the highly successful international chain of cosmetics shops run by the environmental campaigner Anita Roddick. To howls of derision from some quarters, Roddick insists that she is dedicated to saving the planet by buying rainforest products to make into foot ointments, massage cream and the rest. Clay also proposes a condom made from natural rubber sold under the slogan: 'Protect yourself and protect the rainforest.'

Prance agrees that such ideas could help revive sustainable economies in the rainforests. Palm trees may be especially valuable. In Brazil, the Mauritia palm produces fruit, the kernel of the palm nut is rich in oil, and the leaves can be used in handicraft. Kernels from the babussa palm produce an oil identical to coconut oil and their shells fuel boilers at a big Amazonian brewery. In the US, thanks to Clay's work, you can now buy 'rainforest crunch' ice-cream, flavoured with brazil and cashew nuts picked by people living in the Amazon. Prance is working on a similar product for Britain.

All these ideas offer hope that, with a little economic common sense and a little science and entrepreneurial flair, the cattle barons and logging companies could be thrown out of the forests as much by commercial logic as ecological zeal. But the third, and most politically difficult, area of commercial exploitation of the biological riches of the rainforests raises new issues. It lies in materials taken from the rainforests and then propagated, bred or genetically engineered abroad into valuable products such as improved crops or pharmaceuticals. This, many believe, is where the real money is.

Most of the genetic richness of the planet is in the poor countries. Outside the rainforests, there are a number of genetic hot spots for myriad varieties of the world's major food crops, such as wheat, maize and rice. These hot spots, known as Vavilov Centres after the Russian scientist who identified them, are in countries such as Mexico, Turkey and Ethiopia. For several years, the Third World nations have been growing angry that the rich world is pillaging the genetic wealth of the poor tropical nations without paying for the privilege. Shadowy scientists with holdalls wander, more or less literally, into the forests, collect the plants and take them home to their laboratories.

The National Cancer Institute in the US has spent $5 million investigating the properties of some 5,000 plants and animals throughout the tropics looking for treatments for tumours and Aids. It is the largest ever search and includes teams of ethnobotanists interviewing native people to find out which plants they use for medicines. Yet neither national governments nor the native people – who have freely divulged what Western scientists might call their 'intellectual property' – have been offered a share in the profits from the development of any new drug.

Profits from an anti-cancer drug developed from the research may for the moment be theoretical. But those from the rosy periwinkle are already accumulating in the bank. The plant is a native of Madagascar, a poor nation which, in an effort to keep afloat, has destroyed most of its forests. The rosy periwinkle, in the hands of American pharmaceutical companies, has been turned into a drug to cure Hodgkin's Disease. Trade in the drug is worth $100 million a year. A study for the WWF concluded, 'If Madagascar had received a significant part of this income, it would have been one of the country's largest (if not the largest) single sources of income.'

If countries can grow rich selling oil from beneath their land, why not make money from their genetic resources, too? Madagascar is one of the genetic treasures of the planet. Even today, says Peter Raven, director of the Missouri Botanical Gardens, the island contains about 8,500 species of plant, 'some 6,500 of which are found nowhere else. All in all, the island is home to about 5 per cent of the total number of species in the world – about 80 per cent of them to be found nowhere else.' It is the biological equivalent of Abu Dhabi or Saudi Arabia.

If an international treaty provided the government there

with a healthy income as a royalty from the products of the rosy periwinkle, then the country could preserve more of its forests, increasing the prospect of scientists one day finding another biological gold-mine there.

There are plenty of examples from the world of plant breeding where wild strains of important crops growing on apparently unproductive waste land have saved commercial markets from oblivion. Robert Prescott-Allen, one of the founders of the *Ecologist* magazine and later author of the IUCN's *World Conservation Strategy*, calculated in the early 1980s that infusions of wild genetic material were contributing $340 million a year in extra yields and disease resistance to the US agricultural industry. A single variety of wheat found growing wild in Turkey, when successfully bred with existing blighted commercial strains, halted an epidemic of stripe rust in the US in the 1960s. The same plant also provided resistance to several other diseases and may be worth $50 million a year to the US. Yet Turkey receives nothing for this. It has no economic incentive to preserve wild varieties.

Similarly, a single, apparently rather feeble wild variety of rice in India turned out to be the only one from 6,000 tested that was able to provide resistance to grassy stunt virus, which devastated paddy-fields of new high-yield rice varieties in India and Indonesia in the 1970s. Today, the crucial genetic component is incorporated in the crops grown on paddies covering more than 100,000 square kilometres of Asia. India received not one penny for this service. Instead, the new improved rice strain is the property of the Philippines, home of the International Rice Research Institute, where it was developed.

Of course, there are limits to the possibilities for genetic royalty payments. Nobody would suggest that the Chinese should receive a cent for every kitten sold in American pet shops; or that American Indians should take a slice of tobacco revenues. Even without any retrospective clauses, a royalty system could be too complex to administer, and the potential benefits too remote to promote conservation. The profits from the rosy periwinkle would come too late to save most of Madagascar's forests. An alternative idea, supported by

Chris Rose, who investigated the possibilities for the WWF, is to impose a large levy on companies every time they send their researchers to explore a piece of forest or wild grassland.

The new world of biotechnology is certain to widen the horizons of biologists and increase the value of genetic resources. Companies in the rich world will seek not just chemicals from plants or new varieties for breeding supercrops, but also genetic material that can be swapped between species. For Rose, the analogy between biological resources and, say, oilfields no longer holds. Genetic material, he says, is more like information: 'Genetic information carried in plants and animals is like an extremely complex intelligent computer programme, plus programmer, plus computer.' Taking such material without payment 'is like being allowed to enter Silicon Valley and plunder the secrets of the microchip industry, ransack the software developments of IBM and kidnap the best computer scientists all without charge, let or hindrance'. So, he says, let's at least charge a fee at the door.

Rose is suspicious of the role of botanical gardens and men such as Prance at Kew in what could become a new era of 'bioimperialism'. (In 1876, Kew stole rubber plants from Brazil, which then dominated the world market, and shipped them east to establish imperial plantations in Malaya.) Today most botanists still insist that, in the interests of science, they should be allowed to remove tropical plants from the wild and take them to their botanical gardens. The removal of plants from their natural habitat and country creates a potential loophole in any law designed to give nations a stake in any riches derived from their genetic resources. Companies may do deals with botanical gardens to exploit the commercial potential of collected plants. But Rose believes that botanical gardens create another equally serious problem for conservation. Once plants are removed from their habitat, 'the wild habitat is essentially no longer the source of the material and the associated value of the habitat thus vanishes, and with it any incentive to conserve the habitat.'

Botanical gardens are not the only places where the genetic resources of the tropics are stored. Gene banks are increasingly important, especially for food crops. The International Board for Plant Genetic Resources (IBPGR), a body set up on the initiative of the World Bank, is charged with collecting and conserving genetic resources, mostly in gene banks in the rich world. A Canadian pressure group called Rural Advancement Fund International (RAFI) uncovered in the mid-1980s that the gene banks are placed in the countries that fund the IBPGR and that the genetic material inside them is also deemed to be the property of those nations. RAFI's central figure, Pat Mooney, estimates that three-quarters of the world's banked wheat seeds are in Western gene banks, even though most of the seeds come from Third World countries such as Ethiopia and Mexico. Overall, he says, 90 per cent of the seeds gathered from the wild come from the Third World, yet the great majority of them are under the control of the West.

Alongside the IBPGR is a network of international agricultural research laboratories investigating the commercial potential for improving everything from Peruvian potato species to West African yams and maize. Between them, these organisations, and their friends inside the large multinational seed and agrochemical companies, masterminded the green revolution, which has transformed agricultural production in the tropics in the past three decades.

The IBPGR opposes any controls on the free movement of plant materials. Countries have no property rights over their own biological resources, it says. As one critic put it, the IBPGR has 'emerged as a major instrument for the transfer of resources from the South to the North'. Rose adds that, by opting for conservation in gene banks rather than rainforests or the hills of Ethiopia and Mexico, 'the IBPGR is not at present helpful to the WWF's interests.'

The world is on the verge of a new international order governing the ownership of genetic material. As the IBPGR works to place this material in gene banks, there is a new initiative to establish an international treaty on biodiversity in the wild. It is certain to have a profound impact on the conservation of the world's wildlands.

In 1988, scientists at the IUCN, under strong prompting

from the US State Department, began to draw up proposals for an international treaty to preserve biological diversity *in situ*. Pat Mooney at RAFI, who has followed the developing politics of seeds and genetic material throughout the 1980s, argues that under the cloak of environmentalism, the biodiversity treaty will ensure that the world's biological resources are held ever more tightly in the hands of the rich nations.

The treaty plan was taken up in 1989 by the UN Environment Programme and then handed back as a contract to the IUCN to draft a treaty for discussion and possible signing in 1992. According to Mooney, the US has in mind a deal under which 'national governments and indigenous peoples' would receive some kind of financial compensation for the benefits enjoyed by the rest of the world from their genetic resources; but there would be a quid pro quo. He says, 'At a specially convened meeting in Geneva in November 1988, a large US delegation pushed to ensure that the draft treaty would also bind the South into surrendering its [genetic resources].' Poor nations would, in other words, be paid; but they would also be forced to sell.

The arguments over the biodiversity treaty are of vital importance to the environment. Everyone involved will espouse the cause of conservation; but their aims and methods will be very different, as will the environmental and political consequence of their proposals. Yet few greens have begun to discuss the issue. One exception is the World Resources Institute. In the mid-1980s, it appointed the former director of the IUCN, Kenton Miller, to formulate its policy on biodiversity. The WRI intends to work with the World Bank, which is planning its own Biodiversity Action Plan. This may eventually excite as much hostility from environment groups in the Third World during the 1990s as the Tropical Forestry Action Plan has – and for the same reasons. It will argue the creed of privatising the planet's biodiversity as the means to saving it. The Institute and like-minded friends in Washington argue that the world's genetic resources must be delivered for their own protection into the hands of large corporations. Thus Roger Sedjo from Resources for the Future in Washington argued in 1989 that 'the absence of property rights [for wild plants] opens up the possibility of excessive exploitation of the resource, a variation on the "tragedy of the commons".'

Nick Hildyard at the *Ecologist* was one of the first radical environmentalists to tackle the proposals. He believes that the multinational companies that will buy control of the planet's genetic resources are only in profit. And the strategies adopted by them for making money are already the prime cause of the loss of genetic resources round the world. Their policies 'have replaced indigenous agricultural and forestry practices, which rely on exploiting a wide variety of species, and thus encouraging maximum genetic diversity, with monocultures which result in genetic uniformity,' he says. In south-east Asia, two-thirds of the paddy-fields are today planted with one rice hybrid, known as IR-36. As RAFI reports, 'Where 30,000 different varieties of rice grew only a few years ago, Indian agronomists now expect that no more than a dozen will soon dominate.' How, asks Hildyard, can such strategies conceivably be good for genetic diversity?

As part of the push to privatise the world's natural resources, the rich nations are increasingly asserting that all nations should adopt the American approach to 'plant breeders' rights'. These give patent protection to new varieties of plants. At international negotiations on a redrafting of the world's main treaty on trade, GATT, the rich nations led by the US spent 1990 attempting to extend free trade into new areas. They want to establish international patent rights over living things, including hybrid plants and those containing engineered genetic material. (Recent American court cases have established that in the US these rights extend also to bio-engineered animals and potentially even to farm animals and household pets.) 'Into the 1990s,' says Mooney, 'the battle over life patents will be one of the most important North-South and moral battles of this century.'

The rich world wants to assert the patent rights of plant breeders and it wants to guarantee corporations from the North a legal right of access to the genetic material of the South. Says Hildyard at the *Ecologist*, 'The fear is that international patent and licensing agreements will increasingly be used to secure a monopoly over valuable genetic materials which can be developed into drugs, food and energy sources – thus ushering in a new era of biocolonialism.'

While many are anxious to harness commerce in the cause of conservation, Hildyard believes such a cure will inevitably kill: 'It fails to recognise biodiversity as having an inherent ecological value in itself. The conservation of biodiversity can only be achieved over the long term by incorporating the principles of conservation into production processes' – as indigenous cultures do. 'The imperative is to reshape current commercial forces to ecological realities, and not vice versa.'

The green revolution of the 1960s and 1970s has banished from the fields of the world tens of thousands of varieties of wheat, rice, maize and many other food crops. The TFAP and now the Biodiversity Action Plan threaten to do the same in the wild lands. From eggplants in Sudan to soya beans in Malaysia, diversity is being replaced by uniformity. That uniformity leaves crops ever more vulnerable to disease and with ever fewer wild strains available to bail them out with a genetic wrinkle. The genetic erosion of food plant varieties is every bit as alarming as the loss of species in rainforests and wetlands. Yet it remains, to put it mildly, a backwater in the environmental debate.

A glimpse at the world of patented, privatised, corporate-controlled farming shows how far it is removed from the traditions of the peasant farmer, let alone the native stewardship of the rainforests. As RAFI puts it, the effect of the current proposals will be that, 'in effect, the vast biological diversity of the Third World could be rendered the intellectual property of private interests. The inevitable losers in this development will be the countries who have (or had) the biological diversity in the first place.'

RAFI predicts that future crops will become sophisticated assemblies of genetic material; 'A new variety could end up with more patents in it than a 747. Each gene could be "owned" by a different company and come with a royalty charge.' Until recently every farmer was a plant breeder, producing and saving his own seed to sow, and so contributing to the huge genetic diversity. But if the rich nations succeed in enforcing their ideas on plant patents round the world, then farmers may lose that right. The farmer's field is today the genetic equivalent of a Xerox machine. And, just as copyright law controls photocopying, so biotechnology companies will control the seed from their crops. Farmers might also have to pay a biotechnology company every time their cows produce offspring. This is the scale of the change now envisaged. And much of it may be packaged in the name of conservation.

In late 1989, the IBPGR announced plans to establish a giant gene bank somewhere in the Arctic, probably in an abandoned mine shaft beneath the Norwegian island of Spitzbergen. It would provide 'extra security against natural disasters'. There were plans for other stores beneath glaciers in the Himalayas and the Peruvian Alps. It is the final element in an extraordinary vision of how the natural resilience of biological diversity in the world's forests and grasslands and the traditional knowledge of farmers is being subverted by the transformation of modern agriculture. In future, we may have to rely for our survival not on nature but on high-security gene banks – not on the instincts and knowledge of millions of farmers, but on the patented and licensed expertise of a few scientists working for giant corporations.

Privatising the planet

Starting as early as the thirteenth century, the landed aristocracy, increasingly squeezed for cash, began to view their estates not merely as ancestral fiefdoms, but as sources of cash revenue. In order to raise large cash crops, they began to 'enclose' the pasture which had previously been decreed common land ... [Eventually] some ten million acres, nearly half the arable land of England, had been 'enclosed' ... It was the means by which England 'rationalised' its agriculture. But there was another crueller side to enclosure. As the common fields were enclosed, it became ever more difficult for the tenant to support himself. At first slowly, then with increasing rapidity, he was pressed off the land.

This summary of the causes and consequences of enclosures in England comes from Robert Heilbroner's *The Making of Economic Society*. Larry Lohmann of the World Rainforest Movement extracted it to introduce his study of the replacement of rainforests by commercial eucalyptus plantations in Thailand. The parallels are striking. What we are seeing in the last decade of the second millenium is nothing less than the final enclosure movement on planet Earth. The last great wildernesses – the rainforests of the tropics, the rangelands of Africa where elephants and lions still roam with the nomads and their cattle, the mountain passes of the Himalayas – all are being enclosed. Where there are no fences they are tamed by property laws or logging and mining concessions. It is the last great round-up; the privatisation of the planet; the triumph of money. The global common lands are being parcelled out not, by and large, to the people who live on them, but to outsiders who claim that they can make more money from them. The cattle barons of Brazil and Botswana take precedence over forest dwellers and Bushmen; Multinational corporations claim the oil beneath the feet of the native people of Irian Jaya and expel 'squatters' to make way for plantations in Thailand; James Wong and his logging friends plough through the ancient burial grounds of Sarawak. Dam makers and coffee, cotton and sugar planters everywhere, all claim their land in the name of development. Individual property rights count for everything. Most traditional communal land rights count for very little. Almost all the great environmental issues of today arise from this central conflict.

Nor does the privatisation of common rights and resources stop at land. Today in many countries life forms themselves can be patented; and the rich nations want to use international trade agreements to ensure that the rest follow. The Law of the Sea is being followed, as Pat Mooney puts it, with the Law of the Seeds and the Laws of Life. Peasant farmers could once rely solely on their land and their local markets; planting seeds from last year's crop and fertilising the land with their own animals. Their capitalist counterparts, the heirs to the green revolution, must now buy fertilisers and pesticides, pay royalties for the genetic additives in their seeds and read the financial press to discover what price they will get for their crops. Those that do not scramble aboard this economic elevator are, in the current phrase, marginalised. The green revolution may have turned India into a grain exporter, but it has also turned millions off their land and into shanty towns or on to plantations, where they work for low wages and buy at the company store.

Is this the price of progress? In England, enclosures led to an 18th-century green revolution in the countryside. The food from the new cash-crop farms was sent to the cities to feed the children of peasant farmers who were toiling in the new factories creating the industrial revolution. Today, their descendants have colour TVs, Japanese cars and a 35-hour week. The mechanised fields of Europe and North America may employ few people, but they produce so much food that the modern farmers are being paid subsidies to let them go fallow, or to plant trees where none have stood for a thousand years. Critics ask how much of this prosperity is built on the cheap cotton, iron ore, rubber, timber and bananas bought at the expense of the freedom of the peasants of the Third World. Who will subsidise their future prosperity? And can the vulnerable soils of the tropics stand the kind of abuse that the temperate lands have taken without disintegrating? Will the greenhouse effect, the one peril that the rich world cannot offload on to the poor, trigger a breakdown of global life-support systems to confound everybody's ambitions?

Here we can divide the world between optimists and pessimists. Environmentalists can be found on both sides of the debate. The optimists view the world on a continuing upward path towards prosperity. Sure, they say, we are destroying many of the planet's natural resources, using up its minerals and pumping ever more chemicals into soils to make them produce more food. But the history of civilisation is the history of such processes. We have been enriched by it so far. Why should that stop? We may have to dig deeper for coal and oil and minerals to run our industrial machine, but our technology has improved so much that those materials are cheaper than ever before. We may no longer allow our land to stand fallow, but chemical inputs are more than making up the loss in natural soil fertility, and the biotechnology revolution promises much more. Of course there are victims, but you can't make omelettes without breaking eggs.

The optimists point to past great changes in human society. They all had their downsides and all distanced humans from their natural environment and its 'free' products. If there had been environmentalists around 10,000 years ago, when hunters and gatherers first suggested domesticating goats and planting crops, they would have protested. Doesn't nature know best how to use the soil? they would have asked. And why should we plant things when we can gather them for free in the meadows and marshes, woods and hills?

Life for hunters and gatherers thousands of years ago was not nasty, brutish and short. It was sophisticated, based on a highly developed knowledge of the environment and involved remarkably little work. We can see it still in the lives of surviving hunter-gatherer communities, such as the Penan in Sarawak. The only advantage of taking up farming was that it allowed more people to live on the land. Gradually most communities began to farm, whether as shifting cultivators in the forests or as tillers of temperate soils. In the more arid lands of the Middle East, for instance, more sophisticated societies formed, based around irrigated farming. It worked so well that cities developed in which people who were not needed in the fields could evolve yet more artificial forms of life, inventing money and books and machines of war. The optimists' case is that man's inventiveness has allowed him to create a world which, while ever more remote from day-to-day contact with nature, nonetheless sustains increasing numbers of humans at an ever better standard of living – or at any rate in the style to which they aspire.

The optimists admit that the room for error is reduced now. We are running out of virgin land. The enclosure of Europe has been followed by the spread of barbed wire across North America and the steppes of Asia. Sedentary farmers are annexing the rangelands of Africa and carving up the tropical forests. Even the parts of the planet we choose to keep wild are coming under lock and key inside national parks, where there is money to be made out of tourism.

Once there were many civilisations, all more or less independent. It mattered nothing to the Chinese or the Andean Indians or the great civilisations of Zimbabwe and Nigeria when Mesopotamia's irrigation system poisoned the fields with salt and its civilisation bit the dust. Today the greenhouse effect or a ruptured ozone layer could get us all. A single pest could run right through the world's wheat fields or rice paddies. But the optimists believe that we are now that much more sophisticated at identifying and handling such problems. When greens complain that the modern world's solution to every problem is a 'technical fix' which creates a new galaxy of side-effects, optimists shrug their shoulders. Hasn't the world always been like that? they ask.

Not all optimists believe all of this. The superoptimists *par excellence* have been right-wing Americans such as the late Herman Kahn, who once proposed that the Amazon rainforests could be turned into a giant reservoir to power the planet, and Julian Simon, who believes that a rising population is good for the planet because the extra brains to think and hands to work will outweigh the extra mouths to feed. The superoptimists, who are also mostly supercapitalists, argue that there are no 'limits to growth'. If we run out of coal, there will be nuclear power or solar energy. If we wreck our soils, the chemists will find another way of feeding us. Simon's views are rigorously thought out and genuinely held, though they are also worn by people who simply find them a convenient cover for making a quick billion.

Green optimists take a more pragmatic and technocratic view of the world, and their optimism is heavily qualified. There may be no immutable limits to growth, but there are serious practical problems along the way. The demands of hungry mouths are rather more immediate than the products of fertile brains. More people may be OK, but so many more people so quickly is disastrous and may force parts of the world into ecological decline. They see this process already in Africa. For the green optimists the way forward is a positive effort to promote the values and virtues of the developed world, and they put electricity and contraception about equal at the top of the shopping list. Economic development will

relieve poverty and stop its consequent environmental damage. Much of the damage caused by the march of development – World Bank dams, mines, eucalyptus plantations – is
seen as inevitable. There are effects to be mitigated, but
development must go on in the best interests of the community
as a whole.

These qualified optimists see global environmental threats
that impinge on the temperate lands as well as the tropics, as
the greatest planetary peril. Top of the list are the destruction
of forests (which could upset world climates) and the greenhouse effect, whose consequences may be most marked at
higher latitudes. They are relieved, however, to see that inefficiency in the world's use of energy is so great that the output
of greenhouse gases could probably be halved through investment in energy conservation in fridges, factories, cars and the
rest. A mixture of international treaties and domestic tax
policies could manage the problem.

This is a very Western-oriented view of things. It embraces
rather than confronts what Jose Lutzenberger calls the
'fanatical religion of consumerism'. It wants, in Goldsmith's
words, to keep on down the main highway rather than take
the alternative winding road signposted by Schumacher,
Lutzenberger and others.

Here we enter the world of the deep green pessimists. To
some they sound like cranks. Cranks, however, have a habit of
proving less cranky on close inspection; and in the world of
environmentalism what has distinguished them is their ability
to identify the issues that will preoccupy mainstream environmentalists in years to come. This suggests that they may be on
to something.

In general, greens are of a deeper hue in the Third World.
They see better the economic roots of much environmental
destruction. While Northern greens often see the population
explosion as the engine of the ecological crisis in the tropics,
Southern greens point instead to the over-use of resources in
the North. The northerner looks at the rainforest and sees
hordes of landless peasants fleeing from shanty towns and
burning clearings in the jungle. The southerner sees instead the
Japanese timber companies and their roads into the forests.

They see the Western-style cities and corrupt governments spending loans from Western development banks and ransacking the countryside to pay the debt. They see the enclosure of the great tropical commons; the privatisation of the biological resources of the planet. Martin Khor, the economist from the World Rainforest Movement in Penang, posed these questions on a visit to London:

Is the ecological crisis a manifestation of the crisis of greed? Are we coming to the limits of the exploitation of the planet? Has nature nothing left to give? If so, then we must convince people that industrial society is incompatible with sustaining life on Earth. To survive, we must have sustainable living in the First World. We have to deindustrialise the North.

His solution may sound extreme, but his fear is widely held.

The human population of the world has reached a crisis in its relationship with the planet. It is a crisis of confidence as much as one of survival. As our population soars past 5 billion and economic development roars on, change has become so fast, and the stresses on the environment in some places so great that apocalyptic fears are gaining ground. A few optimists still believe in progress and the power of humans to solve their problems. But many more people have come to fear that we are on a roller-coaster to disaster.

My own view is that both the optimists and pessimists may have missed a crucial point. The storm of development, which the optimists love and the pessimists loathe, may eventually blow itself out. The history of human civilisation shows a series of surges in world population that have coincided with technological revolutions. The first occurred perhaps a million years ago, with a revolution in tool making that made hunting a more productive activity. It saw the world's population rise above a million for the first time. The second, 6,000 to 8,000 years ago, after the end of the last ice age, occurred when humans took up agriculture, and this saw us past 100 million. The third, the industrial revolution, is still in full swing. It has seen humans enter an era in which they appear overwhelmingly to dominate activity on the surface of the planet, and in which human society is organised under one economic and political umbrella. Private property is the rule. The common lands are being enclosed; wild animals are being rounded up.

At the end of the 20th century, we are perhaps at the height of this revolution, which some scientists have called the Third Great Climacteric. It is a moment of great danger for our civilisation and our planet: much more so than past periods of rapid change, because of the global reach of our activities. We may all sink or swim together this time. But, provided we don't sink, the moment will pass. In the fury of change we forget that Great Climacterics have not been the norm in the past. Revolutions cause great changes, but they are passing phenomena, and there is no reason to think the present one need be any different. Rates of growth in the world's human population have begun to fall in the past 15 years. There is a growing consensus that population numbers will stabilise, at perhaps ten billion people, around the year 2100. With demographic stability may come economic and ecological stability.

The superoptimists, such as Julian Simon, are right in the broader sense that we cannot go back, only forward. They may even be right that much of the past must vanish as the world finds ways to accommodate the extra billions of people; that we must embrace the change rather than shrink from it. But the pessimists must also be right to show that the kind of economic activity being wished on the rest of the world by the nations that industrialised first is not a kind that can last. It makes no sense to destroy the only cultures that know how to make sustainable use of the rainforests and the grasslands of Africa. The destruction of the forests of south-east Asia to provide plywood for Japanese furniture is crazy. Still worse is the land speculation that drives the destruction of the Amazon forests.

Simon may be right that more brains to think and hands to work will triumph over more mouths to feed. I think he is. But he is wrong to believe that the world's current economic and political systems are capable of harnessing the brains and hands. From the shanty towns of Mexico City to the transmigration camps of Indonesia and the shambles of the Amazon rainforest, we see that they cannot. The Indians of Brazil have more to offer the 21st century than all the junk bond dealers on

Wall Street. Our survival through the next century may depend on finding a new global order that encompasses such obvious facts.

Goldsmith makes perfect sense when he despairs of the mess that human society makes of the planet. To go forward, as Simon desires, we may need the biospheric ethic for which Goldsmith yearns. I see no reason why it cannot happen. The signs of a beginning are all around us. Native crafts and ways of living strike increasing chords in the suburban heartlands of the West. People look for quieter, more restrained ways of living. They smoke less, eat less, turn vegetarian in droves, buy a bicycle, bake their own bread, hope to live in the countryside. Lutzenberger's Messianic religion of consumerism may be on the wane. At present, change is slow and concerned largely with personal lifestyle. But as the Third Great Climacteric wanes, the same feelings may lead to quieter, less aggressive, more contemplative politics and economics. George Bush became US president with a promise to bring a 'gentler America'. Goldsmith would call it more aesthetic and he may not be far wrong.

The new biospheric ethic is already at work in our attitude to animals, to leg traps and whalers' harpoons. The days when Aristotle Onassis took his clients on joyrides to watch the slaughter of whales seem long gone. We abhor the chopping down of trees and the polluting of rivers. Television is good at showing their horrors. We are less good at recognising the ills done to our fellow humans or at understanding the economic processes that destroy our environment. But, as this book shows, there are plenty of people around who are working to help us do so.

The naive stirrings of the green consumer may, despite the best efforts of many firms to subvert them, lead to a greener world. If environmentalists are here merely to wave their arms uselessly as human civilisation heads over the cliff, then they may as well not bother. The best of them, however, in many different guises and from many different perspectives, do offer a new way. The challenge for many of them is not to be timid. The World Wide Fund for Nature should not bury itself in its nature reserves and parks, emerging only to take pot-shots at poachers. It must take its knowledge of the biosphere out to meet the people. We cannot, at this moment above all others, separate humans from nature; we must find new ways to live with nature. Greenpeace must not hide behind its corporate persona and its market research. It ought to look afresh at what it thinks about the world.

Friends of the Earth, perhaps by being more democratic than most groups, has, I believe, found a better mix in its work between ethics, lifestyle and politics; but it too must be bold. It must not be seduced by the trappings of power at the International Tropical Timber Organisation or the World Bank. The real power for change is in the streets of small-town America, on the plains of India, and in the hearts of the East Europeans.

As the Third Great Climacteric begins to wane, the consequences of its excesses are becoming more visible. We can today begin to comprehend the brutality of our assaults on the planet in the past two centuries, but we are far from finding ways to halt the destruction. With Simon's optimism and Goldsmith's ethic, there may be hope. Green Warriors are showing the way.

ACKNOWLEDGMENTS

I have tried to tell the stories of the Green Warriors through their own mouths, where possible. So many of the people who helped me along the way are acknowledged in the text. But special thanks are due to the people at the *Ecologist*, especially Teddy Goldsmith and Nick Hildyard, and to Larry Lohmann and Marcus Colchester, many of whose ideas underpin my own thoughts. The wisdom and knowledge of Chris Rose of Media Matura was also important and several chapters bear the mark of Pat Adams and Phil Williams. The brave campaigners of Malaysia, especially Chee Yoke Ling, Martin Khor and Harrison Ngau, provide precious links between warriors of the pen and warriors of the spear and made me believe that greens could be a force for good in the Third World. In the months before the people took to the streets of Eastern Europe, Janos Vargha and his many extraordinarily hospitable friends and relations in Budapest showed me that green was an important colour in their revolution.

Thanks too for many insights from Koy Thomson, Richard Sandbrook, Tom Burke, Graham Searle, Jeremy Leggett, Pete Wilkinson, Alan Thornton, Martha Belcher, Walt Patterson, Phil Hurst, Stewart Boyle, Liz Hosken and to Roger Milne, Omar Sattaur, Debora MacKenzie and Catherine Caufield for ploughing the same field.

Robert Hunter's writings, notably in his book the *Greenpeace Chronicle*, were invaluable on the early days of Greenpeace; Pat Mooney was a shining light on seeds; Vandana Shiva shed light on many things. I regret having failed to meet them in person. At The Bodley Head, Jill Black accepted a manuscript rather different from the original proposal and Julia Hall edited with such gentle precision that I barely noticed.

Useful Addresses

INTERNATIONAL
Friends of the Earth International
26–28 Underwood St
London N1 7JQ
England

Greenpeace International
Keizersgracht 176
1016 DW Amsterdam
Netherlands

WWF International
Avenue du Mont Blac
Gland 1196
Switzerland

ARGENTINA
Amigos de la Tierra
cc 3560
1000 Buenos Aires

Fondation pour la Protection de
    l'Environnement
Casilla de Correo 83
Correo Central
5000 Cordoba

Greenpeace
Junin 45, 3 Piso
1026 Buenos Aires

AUSTRALIA
Friends of the Earth
PO Box 530 E
Melbourne, Victoria 3001

Greenpeace
Private Bag 6
134 Broadway
Sydney, NSW 2007

Rainforest Information Centre
PO Box 368
Lismore
NSW 2480

Tasmanian Wilderness Society
130 Davey St
Hobart 7000

WWF
Level 17, St Martin's Tower
31 Market St
PO Box 528
Sydney
NSW 2001

AUSTRIA
Die Grune Alternative
Millergasse 40/9
1060 Vienna

Friends of the Earth
Rheinglasse 34128
1140 Vienna

Greenpeace
Mariahilfer Gurtel 32
1060 Vienna

WWF
Ottakringererstr. 114–116/9
Postfach 1
1162 Vienna

BANGLADESH
Centre for Research and Action
    on Environment and
    Development
17 Elephant Rd
PO Box 5007
New Market
Dhaka-1205

Friends of the Earth
PO Box 4222
Dhaka 1000

BARBADOS
Caribbean Conservation
    Association
Savannah Lodge
The Garrison
St Michael

BELGIUM
European Environmental Bureau
rue de Luxembourg 20
1040 Brussels

Les Amis de la Terre
Place de la Vingeanne
5158 Dave

Greenpeace
Waversesteenweg 335
1040 Brussels

WWF
608 Chaussée de Waterloo
1060 Brussels.

BOLIVIA
Fundacion Natura
c/o LBII
Calle Bolivar 967
La Paz

BRAZIL
Amigos da Terra
Rua Miguel Tostes 694
Porto Alegre RS 90420

Partido Verde (Green Party)
Rua Dr Francisco Muratori 45
Lapa, Rio de Janeiro

CANADA
Green Party of Canada
831 Commercial Drive
Vancouver
British Columbia V5L 3W6

Friends of the Earth
Suite 701
251 Laurier Ave W
Ottawa, Ontario K1P 5J6

Greenpeace
578 Bloor St West
Toronto
Ontario M6G 1K1

Pollution Probe
12 Madison Ave
Toronto
Ontario M5R 2S1

Probe International/Energy Probe
225 Brunswick Ave
Toronto
Ontario M5S 2M6

WWF
60 St Clair Ave East
Suite 201
Toronto
Ontario M4T 1N5

CHILE
Instituto de Ecologia Politica
Londres 88 Depto 20
Santiago

COLOMBIA
Fundacion Natura
Calle 90, No 10–61
Oficina 201
Bogota 55402

CYPRUS
Friends of the Earth
Maroni
Lanarca District

DENMARK
Friends of the Earth (NOAH)
Studiestraede 24
1455 Copenhagen

Greenpeace
Thomas Laubs Gade 11–13
2100 Copenhagen

De Gronne
Voonporten 14–108
1220 Albertslund

WWF
Osterbrogade 94
2100 Copenhagen O

ECUADOR
Fundacion Natura
Av 6 de Diciembre 5043
Casilla 253
Quito

Tierra Viva
Casilla 1891
Cuenca

FIJI
South Pacific Action Committee
on the Human Environment and
Ecology
PO Box 1168
Suva

FINLAND
Green Union
Latinen Papinkatu 2–4
00530 Helsinki

WWF
Uudenmaankatu 40
00120 Helsinki 12

FRANCE
Ecoropa
24 rue d'Amitage
Paris 20

Les Amis de la Terre
15 rue Gambey
75011 Paris

Les Verts
90 rue Vergniaud
75013 Paris

WWF
14 rue de la Gare
75016 Paris

GERMANY
Bund
Postfach 300220
5300 Bonn 3

Die Grunen
Colmantstrasse 36
5300 Bonn

Greenpeace
Vorsetzen 53
2000 Hamburg 11

Institute for European
Environmental Policy
Aloys-Schulte Strasse 6
5300 Bonn

WWF
Sophienstrasse 44
6000 Frankfurt 90

GHANA
Friends of the Earth
PO Box 3794
Accra

HONDURAS
Assoc Hondurena De Ecologica
Apartado Postal T-250
Tegucigalpa

HONG KONG
Friends of the Earth
One Earth Center
61 Wyndham St M/F

HUNGARY
ERTE Nature Conservation Club
Egyetem ter 1–3
1035 Budapest

Danube Circle
Bocskai ut 31
1113 Budapest

INDIA
Centre for Science and the
    Environment
807 Vishal Bhavan
95 Nehru Place
New Delhi 110019

Chipko Information Centre
Parvatiya Navjeevan Mandal
Silyara
Tehri-Garhwal
249155 Uttar Pradesh

Environmental Action Group
1 Court Rd
Delhi 110054

Lokayan
13 Alipur Rd
Exchange Store Building
Old Delhi 110054

Narmada Dharangrast Samite
PO Box 52
Dhule 424001
Maharashtra

Research Foundation for Science,
    Technology and Natural
    Resource Policy
105 Rajpur Rd
Dehra Dun 240001

WWF
c/o Godfrej & Boyce
Lalbaug Parel
Bombay 400 012

INDONESIA
Irian Jaya Development
    Information Service Centre
PO Box 52
Jayapura
Irian Jaya

SKEPHI
Jalan Tebet Salam IG/35
Jakarta Selatan 12810

WALHI
Jalan Penjernihan 1
Kompleks Keungan 15
Pejompongan
Jakarta 10210

IRELAND
Earthwatch
Harbour View
Bantry
Co Cork

Greenpeace
29 Lower Baggot St
Dublin 2

ITALY
Amici della Terra (FoE)
via del Sudario 35
00186 Rome

Greenpeace
28 viale Manlio Gelsomini
00153 Rome

WWF
via Salaria 290
00199 Rome

JAPAN
Friends of the Earth
801 Shibuya Mansion
7–1 Uguisudani-cho
Shibuya-ku, Tokyo 150

Japan Tropical Forest Action
    Network
801 Shibuya Mansion
7–1 Uguisudani-cho
Shibuya-ku, Tokyo 150

WWF
Nohonseimei Akabanebashi
Bldg 7F, 3-1-14 Shiba
Minato-ku, Tokyo 105

KENYA
African Wildlife Foundation
PO Box 48177
Nairobi

Green Belt Movement
c/o National Council of Women
    of Kenya
Moi Avenue, PO Box 67545
Nairobi

Environmental Liaison Centre
International
PO Box 72461
Nairobi

African NGO Environmental
Network
PO Box 53844
Nairobi

LUXEMBOURG
Greenpeace
Postbox 229
L-4003 Escg/Alzette
Luxembourg

MALAYSIA
Consumers' Association of
Penang
87 Cantonment Rd
10250 Penang

Environmental Protection Society
of Malaysia
17 Jalan SS 2/53
PO Box 283
Petaling Jaya 46740

International Organisation of
Consumer Unions
Asia/Pacific Office
PO Box 1045
10830 Penang

Sahabat Alam Malaysia (Friends
of the Earth)
43 Salween Rd
10050 Penang

and: PO Box 216,
Marudi
Baram, Sarawak 98050

WWF
10th floor, Wisma Damansara
Jalan Samantan
Kuala Lumpur 50490

NETHERLANDS
Air Pollution Action Network
PO Box 5627
1007 Amsterdam

Friends of the Earth
Damrak 26
1012 Amsterdam

Foundation for Environmental
Contact Poland/Netherlands
PO Box 5627
1007 Amsterdam

Greenpeace
Damrak 83
1012 Amsterdam

International NGO Forum on
Indonesia
PO Box 11609
2502 The Hague

IUCN
Damrak 28–30
1012 Amsterdam

Society for Environmental
Protection
Donkerstraat 17
3511 Utrecht

WWF
Postbus 7
3700 Zeist

NEW ZEALAND
Friends of the Earth
PO Box 39–065
Auckland-West

Greenpeace
Private Bag
Wellesley Rd
Auckland

WWF
PO Box 6237
Wellington

NORWAY
Greenpeace
St Olavsgt 11
PO Box 6803 St Olavsplass
0130 Oslo 1

WWF
Hegdehaugsveien 22
0167 Oslo 1

PAKISTAN
Environment Management
 Society
141-A, SMCH Society
Karachi 3

WWF
PO Box 1312
Lahore

PAPUA NEW GUINEA
Friends of the Earth
PO Box 4028
Boroko

PHILIPPINES
Haribon Foundation
Suite 306
Sunrise Condominiums
226 Ortigas Ave
San Juan
Metro Manila

POLAND
Polish Ecology Club
Palac Pod Baranami
Rynek GI 27
31010 Krakow

Polish Green Party
Zygmunt Fura
PO Box 783
30960 Krakow

PORTUGAL
Amigos da Terra
Rua Pinheiro Chagas 28
2nd floor
1000 Lisbon

SPAIN
Amigos de la Tierra
Avenida Betanzos 55
Madrid 28029

Greenpeace
C/Rodriguez San Pedro 58, 4 Piso
28015 Madrid

WWF
6 Sanata Engracia
Madrid 10

SRI LANKA
Wildlife and Nature Protection
 Society
Chaitiya Rd
Marine Drive, Fort
Colombo 1

SWEDEN
Friends of the Earth
Fjallgaten 23A
Stockholm

Greenpeace
PO Box 7183
S-402 34 Goteborg

Swedish NGO Secretariat on Acid
 Rain
Miljovard
PO Box 33031
S-400 33 Goteborg

WWF
Ulriksdals Slot
171 71 Solna

SWITZERLAND
Greenpeace
Muellerstrasse 37
Postfach 4927
8022 Zurich

WWF
Forrlibuckstrasse 66
Postfach 749
8037 Zurich

Fruende der Erde
Engelgasse 12a
9000 St Gallen

TANZANIA
Tanzania Environmental Society
PO Box 1309
Dar es Salaam

THAILAND
Project for Ecological Recovery
1705 Rama IV
Bangkok 10500

Siam Environment Club
Chulalongkorn University
Bangkok 10500

UNITED KINGDOM
Ark Trust
500 Harrow Rd
London W9 3QA

Ecologist
Corner House
Station Rd
Sturminster-Newton
Dorset

Environmental Investigation
   Agency
208 Upper St
London N1 1RL

Friends of the Earth
26–28 Underwood St
London N1 7JQ

and: 15 Windsor St
      Edinburgh EH7 5LA

Gaia Foundation
18 Well Walk
Hampstead, London NW3 1LD

Green Party
10 Station Parade
Balham High Rd
London SW12 9AZ

Greenpeace
30–31 Islington Green
Londin N1 8XE

International Institute for
   Environment and Development
3 Endsleigh St
London WC1H 0DD

Lynx
PO Box 509
Dunmow
Essex CM6 1UH

Oxfam
274 Banbury Rd
Oxford OX2 7DZ

The Panos Institute
8 Alfred Place
London WC1E 7EB

Survival International
310 Edgware Rd
London W2 1DY

WWF
Panda House
Weyside Park
Godalming GU7 1XR

USA
Bank Information Center
731 8th Street SE
Washington DC 20003

Cultural Survival
11 Divinity Avenue
Cambridge, MA 02138

Debt Crisis Network
15 Rutherford Place
New York

Earth Island Institute
Suite 28, 300 Broadway
San Francisco

Environmental Defense Fund
1616 P Street NW
Washington DC

Friends of the
   Earth/Environmental Policy
   Institute/Oceanic Society
218 D Street SE
Washington DC

International Rivers Network
301 Broadway
San Francisco

Greenpeace
1436 U Street NW
Washington DC

National Wildlife Federation
1412 16th Street NW
Washington DC

Natural Resources Defense
    Council
1350 New York Ave NW
Washington DC

Rainforest Action Network
301 Broadway, Suite A
San Francisco

Rainforest Alliance
295 Madison Ave
Suite 1804
New York

Sierra Club
703 Polk St
San Francisco

Worldwatch Institute
1776 Massachusetts Ave NW
Washington DC

World Resources Institute
1709 New York Ave NW
Washington DC

USSR
Estonian Green Movement
8 Veski St
Tartu 202400
Estonia

INDEX